Manfred Kochen:
PRINCIPLES OF INFORMATION RETRIEVAL

Dagobert Soergel:
INDEXING LANGUAGES AND THESAURI: CONSTRUCTION AND
MAINTENANCE

Robert M. Hayes and Joseph Becker:
HANDBOOK OF DATA PROCESSING FOR LIBRARIES, Second Edition

Andrew E. Wessel:
COMPUTER-AIDED INFORMATION RETRIEVAL

Lauren Doyle:
INFORMATION RETRIEVAL AND PROCESSING

Charles T. Meadow:
APPLIED DATA MANAGEMENT

Andrew E. Wessel:
THE SOCIAL USE OF INFORMATION: OWNERSHIP AND ACCESS

Hans H. Wellisch:
THE CONVERSION OF SCRIPTS: ITS NATURE, HISTORY, AND
UTILIZATION

Eugene Garfield:
CITATION INDEXING: ITS THEORY AND APPLICATION IN
SCIENCE, TECHNOLOGY, AND HUMANITIES

Frederick W. Lancaster:
INFORMATION RETRIEVAL SYSTEMS: CHARACTERISTICS,
TESTING, & EVALUATION, Second Edition

Andrew E. Wessel:
IMPLEMENTATION OF COMPLEX INFORMATION SYSTEMS

William B. Rouse and Sandra H. Rouse:
MANAGEMENT OF LIBRARY NETWORKS: POLICY ANALYSIS,
IMPLEMENTATION, AND CONTROL

Charles T. Meadow and Pauline A. Cochrane:
BASICS OF ONLINE SEARCHING

Basics of
Online Searching

Basics of
Online Searching

Charles T. Meadow

Drexel University
Philadelphia, Pennsylvania

Pauline (Atherton) Cochrane

Syracuse University
Syracuse, New York

A WILEY-INTERSCIENCE PUBLICATION

JOHN WILEY & SONS
NEW YORK • CHICHESTER • BRISBANE • TORONTO

Library of Congress Cataloging in Publication Data

Meadow, Charles T
  Basics of online searching.

  (Information sciences series)
  "A Wiley-Interscience publication."
  Includes index.
  1. On-line bibliographic searching. I. Cochrane,
Pauline, 1929– Joint author. II. Title.

Z699.3.M395   025'.04   80-23050
ISBN 0-471-05283-3

Printed in the United States of America

10 9 8 7 6 5 4 3 2 1

This book is dedicated
by CTM to his joyful daughter Alison,
and by PAC to Karen, who still has a half century of online to go

Information Sciences Series

Information is the essential ingredient in decision making. The need for improved information systems in recent years has been made critical by the steady growth in size and complexity of organizations and data.

This series is designed to include books that are concerned with various aspects of communicating, utilizing, and storing digital and graphic information. It will embrace a broad spectrum of topics, such as information system theory and design, man-machine relationships, language data processing, artificial intelligence, mechanization of library processes, non-numerical applications of digital computers, storage and retrieval, automatic publishing, command and control, information display, and so on.

Information science may someday be a profession in its own right. The aim of this series is to bring together the interdisciplinary core of knowledge that is apt to form its foundation. Through this consolidation, it is expected that the series will grow to become the focal point for professional education in this field.

Preface

The purpose of this book is to teach the principles of interactive bibliographic searching, or information retrieval, to those with little or no prior experience. The major intended audiences are students, working information specialists and librarians, and end users, the people for whom all this searching is done.

For student use, this book can be a text appropriate for introductory courses in schools of library and information science. Working information specialists and librarians whose backgrounds have not yet included instruction in online searching should find this a useful self-instruction manual, but it must be coupled with practice and the use of prepared exercises and search service users' manuals. Finally, many who are today end users of online information systems may wish to learn how to do their own searching or even just to prepare themselves to work with the professional searcher, and they will find the book useful toward those ends.

This book is *not* intended as a substitute for search services' users' manuals. We have not attempted to cover all commands or contingencies and it would be impossible for us to write a book that is continuously up to date with their changes. Had we tried, the book would have had to be about 1000 pages in length and packaged in looseleaf form. Indeed, it was a struggle to keep up with the changes made while writing was in progress!

It is our intent to teach principles, rather than the detailed mechanics of any particular search system. Our examples are based on the Bibliographic Retrieval Services, Inc. (BRS), DIALOG, and ORBIT search services. We intend no endorsement of these systems nor any contrary indication by our omission of examples from other services. We have selected BRS, DIALOG, and ORBIT because they are the most commonly found services in most libraries. There are many other fine systems, such as the New York Times Information Bank, the National Library of Medicine's MEDLINE, Mead Data Central's LEXIS, and West Publishing Co.'s WESTLAW. Our objective is to teach you, the reader, what searching is all about and how to compare different services. Giving equal space to all services is not a part of our aim, so we urge you not to count lines of text devoted to, or numbers of citations of, each service. We see them as being not too dissimilar—probably more alike than their sales literature would admit. We feel a student can learn the principles from any of them and transfer them to any other.

We have used, throughout, masculine pronouns when referring to a person unknown or to a hypothetical person. Since one of the two authors is a woman and since anyone in the field recognizes that a large, probably predominant, fraction of its membership is female, we hope that readers realize we know this and intend no slight by this usage. We feel it is conventional English and a means of avoiding cumbersome constructions, such as s/he.

Typographically, we use italics in the text to represent a user's input to a computer, such as *select italics*. Capital letters indicate the computer's messages, such as HELLO FROM ORBIT. We have shown logical connectives such as *and, not,* and *or* in boldface italics simply to make their use evident to the reader. In actual computer input, they are not set off in any manner.

We are grateful for help in preparing and criticizing early drafts of this book provided by Trudi Bellardo, Charles P. Bourne, Michael R. Halperin, Sara D. Knapp, Karen L. Markey, and Judith Tessier.

The index was prepared with the assistance of D. Joan Joyce, a doctoral student at Syracuse. Her work is much appreciated, but any errors in the index should be placed at the door of the second author who prepared final index copy when Joan had to return to Australia.

CHARLES T. MEADOW
PAULINE (ATHERTON) COCHRANE

Philadelphia, Pennsylvania
Syracuse, New York
March 1981

Contents

Chapter 8

Chapter 9

Chapter 10

Chapter 11

Chapter 12

Appendix A

Appendix B

Appendix C

Basics of
Online Searching

One

Introduction

1.1 SOME BASIC DEFINITIONS

The purpose of this book is to tell you about searching *data bases* with the aid of a computer. We are emphasizing *bibliographic data bases* and the computer environment of *online, interactive searching*.

A *bibliographic data base* contains a file of document descriptions that are records you can use for deciding whether to search for the document itself. The documents, as we define them, may be journal articles, reports, patents, books, or the like. The descriptive information in these records contains such information as title, author, publisher and date, and subject information, which may include subject classification *terms* or key words and may also include an abstract. We use the word *term* to mean any one of the descriptive elements except title or abstract. A *descriptor* is a special term cited to describe subject content that is assigned to the document by an indexer.

Online searching means that the searcher is in direct communication with the search program on a computer. More technically, it means that the *terminal*, the device the searcher uses to send messages to and recieve them from the computer, is connected either directly or by telephone. An *interactive* search is one in which the searcher and computer talk back and forth to each other, exchanging information and asking questions. A computer-based search system cannot really be *interactive* without being *online* because if it is not online the exchange of messages would take too long—like exchanging messages by telegram instead of by telephone conversation. Since the two characteristics are so often found together, the word *online*, in common usage, has taken on the meaning of interactive as well. We'll get more into the technicalities later.

The field is only about a decade old, and it is growing fast. Some of the data bases we now deal with are not restricted to bibliographic information, but may contain statistical information as well. Some day, we can look forward to

1

searching and retrieving the entire document, instead of just a summary description.

If you are not familiar with the terms used in this field, or the names of the companies, services, products, and major users involved in it, you might consult such publications as *Online, Online Review, Data Base,* or *The Information Manager.* Most of the companies in the online bibliographic searching business advertise in these journals. Their free brochures (and books like this) should help you venture into this field, which is moving very rapidly. Many of these companies exhibit at professional meetings such as the American Library Association annual conference.

In *The Information Manager,* for example, you would be greeted by a great array of advertisements that announce many *information systems* and *services, data banks* and *data base suppliers,* and even firms of *information specialists* who are expert in "vocabularies for indexing systems." There is an expanding job market in this field.

One ad describes online searching in this way:

> *"Computerized literature searching*—locate meaningful information in minutes; organize the results in easy to read form; speed delivery of complete source documents, and pay only for usage, . . . access worldwide literature in a broad range of subject areas using a *terminal* and *telephone* located in your own organization."*

Another ad in this same issue does not mention computers, but it shows a picture of library stacks with a *terminal* superimposed and it speaks of their "information retrieval system" as the "world's leading *online retrieval service,* which offers more than 70 *data bases* and more than 18,000,000 *document references,*" and "for libraries, we offer many advantages."

Names like Lockheed's DIALOG retrieval service, System Development Corporation's (SDC) Search Service ORBIT retrieval system, Enviroline, CIS, and the Information Bank crop up all through this trade publication "intended for people involved in integrating many of the various information handling technologies into a total system."

Hopefully, this book will enable you to *read and understand* the ads and articles in journals such as *Online,* or *The Information Manager,* as well as help you become a self-sufficient online searcher.

1.2 SEARCH SERVICES

The organization that provides the computer and supporting services that enable online searching to be done is called a *search service.* These are often private companies (vendors), sometimes government agencies, and university

---

Information Manager, August 1978.

centers. The data bases generally are created by another organization, again a private firm, government agency, or professional abstracting group. They provide their data bases to the search services on a lease and/or royalty basis. Examples of data base suppliers are Chemical Abstracts Service, a branch of the American Chemical Society, the Central Abstracting and Indexing Service of the American Petroleum Institute, and the Educational Resources Information Center (ERIC) of the U.S. Office of Education. Chapter 6 and Appendix C give details about other data bases and their documentation.

The search service provides the computer whose use can be shared simultaneously among many users. They assemble data bases from many suppliers (Lockheed Information Systems' DIALOG search service offers over 100 data bases), make them available to users, and provide supporting services, such as training, documentation, and consulting. The search service also serves as agents for arranging the communications between user and the search computer. The major online search services used by libraries and other information centers are the following:

1   DIALOG (Lockheed Information Systems).
2   ORBIT (System Development Corporation—SDC).
3   BRS (Bibliographic Retrieval Services, Inc.).
4   MEDLINE (National Library of Medicine).
5   New York Times Information Bank (New York Times).
6   LEXIS.

In this book we will try to be *general* in our descriptions of how to search, but we will *illustrate with examples* from DIALOG, ORBIT, and BRS.

The major buyers of a search service today are libraries—academic, special, public, and even school libraries. They may resell the service to their clients, provide it free, or share the costs. Some, but not all, libraries encourage their users to learn to search for themselves. Most, however, employ highly trained specialists who may be called by such titles as search specialist, information specialist, or data systems librarian. These *intermediaries* assist the user or perform the search for the user. Our emphasis in this book is on the process of online bibliographic searching, which includes the use of a professional intermediary between the search service and the user.

1.3   USING ONLINE SEARCH SERVICES

Promotional brochures and posters around a library's reference desk usually point the user to the staff responsible for online bibliographic searching. These signs may advertise "Computer Assisted Research," "Online Data Base Searching," "Bibliographic Counseling Services," "Custom-Made Bibliography Service," or "Information Retrieval." The service is usually considered an extension of traditional reference service and may be available at different service points, for example, the Chemistry Library, the Medical Center Library, and the Reference Department. The brochures usually describe the data bases which can be searched as well as the search service they will be using.

If a fee is to be charged for the service, this will be explained to the user beforehand because the size of the fee may depend on whether the library is trying for full or partial cost recovery and what limits the user will put on the data bases to be searched, on the size of putout, or on the time online.

Occasionally, libraries will offer their users some type of bibliographic instruction. In these classes, if they do perform online searches, the libraries will demonstrate this service and explain all the details.

Besides libraries, there are information service agencies or "information brokers" in most large cities that offer to perform online searching for a fee. They are probably listed in the yellow pages of the telephone directory. They operate in much the same way as the library service described earlier.

1.4 SOME VOCABULARY

Like all new fields, online searching specifically and information management in general (or information storage and retrieval as it used to be called) have terminological problems. Many words are used interchangeably. Some *concepts* have several *names* attached to them. Many "synonyms" have been derived from different aspects or developments. If we do not define all concepts adequately, maybe our Tables of Equivalents (Table 1.1 and 1.2) will help you when you read other authors' work.

The tables should help you see how synonymous various terms are. Strictly speaking, for example, *computer, interactive,* and *online* are not synonyms because the latter two words describe aspects of a computer system, but in the field of *online bibliographic retrieval,* which is the focus of this book, these words are used interchangeably as *adjectives* to describe a computer-based *system* or *service* in the field.

The intention of the words in column 1 of Table 1.1 is to imply that the service or system (column 2) is computer-based, using the most modern form of computer system, which allows the user to *interact* or even interrupt the computer while using it and to stay connected (*online*) rather than submit a job and sign off, having to wait to receive the finished job offline later. So some authors use the adjective *online,* others use *interactive,* and still others say *automated* or *computer-based.*

Each column of Table 1.1 contains "synonymous" terms. A word from one column can be combined with a word or phrase in an adjacent column to form a larger concept. Recognizing a term in a column that you can define may help you to scan the column to see what other terms are near synonyms. For example, an article on the subject could contain the following sentences: (1)

Table 1.1   Table of Quasi-Equivalent Terms Used to Describe Concepts in Online Bibliographic Retrieval

(1)	(2)	(3)	(4)	(5)	(6)
Machine	System	Data base	Documents	Data elements	Descriptors
Computer	Service	Data bank	References	Fields	Words
Computer-based	Search	File	Records	Information fields	Text
Automated	Search service	Indexes	Bibliographic records	Citation elements	Search terms
Computerized	Retrieval	Data set	Items	Access points	Element labels
Online	Information system	(Library catalog)	Data	Searchable fields	Keywords
Interactive	Retrieval system	(Abstracting service)	Unit records	Record structure	Controlled language
Mechanized	Retrieval service	(Book index)	(Catalog cards)	Tags	Concepts
Remote terminal	Bibliographic retrieval	(Literature)		(Catalog entries)	Free text/natural language
	Literature searching			(Elements of a catalog card)	(Subject headings)
	Literature service				
	Vendor				
	Supplier				
	Information retrieval				
	(Reference service)				

Table 1.1 (continued)

(7)	(8)	(9)	(10)	(11)	(12)
Dictionary	Commands	Intermediary	User	Search	Output
Vocabulary	Dialogues	Online searcher	End-user	Request topic	Search results
Basic Index	Functions	Search analyst	Searcher		Source documents
Inverted file	Search language	Information specialist	Requester		(Library collection)
Thesaurus	Computer software	(Reference librarian)	Client		(Books)
List	Protocols		(Library patron)		(Journal articles)
Search words	Search logic				(Reports)
(Library catalog entries)	Set combination				
(Indexing system)	Set of search statements				
	System features				
	Search strategy				
	(Catalog search)				

Note:

A Each column (1–12) lists terms or phrases which are used ***almost interchangeably*** by diverse authors writing in this field.

B In the literature of the field, words in one column have been combined with words in adjacent columns to form wider concepts, or provide some detail about the overall system being described. For example, words in columns 1–2 label the field overall; words in columns 3–4 describe what is *in* the system; words in columns 5–7 describe what is in those files and from what they are derived; words in column 8–11 describe what is done by whom for whom; and words in column 12 describe the output.

C Words in brackets link this "current" list with older terms from library science literature which are quasi-synonymous. For example, a *data base* or *file* (Column 3) is similar to a library's catalog or a book's index; a *descriptor* (column 6) is like a subject heading; *searchable field* (column 5) is like a catalog entry; an *intermediary* (column 9) is like a reference librarian, and so on.

6

Table 1.2 **Examples of Synonymous Terms and Phrases in Combination**

Column Number (see Table 1.1)	Explanation of Concept	Examples of Synonymous Phrases
A Concept 1 + 2:	Name of the field or service	A1 Computer-based search service A2 Automated information retrieval A3 Online vendor or supplier
B Concept 3 + 4:	What is *in* service	B1 File *of* bibliographic records B2 Data base *of* documents
C Concept 5 + 6 + 7:	What is in the File and how is it accessed	C1 Fields *of* search terms *from* basic index C2 Access points of keywords *from* inverted file
D Concept 8—11:	What is done by whom *for* whom	D1 Search logic is developed *by* intermediary *for* the end-user's topic D2 System features allow the information specialist to handle the client's topic

computer-based (2) *literature searching device* (3) with *data bases* of (4) *bibliographic records* (5) assessed by means of (5) *descriptors* from a (6) *thesaurus* as well as other (7) *searchable fields.* (8) The *search language* allows the (9) *intermediary* to aid the (10) *end-user* find (11) *source documents.*

These two sentences could be written using other terms or phrases in each of the 11 columns and would have the same meaning for some readers, slightly different to others. (See Table 1.2) The bracketed words in each column are of an older vintage representing the world of libraries before computers.

If this doesn't totally confuse you, find some consolation in the fact that the much abused term *information* itself has been around for 600 years without being adequately defined. (It was first used in 1387, according to the *Oxford English Dictionary*.) Back then it was spelled "informacioun"! There are now many definitions of this single word and surrounding concepts.

The field of information is undergoing many changes each decade. With home computers, computer stores, videodiscs, and Viewdata systems coming into being, we can expect even more rapid changes from now to the end of the century.

About all we can hope to do in this book is hold on to the tail of this whirlwind field. For us, in this book, our definitions and explanations will be primarily about *bibliographic information*, that is, systems that access citations or references to literature (books, journal articles, reports, and the like). However, we do not mean to limit ourselves to information about printed matter alone. Bibliographic information can refer to films, recordings, phonotapes, and other media as well.

The computer-based retrieval systems we will be discussing can be used, with some additional or different steps, to access *numeric data* as well, but it is not our primary intent to describe all information retrieval systems. Our focus in this book is the focus of the present bibliographic retrieval services. The world of online information services is expanding rapidly and we know *online bibliographic retrieval services* are probably a precursor to *online fact retrieval* and *online question-answering* systems. So before you read this book, know that someone may be writing a sequel to it. In the meantime, we hope this book will help to describe what some people have called the "online revolution."

This book can be described as being in four parts. After this introduction, Chapters 2–4 explain the preliminary operations on the terminal and elementary skills needed for online searching. This is followed by Chapters 5–8, which introduce the basic elements that one works with—the files (or databases) and the command language in the computer-based system. The last part goes into more detail about the search language and system features and provides guidance in search strategy. The appendices contain brief descriptions of some of the most popular files and retrieval systems.

Two

Elements of
Interactive Searching

2.1 HOW DATA BASES ARE ORGANIZED

You cannot be an accomplished library researcher without a good understanding of how books are organized; what kind of books, journals, and other documents are available in a library; how these are arranged; and what catalogs and indexes are available to assist you in searching. Similarly, in searching with a computer it is necessary to know something about how the records you are searching are organized: what smaller information elements the records consist of and how they are defined, represented (codes, abbreviations, syntax), and ordered relative to each other in storage.

To use a library's card catalog you need to know what information elements (such as title, author, subject) may be found as access points in the alphabetic sequence of cards in the file. Most users know they normally cannot look up a Library of Congress classification in the catalog, or a publisher, unless the publisher's name is also a subject or title. But, *classification* and *publisher* are elements of the record printed on the card. Thus we know that if we want to search the card catalog on what McGraw-Hill has published on computers, we must start our search with *computers*, not with *McGraw-Hill*.

Computer search systems have analogous restrictions, but not necessarily the same ones. Any bibliographic record may be thought of as divided into *elements* or *fields*. A record to be stored in a computer has approximately the same fields as a catalog card, although the typical entry in a mechanized information retrieval system has more information than a catalog card, which permits finer distinctions to be made between documents on closely related subjects and hence enables you to separate them from each other. The computer record often contains an abstract, which is hardly ever present in a catalog card.

Figure 2.1 shows the contents of a typical record in a machine bibliographic file. In Chapter 6 we will present more information about record content and structure.

In addition to what is in a record, we need to know something about how records are ordered. A collection of records, in data processing terms, is called a *data set* or *file*. We shall use the latter term. *Data base* is a term without a strict and commonly used definition, but we may take it to refer to a set of related files that are stored and searched together. For example, the ERIC data base consists of several files differing from each other in subject matter and source of material, but all related to education. *Data bank* is even less well defined. Some treat this term as a synonym for data base; some use it to refer to a data base or file of numeric data or other forms of nonbibliographic information.

Online bibliographic files are usually in order by date or by order of entry of records into the file, which is closely correlated with date. New records are generally added to the end of a file and, depending on how these are handled before being introduced into the computer, this may or may not put the resulting machine file in strict date order. Even if a file is said to be in date order, the user must become sensitive to such questions as *date of what?* Publication? Receipt of the record? Entry of the record into the file? Announcement of the document in a printed abstract journal? Do later dates precede or follow earlier ones?

ID NO.- E1791187122   987122
METHANOL-BASED HEAT PUMPS FOR STORAGE OF SOLAR THERMAL ENERGY.
Anon
EIC Corp, Newton, Mass
Energy Technol: Proc of Therm Energy Storage Contract Inf Exch Meet, 3rd Annu, Springfield, Va, Dec 5-6 1978 Organized by Sandia Lab, Livermore Calif for DOE (CONF-781231), Washington, DC, 1978. Available from NTIS, Springfield, Va p 425-432
The basis of the heat pump storage system is a chemical reaction that proceeds in one direction at high temperature and in the opposite direction at low temperatures. A gas-solid reaction maximizes storage energy density and provides ready separation of the chemical products. Methanol is particularly suited as the vapor due to its low freezing point, high entropy vaporization, and relative freedom from hazards. Twenty inorganic salts were screened in a specially designed thermogravimetric analyzer (TGA) employing fixed $CH//3OH$ vapor pressure and slowly varying temperatures. Appreciable reaction was found for a dozen salts, and four salts were found to have thermodynamic and kinetic behavior approximately suitable for use in a heat pump: $MgCl//2$, $FeBr//2$, $CoBr//2$, and $CaCl//2$. The use of the reaction between $CaCl//2$ and $CH//3OH$ vapor in a thermally activated heat pump for solar storage, heating and cooling appears promising for residential use. 2 refs.
DESCRIPTORS: (*HEAT PUMP SYSTEMS, *Design), (SALTS, Energy Storage), (HEATING, Solar), CARD ALERT: 643, 505, 901

Figure 2.1 A typical record in a bibliographic data base. Illustrated is a single record from Compendex, the data base of Engineering Index, Inc. Data elements include document identification number, title, author (in this case, anonymous), corporate source, publication information, abstract, and descriptors.

If records are ordered by date (any of the dates questioned above) and you want to search on an author's name, it would clearly be a tedious thing to search every record of a file, from oldest to newest, to see if it contains a work by the given author. More than tedious, the search through a million records, a number not uncommon in modern computer-based bibliographic files, takes large amounts of time and money. Therefore, there is usually a second file generated, called an *inverted, dictionary,* or *index file.* It is in order by word, term, or descriptor and, for each word, tells in which documents that word is found. While the records of the main file appear as shown in Figure 2.1, a dictionary file will be similar to what is shown in Figure 2.2. A data base may be said to consist of a *main file* of bibliographic records and its associated *dictionary file.*

It is possible to put every word or code from every field of the original record into the dictionary, (except for such common words as *the, and, but,* . . .). More commonly, search systems select only the more useful fields for inclusion in the dictionary. Obviously, you as a searcher must know which fields are searchable in the dictionary, just as the card catalog searcher must know for what kinds of terms entries are generated. There are probably as many variations in record structure and dictionary make-up as there are combinations of search services and data bases.

NO:	1
TI:	ALGEBRA
AU:	BOOLE
SU:	MATHEMATICS

NO:	2
TI:	BIOLOGY
AU:	DARWIN
SU:	EVOLUTION

NO:	3
TI:	CALCULUS
AU:	COURANT
SU:	MATHEMATICS

(a)

ALGEBRA	1
BIOLOGY	2
CALCULUS	3
DARWIN	2
EVOLUTION	2
MATHEMATICS	1 3

(b)

Figure 2.2 The use of a dictionary file simplifies and speeds the process of searching for the occurrence of a particular word or field value, by permitting an alphabetic search for the word, itself, rather than a full search of every record of the main file. (a) A main file consisting of records containing a record number (NO), title (TI), author's name (AU) and subject (SU). (b.) The inverted dictionary file, which lists the contents of selected fields together with the numbers of the records in which the values occur.

2.2 CONNECTING USER AND DATA BASE

Prior to beginning a search, there is a certain amount of what we might call overhead work required that is not directly related to the search, but is necessary in order to perform one. A user employs a communications *terminal*, a communications *network*, and the *search computer*. The terminal (from *terminus*—end—the end of a communications network) is an electric-typewriter-like device linked, as we shall see, to the computer through the telephone system. The keyboard resembles that of a typewriter, but the medium for displaying information may be paper or an electronic display screen or video display unit, much like a television screen. Other aspects of terminals are discussed in Chapter 4.

The terminal is linked to the telephone system, and then it is either directly linked to the search computer or it makes use of a special combination of telephone lines and small computers called a *digital communications network*, also to be described more fully in Chapter 4. Most searching places relatively low demands on a communication system, transmitting alphabetical and numeric characters at a rate slower than the maximum the system could carry. The line connecting a computer and a user terminal is often idle while the user thinks about what he has retrieved or the computer works at carrying out a user request. Because of this low rate of usage, the network, through its computers, is able to combine the messages of many users onto a single communication circuit. Thus over a single telephone line, say from Philadelphia to Los Angeles, the network can appear to carry many messages simultaneously, because each user ties up so little of the system's capacity. Basic network concepts are illustrated in Figure 2.3. This lowers the cost of

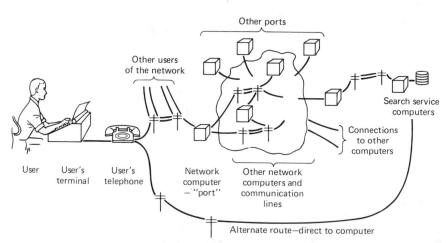

Figure 2.3   Basic digital communications network.

communication and makes possible the economical use of computers thousands of miles distant from the end-user. At present, digital communications (that is, the transmission of codes for letters and numbers, rather than the sound of the human voice speaking words) costs less for long distance callers through such a network than does a conventional, single-user telephone call, which ties up a circuit for the duration of the call.

The computer operated by the search service has stored within it all the data bases the service offers. Its computer programs receive user requests and carry them out. *How* the computer functions is outside the purview of this book, but is covered in references 2–5. The computer, like the communications network, must serve a number of users simultaneously. The cost of operating a computer for a single user at a time would be prohibitive. Multiple simultaneous use of a computer is called *time sharing*, a procedure that makes online searching, as well as many other computer services, an economic possibility.

The user tends to be unaware of all the bustling, sharing activity of which he is a part. Generally, he is aware only of his own use of the computer. The network and other users are what computer scientists call *transparent*, not visible to or able to be sensed by the user. Experienced users learn, though, to notice that at some times the computer does not respond to requests as rapidly as at others. This is usually the result of crowding—a large number of people using the computer at one time.

There is a certain ritual to be followed in order to link the user's terminal with the computer. Roughly, it is analogous to calling a friend in a large office through the telephone system. You dial a telephone number, not of the search computer, but of one of the network's small computers in or near your city. Treating this computer somewhat as the telephone operator at your friend's office, you "tell" it whom you want to "talk" to—all in code. The network computer then connects you to the appropriate computer, to which you now identify yourself. You do this by giving a password, rather than your name. The password identifies you as a valid user and implies authorization for the search service to bill you for the computer time you are about to use. You will also be billed for the use of the network through your search service. The network, in other words, treats the search service as its customer, and the search service resells network services to the consumer. Figure 2.4 shows a log of the conversation between a user and a network computer up to the point where the search service computer takes over.

When your terminal is finally connected to the computer you want to use (networks usually serve many different computer services; connection to the network is not the same as connection to the computer) and you are identified as a valid user, your overhead functions are completed. The actual search begins with you telling the computer what file you want to search. Then, you are ready to begin searching.

```
① TELENET
215 8D

② TERMINAL=

③ @C 415 20

④ 415 20 CONNECTED

⑤ ENTER YOUR DIALOG PASSWORD
Ж Ж Ж Ж Ж Ж    LOGON Filel Tue 29apr80 10:15:40 Port65F
```

Figure 2.4 The log-on conversation. This is a transcript of the conversation that results in a user linking his terminal to DIALOG via the TELENET network. (1) TELENET identifies itself and the particular line by which you are connected to it (line 8D in area code 215). (2) TELENET asks for a code, which does not print, to identify the type terminal in use. (3) The user, again in code, identifies the computer wanted, computer number 20, in area code 415. (4) When TELENET establishes the link to DIALOG, it tells us that the requested computer is connected. (5) DIALOG begins to send messages, here asking for the user's password.

2.3   SELECTING TERMS

Customarily, an online search begins with the user looking up information on individual terms or phrases. These may be subject terms such as descriptors assigned by an indexer, author names, titles, or individual words occurring in a title or abstract or other field of the record. There are two ways to seek and retrieve term information: look up a term in a dictionary or thesaurus or search for all records containing the term, retrieving those that do. Those are shown in Figure 2.5

The results of a dictionary search vary from search service to search service and data base to data base. Generally, however, you get a list of terms, some preceding and some following your term in alphabetical order, together with a count of how many times that term appears in the main file—and how many records contain it. You will not be shown the list of record numbers, just a count of the list's length. There may also be information about related terms. It is the subject interrelation of terms that characterizes a thesaurus. If there is a thesaurus, then you can find out not only what terms are spelled like your search term in the alphabetic sequence, but which ones have similar meanings. Figure 2.6 shows the result of a dictionary search of several different search services.

A dictionary search merely tells you something about the terms you search on. The next step is to retrieve all records containing that term, a necessary step if you eventually want to browse through these records or print them at your terminal. If you ask for retrieval on the basis of a single term, a *set* is created that consists of all the records meeting your search criterion; that is, this set contains the term you specify. At least, that is a good way to visualize what a set is. What actually happens is more likely to be that the machine will

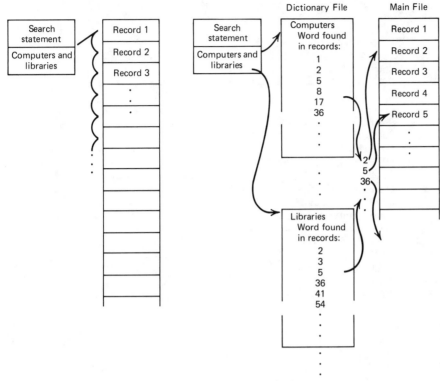

Figure 2.5 Basic methods of search. (*a*) *Serial search.* Each record of the file is compared with the terms in the search statement. The entire file must be seached to insure that all records in it will be retrieved. This method is simple in logic and execution, but requires the searching of a large number of records. (*b*) *Inverted file search.* The terms in the search statement are looked up in a dictionary file, whose records tell which records in the main file contain these words. The lists of records are combined and only a few of the records in the first list are retrieved from the main file. This method is more complex but significantly reduces the number of records that must be examined.

retrieve a list of *record numbers,* rather than the complete records. This list is what is set aside and you are told the set number (sequential number of the set in the order created, first one, second two, and so on) and how many record numbers there are. A typical sequence (see Figure 2.7) might be to search the dictionary for *computer* and as a result discover that there are no, or very few, records containing that term, but that the more commonly used term is the plural form, *computers.* Then, you would create a set of the numbers of the records containing the term *computers.* You might then go on to look up *library* or *libraries* in the dictionary. Had you looked up either *computer* or *library* in the printed thesaurus that accompanies the data base, you might have discovered the correct form of the term without need for the computer

```
? expand computers

Ref        Index-term                                                            Type Items RT
E1         COMPUTERIZED VOCATIONAL
              INFORMATION SYSTEM------------------------------------------------------    4
E2         COMPUTERIZING-------------------------------------------------------------   22
E3         COMPUTERLESS -------------------------------------------------------------    2
E4         COMPUTERLIKE -------------------------------------------------------------    1
E5         COMPUTERN-----------------------------------------------------------------    2
E6         -COMPUTERS---------------------------------------------------------------- 3879    31
E7         COMPUTERS ASSISTED
              PLACEMENT SCHEME -----------------------------------------------------    1
E8         COMPUTERS IN EDUCATION----------------------------------------------------    1
E9         COMPUTERS . . . YOU-------------------------------------------------------    1
E10        COMPUTERSPELLED ----------------------------------------------------------    1
E11        COMPUTERUNTERRICHT -------------------------------------------------------    1
E12        COMPUTERUNTERSTUTZEN------------------------------------------------------    1
E13        COMPUTES------------------------------------------------------------------   32
E14        COMPUTEST ----------------------------------------------------------------    1
E15        COMPUTING ----------------------------------------------------------------  663
E16        COMPUTOR -----------------------------------------------------------------    2
E17        COMPUTORIZED--------------------------------------------------------------    1
E18        COMPUTRAC-----------------------------------------------------------------    2
                                                                                      -more-

? expand e6

Ref        Index-term                                                            Type Items RT
R1         COMPUTERS-----------------------------------------------------------------  3879    31
R2         ANALOG COMPUTERS--------------------------------------------------------N     62     3
R3         DIGITAL COMPUTERS ------------------------------------------------------N    163     3
R4         EQUIPMENT --------------------------------------------------------------B  11428    67
R5         ARCHITECTURAL RESEARCH-------------------------------------------------R     96    11
R6         ARTIFICIAL INTELLIGENCE -----------------------------------------------R    153     9
R7         AUTOMATION ------------------------------------------------------------R   1787    20
R8         COMPUTERASSISTED
              INSTRUCTION--------------------------------------------------------R   3960    18
R9         COMPUTER BASED
              LABORATORIES-------------------------------------------------------R    143     2
R10        COMPUTER ORIENTED
              PROGRAMS ----------------------------------------------------------R   2188     9
R11        COMPUTER OUTPUT
              MICROFILM ---------------------------------------------------------R     69     6
R12        COMPUTER PROGRAMS -----------------------------------------------------R   2815     8
R13        COMPUTER SCIENCE ------------------------------------------------------R   1003    14
R14        COMPUTER SCIENCE
              EDUCATION ---------------------------------------------------------R    514     9
R15        CYBERNETICS------------------------------------------------------------R    273    17
                                                                                      -more-
?
```

Figure 2.6 Dictionary searching. DIALOG gives the most elaborate display. Shown here is a request for information on *computers*, which shows 3879 documents under this term and 31 related terms. A second command, *expand e6* asks for more information about the term on line e6, and the resulting display shows some of the 31 terms related to *computers*.

```
SS 1 /C?
USER:
nbr computer-assist

PROG:
POSTINGS              TERM
     1               COMPUTER WORD PROCESSING/IT
     1               *COMPUTER WORD PROCESSING/IT
     2               COMPUTER-ASSISTED INSTRUCTION/IT
     1               *COMPUTER-ASSISTED INSTRUCTION/IT
     1               COMPUTER-ASSISTED REVIEW LESSONS ON/IT
UP N OR DOWN N?

USER:
down 6

PROG:
POSTINGS              TERM
     1               COMPUTERANWENDUNGEN/TI
     1               COMPUTERANWENDUNGEN/BI
     1               COMPUTEREINSATZ/TI
     1               COMPUTEREINSATZ/BI
     1               COMPUTEREZED/BI
     1               COMPUTERIMAGES/BI
UP N OR DOWN N?

USER:
```

Figure 2.6 (continued)   The ORBIT dictionary search command is *nbr* (neighbor). It retrieves five lines of data showing how often the term occurred in various fields (IT means index term). The question "Up *n* or down *n*" asks the user if he wishes to see more information and in which direction he wishes to move—terms preceding those shown or following them.

```
    3__:  r o o t  c o m p i l
          COMPIL$
R1        COMPILABLE                                4 DOCUMENTS
R2        COMPILATED                                1 DOCUMENT
R3        COMPILATION                             368 DOCUMENTS
R4        COMPILATIONS                             38 DOCUMENTS
R5        COMPILATORY                               1 DOCUMENT
R6        COMPILE                                 100 DOCUMENTS
R7        COMPILED                                499 DOCUMENTS
R8        COMPILER                                431 DOCUMENTS
R9        COMPILER'S                                2 DOCUMENTS
R10       COMPILERS                               185 DOCUMENTS
R11       COMPILES                                 14 DOCUMENTS
R12       COMPILING                                94 DOCUMENTS
```

Figure 2.6 (continued)   The BRS command *root* gives a result similar to ORBIT's *nbr* command.

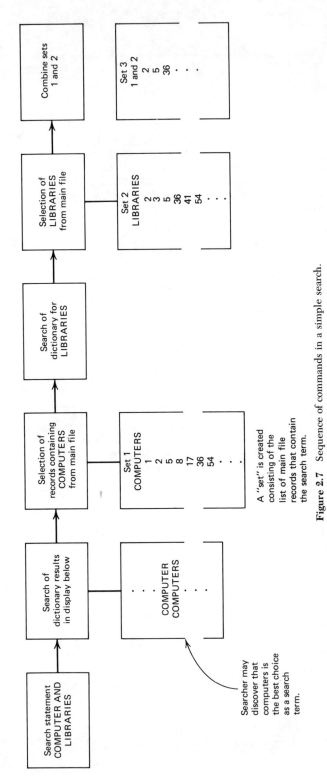

Figure 2.7 Sequence of commands in a simple search.

18

dictionary search, and you might have created the set directly. The printed form tells you the correct term to use; the computer form of the dictionary tells you that, plus how many times each term occurs, and how often terms with similar spellings occur. All this is described in more detail in Chapter 7.

2.4   COMBINATORIAL LOGIC

In Section 2.3 we discussed how to create sets based on individual descriptors or terms. What to many people is the heart of online searching comes when we combine these single-term sets. Suppose we have created a set based on the term *computers,* another based on *libraries,* and yet another based on *circulation.* If the intended subject were the use of computers in library circulation systems, we might well assume that each of the three descriptors must be present in the record for any relevant document. Thus we would ask the computer to find all record numbers that are in each of the three individual sets, as shown schematically in Figure 2.8.

We might have been interested in the use of computers in library

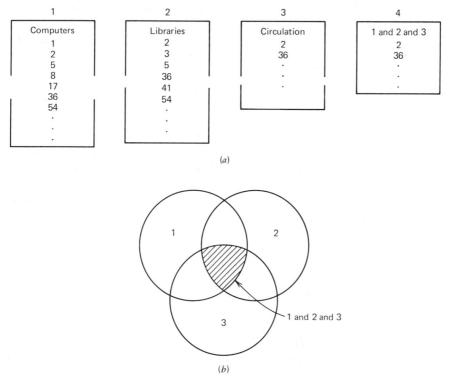

(a)

(b)

Figure 2.8   A tabular *(a)* and graphic *(b)* portrayal of the concept of the intersection of three sets.

circulation *or* reference work. Then we would want to insure that *both computers and libraries* were in any record selected as well as *either circulation or reference*. This is illustrated in Figure 2.9. Notice that combining sets creates new sets just as the initial selection of individual terms does. Once a set is created, whether by specification of a term, by combination of existing sets, or by a combination of these techniques, the new set has a set number and can be used to make future combinations, if desired.

Anyone who has ever searched files of any kind has certainly performed these kinds of operations. They are almost second nature to a librarian. Sometimes, when we stop to think about how we do some ordinary task, such as walking, hitting a tennis ball, or combining file sets, it suddenly seems complex and mysterious. Set combination is made all the more so because there is a mathematical way to express these concepts and the name of the concept and appearance of the symbols can be intimidating to those not used to mathematics.

In mathematics *Boolean algebra* (after George Boole, 1815–1864) is concerned with relationships among sets and operations upon them. We will introduce the operations of Boolean algebra in Chapter 7. We will try to make as little use of unfamiliar symbols as possible, but some use is helpful in searching.

If we want selected records to be in *both* sets A and B, then we define a new set which is the *intersection* of A and B. Verbally, the operation of intersection is described using the word *and.* We say the new set C is made up of A *and* B. If we want to create a set of these records that are either in A or in B or both, we call this the *union* of sets A and B.

When you have in mind possible synonyms for some term, the thing to do is form their union or, in the jargon of searching, "*or*" them together, as *computer or data processor or automation*. The terms need not be synonymous in all contexts, just the one you have in mind. The terms *computer* and *automation* are not synonyms, but either might lead to documents on the automation of library circulation systems, because a computer is usually at the heart of such a system.

When you have different concepts and want material that is about all of them use, "*and.*" For example, *computer and library* combines two dissimilar terms. These two rules are somewhat oversimplified, but are intended to serve as a start.

The term *strategy* is sometimes applied to a set combination expression, such as *A and B or C*. We feel this is a misnomer. Our ideas on strategy are found in Chapter 12. We think the proper word to describe a combination is *expression*, which is used in mathematics and in computer programming to describe exactly this concept, or *search formulation*.

So far, we have talked about choosing a file, searching a dictionary, creating some sets on the basis of simple terms, and combining the original sets into other sets based on a combination of term presence or absence. It is not always immediately apparent what combination of sets will best achieve a

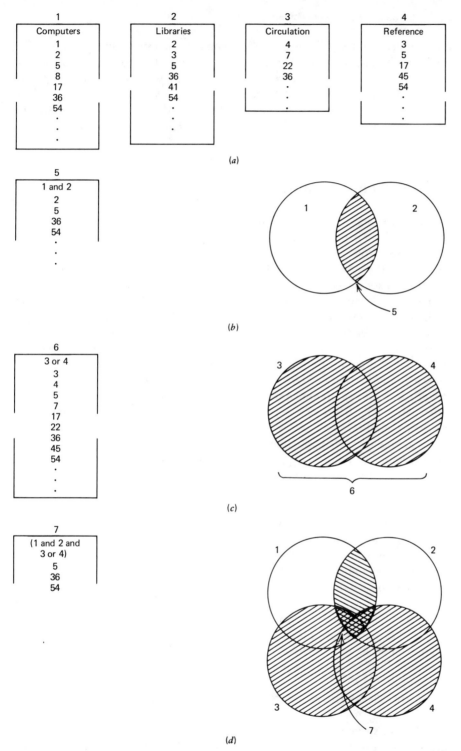

1	2	3	4
Computers	Libraries	Circulation	Reference
1	2	4	3
2	3	7	5
5	5	22	17
8	36	36	45
17	41	.	54
36	54	.	.
54	.	.	.
.	.		.
.	.		
.			

(a)

5
1 and 2
2
5
36
54
.
.
.

(b)

6
3 or 4
3
4
5
7
17
22
36
45
54
.
.
.

(c)

7
(1 and 2 and 3 or 4)
5
36
54

(d)

Figure 2.9 The intersection (b), union (c) and intersection (7) of an intersection with a union (d) of the sets, shown in (a).

21

search objective. Usually, several tries are made, each successive trial using the results of the previous one. This is why we use adjectives such as *iterative* and *interactive* to describe the process. Sooner or later, we have to stop relying on our intuitive idea of what combination is best or of how many records should be in a set. We want to look at some of the records of a set, to browse the collection—a fine, old, precomputer library concept just as important now as it ever was.

2.5   BROWSING AND PRINTING

One of the major advantages of online searching is that you do not have to be content with an expression of set relationships or a count of how many records are in a set. You can at any time examine the records that constitute a set. (Recall that the actual set is a collection of *record numbers.* Saying that records constitute a set is a convenient usage that is not literally correct.) Suppose, for example, you have created a set consisting of 120 records, defined as consisting of the terms *computer* **and** *library.* Now you would like to see whether any of these articles actually suit your needs and, if so, which are the best ones. All search systems have commands that enable the user to display selected records and to select those portions of the record to be displayed. Usually, records will appear in inverse date order, most recent first, so that asking for the first five records in a set gets the most recent five. Some computer systems permit you to specify which fields of a record you want to see; others offer a variety of predetermined formats.

There is always a distinction between printing or displaying information on your terminal (online) and printing at the search service's computer center (offline). Local viewing on your own terminal is done for reviewing, to verify that you are getting what you want, or to get ideas on how to improve set definition and how to ensure fastest delivery of your results. However, printing of a large number of records in this way can be expensive. For this reason, the general convention is that once you have decided you have the set you want, have its records printed at the computer center and mailed to you. Printing at the computer center is done at a much higher rate of speed and lower cost than is possible on a remote terminal and does not require use of the telephone network.

Browsing can be expensive, but its skilled use is required and can be expected to pay off in terms of better quality retrieval and possibly lower overall charges in order to achieve an objective.

2.6   VARIATIONS IN COMMAND LANGUAGES

In this brief survey of interactive searching, we have avoided use of any actual commands, except in the figures, to illustrate principles. These will be introduced later. One reason for avoiding them now is the unfortunate fact that all the major systems use different command languages for users to communicate with the computers. It is approximately like the situation we might have if every manufacturer of electric light bulbs or lamps used his own version of the diameter and thread pitch of the base of the bulb. All the search services offer just about the same service and perform about the same functions. The differences may appear major to some and relatively insignificant to others, but they can be confusing. Therefore, our approach is to present search concepts separately in terms of *function* to describe how some of the search services allow you to request particular functions and then, in the appendices, to provide detail on the various languages.

2.7 THE COST OF ONLINE SEARCHING

How expensive is online searching and how can ordinary people afford to use a large computer that might be 3000 miles away? We have partially answered these questions: multiple, simultaneous use of telephone circuits and time sharing of the computer reduce the cost per minute to each user. The net cost is affordable to many individuals and organizations. The general trend in search services has been for prices to hold fairly steady, even in a generally inflationary economy. The same is true for computers and communications, independently. Network communications costs have tended to go down with increasing sophistication of the technology.

The absolute cost of searching varies and we can only give the major components of cost and a range of prices. The constituents of cost are:

1 Terminals (equipment, maintenance, supplies).
2 Computer operation, as described above.
3 Communications circuits, the use of which was described above.
4 Acquisition of the data bases. Search services normally pay, and pass on, a royalty to the compilers of a data base, just as publishers do.
5 Supporting services. Search services must load data bases into their computers and offer training courses, users' manuals, and telephone troubleshooting consultation.

The user usually pays the search service on the basis of *connect time,* the actual amount of time the user's terminal is connected to the service's computer through a communications network. During some of this time the computer is working furiously on the user's requests, searching files and setting up sets. At other times, it is idle while the user reads displayed records or merely thinks about what to do next. All these variations are averaged in arriving at the price charged, which is then rendered in terms of connect hours, or portions thereof, including communications. Because royalties paid to data base suppliers vary considerably, as do the amount and quality of support services, the rate the user pays for different data bases also varies considerably.

Typically, for commercial services, the minimum rate is about $15 per hour and the maximum around $125 per hour. Rates for government subsidized systems, such as MEDLINE, may be as low as $8−10 per hour. Communications, through a data communications network, may add $5 to 10 per hour. The time required to perform a search is also a variable. In many libraries, a search will be done in less than five minutes under normal circumstances, thus costing roughly one to ten dollars. Such a search may involve little more than defining a few sets, combining them, and displaying a few records. A search involving a great deal of browsing and redefinition of sets may take half an hour, costing typically $15−50.

Terminals can cost from less than $1000 to several thousand dollars plus maintenance, which is about 10% of purchase price per year. They may rent for a price that would cover purchase price in about two years. On an hourly basis, they account for but a small fraction of total cost.

The question of whether the cost is worth it clearly depends on the individual searcher and the value he places on the information retrieved and speed of the service. Although most people are unused to paying anything at all for library services, many find the fees modest enough, considering the time that can be saved. Corporations, government agencies, and law firms may find the speed and completeness of computer-based searching to be necessary to their operation.

REFERENCES

1   Atherton, P. and Christian, R., *Librarians and Online Services*, White Plains, N.Y., Knowledge Industry Publications, 1977.
2   Lancaster, F.W. and E.G. Fayen, *Information Retrieval On-Line*, Los Angeles, Melville Publishing Co., 1973.
3   Lancaster, F.W., *Information Retrieval Systems*, New York, John Wiley & Sons, 1978.
4   Meadow, Charles T., *The Analysis of Information Systems*, 2nd ed., Los Angeles, Melville Publishing Co., 1973.
5   Meadow, Charles T., *Applied Data Management*, New York, John Wiley & Sons, 1976.

Three

The Presearch Interview

3.1. IN THE BEGINNING . . . GETTING HELP FROM AN INFORMATION SPECIALIST

The presearch interview that takes place between an information requester and the information specialist who will search online is a conversation similar in some ways to that which occurs at most library desks when a user asks a reference librarian for assistance, but there are important differences. In both cases, an attempt is made to understand the information needs of the user so that a search in the library's catalog or one of many reference sources will be successful. The *object* in *all* library research is to locate the needed information or to find out where the needed information can be found. The *process* of searching conventionally in the library is quite different from searching online.

In the case of computer-based search services, the user almost always delegates the search to the information specialist. In cases not involving computers, the *user* usually does the search in the library *alone* before or after some explanation or direction from the librarian.

The conversation between the librarian and the user, before any search is undertaken, may begin with a question like "What do you have on psychology?" and it may end with the librarian learning that the user really wanted information about "the use of behavior modification techniques in the classroom." The interviewing skill, professional knowledge, and experience of the librarian helps to make the transition from *first* to *best* question so that the search by either the requester or the librarian can be more successful and efficient. If this conversation is successful, the librarian can direct the user to the best library reference material available for the specific question, or the search online can be right on target and focused. If the conversation does not clarify the request, much time and money can be wasted.

Because the user's request will probably be searched online by the librarian and not the user, the training of librarians and other information specialists for online bibliographic searching must include instruction in their role as *intermediaries* for the information requester. The online computer-based literature searching services used, such as BRS, DIALOG, ORBIT, CAN/OLE, and MEDLINE, are searching tools providing access to data bases, but to use them properly, users of these systems must come to understand the request made by the end user or information requester.

In library research, the librarian knows what the library contains, how the collection of resources is organized, and how to complete an interlibrary loan, if necessary, to fulfill a request. To the requester, the subject headings in the catalog may appear difficult to use, but the librarian can get around them and knows when to look beyond the catalog for additional information. Usually some of this knowledge and body of skills are passed on to the library user in a quick tutorial. This will help when the library tools are used later. For example, once the library catalog or printed abstracting service is explained, it is easy to use it again and again.

However, for the online search, special skills that are time-consuming to explain to the user need to be employed. Today, the requester is rarely given instructions on how to do the search online alone. What librarians know about data bases and online systems will help them perform a better search for requesters, but the librarians also need to understand the request quite clearly for *they* will do the searches. This is one of the fundamental differences between traditional library reference service and online searching as usually practiced today. In the future, we can expect to see a steady increase in self-searching by users. Our discussion in this chapter concerns the conventional *intermediated* search.

3.2 STEPS IN CONDUCTING THE INTERVIEW

In the use of computer systems for online bibliographic searching, the information specialist (or librarian) usually performs as the *intermediary* between the "end-user" and the retrieval system. Thus the transfer of the searching function from the requester to the librarian (or information specialist) makes the conversation between librarian and requester before the search a very important step in the search process. During their conversation, it is necessary to:

- *Negotiate* the request for information.
- *Transform* it into search statements which the online system and file can handle.

They must discuss:

- Objectives to strive for.
- Choice of terms.
- Search strategy.

All these steps or tasks in the presearch interview can occur in any number of sequences and may even continue while the intermediary and requester are working together online, if that is a customary practice. Sometimes, but not always, the requester may be at the computer terminal when the online search is done. Not all steps will occur in every interview. Some may be more essential than others, depending upon the request. Some steps take more time than others.

Of the eight steps enumerated in Figure 3.1, some typically occur only in the presearch interview, for example, identifying data bases and compiling search terms. Other steps can occur then as well as when the online search is going on, for example, formulating search logic and ordering output. Step 8 is usually a postsearch activity.

Some of these steps will be discussed here; other steps will be discussed in the following chapters. They are important steps that must be understood, to some extent, by both the requester and the intermediary.

The requester is usually asked by the information specialist to prepare for the online search ahead of time—even before the formal presearch interview takes place. Some people in charge of computer-based search services use forms (such as that in Figure 3.2) to elicit the required information in Steps 1 and 4 (Clarification and Negotiation of Need, and Search Objectives; and Compiling Search Terms) from the requester *before* the presearch interview takes place. It can help both persons save time if such a form is completed or used to guide the line of the interview. Occasionally the procedure may be for such a form to *replace* the interview entirely! One can readily see how items 11, 12, and 17 in Figure 3.2 relate to Steps 1 and 4 in Figure 3.1 and how items 14, 15, and 18 relate to Steps 5 and 6.

Relationship of Steps in Interview and Information Sheet from Requester

Step 1 Clarifying and Negotiating the Information Need and Search Objectives

Step 4 Compiling the Search Terms

Info Sheet Items:
11 Search Topic
12 Key Words
17 Scope of Search

Step 5 Making Output Choices

Step 6 Conceptualizing the Search as Input to the Retrieval System

Info Sheet Items:
14 Languages
15 Range of Years Wanted
18 Fee Limit

The information specialist or intermediary is trained to do Steps 2 (Identify Relevant Data Bases), 3 (Plan Search Strategies), 5 (Ordering Output), and 6 (Preparing Search as Input to System) once there is a clear understanding of the requester's need and requirements. By reading books like this, studying data base descriptions and user manuals, and by receiving training in online searching, the online searcher achieves the skills to perform these steps efficiently.

Steps (not in Fixed Order)

1   **Clarifying and Negotiating the Information-Need and Search Objectives**
    Interviewing the information requester clarifies the narrative form of the *request* and determines *search objectives:*
    (a)   retrieve *all* relevant items (high recall);
    (b)   retrieve *only* relevant items (high precision);
    (c)   retrieve *some* relevant items.
    Identify constraints (e.g., books only as output or only in English, or only if published after 1975)

2   **Identifying Relevant Online System and Data Bases**
    Determining which online system and data base to use first, which next, etc.

3   **Formulating Basic Search Logic and Planning Search Strategies**
    Analyzing the search topic into parts called facets or concept groups. Planning approaches to search strategy for combining concepts of the topic.

4   **Compiling the Search Terms**
    Choosing indexing terms from the data base's thesaurus or other printed word lists.
    Selecting terms for free text searching of the subject-conveying fields (title, abstract, etc.).
    Deciding to use thesaurus and alphabetic word lists online.

5   **Making Output Choices**
    Choosing limits on, and printing of, output.
    Selecting an approach to search strategy that best satisfies the search objectives expressed by the requester.

6   **Conceptualizing the Search as Input to the Retrieval System**
    Arranging the search terms into concepts or facets for search strategies using features of the retrieval system, for example, truncation, word proximity.
    Noting most important and less important concept groups and deciding on sequence of input to access these concept groups efficiently.
    Restricting or limiting output based on search objectives.

7   **Evaluating Preliminary Results**
    Reviewing search results, step by step.
    Considering alternative search strategies to meet search objectives (recycling Steps 1–6).

8   **Evaluating Final Results**
    Determining requester's satisfaction with search results.

Figure 3.1   Steps in the presearch interview and the online search.

Step 2, identifying relevant online search system and data bases, can be a difficult task because over 100 data bases can now be searched online, many on several online systems. If the search request seems to cross several fields of study, it can be extremely difficult to choose which one to search first. As most of the data bases correspond to some printed abstracting or indexing service, the information specialist or subject expert may be familiar with the coverage. If not, a quick check of the journal list covered by the printed service may help decide if one data base will be searched before another. Because this is not always possible, the retrieval services have produced subject lists for the data bases they have made available online. Occasionally these indexes to broad subject categories covered in the data bases are themselves online.

(20 Items)

Library Use Only (1-5)

1. Search No. _____
2. Library _____
3. Accepted _____
4. Searched by: _____
5. Data Bases _____

6. Name _____

7. Department _____

8. Mail Address (if different from above)

_____

9. Home Phone: _____ 9a. Business Phone: _____

10. User:_____ Faculty,_____ Grad. Student (_____ Ph.D.), _____ Staff

_____ Undergraduate,_____ Other_____ Affiliated:_____

11. SEARCH TOPIC: Describe the subject/topic you want searched. Please state your description in prose. Here is an example: *Citations that deal with the effects of any mutation on the eye color of the fruit fly (Drosophila celanogaster)."*

12. KEY WORDS: List key terms, phrases or concepts that describe your topic or research. Give synonyms and spelling variations. Specify terms you do *NOT* want used in retrieving items.

13. SAMPLE CITATIONS: List 2 or 3 citations on your topic, if known or easily available.

_____

14. LANGUAGES:_____ English only,_____ Any language. _____ Languages in addition to English _____

15. RANGE OF YEARS WANTED:_____ All years available,_____ No items before 19_____ .

16. ABSTRACTS NEEDED (if present in file searched)_____ yes. _____ no.

17. SCOPE OF SEARCH: Check the kind of search you want.

_____ COMPREHENSIVE: In which an attempt will be made to retrieve the maximum number of items with the possibility that there may be a relatively high percentage of nonuseful items.

_____ LIMITED: In which an attempt will be made to retrieve a minimum acceptable number of items with the possibility a number of items that would be in a comprehensive search will not be retrieved.

18. FEE LIMIT: Give the approximate amount acceptable as a maximum fee. This will guide the searcher in the selection of data bases and in determining the scope of the search.

$_____

PLEASE NOTE: THE FEE PAYS FOR A SEARCH. IT IS POSSIBLE THAT NO RELEVANT CITATIONS WILL BE FOUND.

19. DEADLINE: State the latest date beyond which the search will not be useful to you.

NOT USEFUL AFTER _____

20. AUTHORIZATION: I authorize the library to perform the search described above and agree to the charges incurred in doing the search. Payment will be made by:

_____ Check, _____ Interdepartment fund transfer,_____ Cash

Signature _____ Date _____

Figure 3.2 Information sheet from requester. Reprinted courtesy of Stanford University.

DIALIST of the Dialog system, a Merged Term Frequency Index, available in microform, allows one to scan for postings of a term representing subject across several data bases in broad subject areas. When you see that the term "automobile," for example, has been used 1436 times in NTIS, 4469 times in Engineering Index (Compendex), and 372 times in INSPEC, it is fairly straightforward to decide to search Compendex first, if you are interested in automobiles. Study of the User Guides for each data base available on the retrieval system to be used also helps the online searcher make an intelligent decision about which to use first, second, and so on. Dialog (DIAL INDEX), BRS (CROS) and ORBIT (Data Base Index) are lists that can be searched online to help decide on which data base to search first.

Steps 3 and 4 are covered in more detail in later chapters.

Steps 7 and 8, Evaluating Preliminary and Final Results, are usually activities for both the requester and searcher and can occur even before the search is completed and paid for. That is why items 18 and 20 (*Limits to Fee* and *Authorization*) are on the form in Figure 3.2.

These steps or completion of these tasks can be reviewed and rated as successful or unsuccessful. Some librarians use a *checklist* of questions (see Figure 3.3) that they try to answer and that they occasionally ask the requester to answer. This is helpful whenever an evaluation of the service is being undertaken. It is difficult to do all the time, however. A careful glance shows how these questions on the check list relate to the steps in the presearch interview (Figure 3.1)—*A* and *B* relate to Steps 1 and 5, *C* relates to Step 4, *D* relates to Steps 3 and 6, and so on. Sometimes, when the two engaged in the presearch interview answer these questions separately, and exchange their answers, they find some areas of disagreement. Such an exchange allows the librarian to clear up any misunderstandings.

3.3 CONCEPTUALIZING THE SEARCH

The following discussion should help both requester and information specialist to prepare for Steps 1, 3, and 6 in Figure 3.1. These are steps that both can do separately and then compare the outcome before going online. Agreement can show that both approaches are compatible and will undoubtedly insure a satisfactory search online.

There may be several different search formulations that give essentially the same performance, but all searchers will agree that a search should be analyzed into facets or concept groups. *Facet* indicates a separate aspect of a query. For example, a query on the effects of TV violence on children can be separated into three distinct concept groups (or facets, notions, sets, parts, components): (1) television, (2) violence, and (3) children.

In order to perform an online search, these three facets or sets are joined using operators such as *and, or, not.* Since all three facets in this request must be present to satisfy the stated information need, the operator *and* is used with the search terms selected to represent the three facets.

The inclusion of more synonymous terms to the set representing *violence*

A.	**Clarification of Request** (Steps 1 and 5 in Figure 3.1)	

Is there an agreement on the narrative statement of the information need?

B   **Request Negotiation** (Steps 1 and 5 in Figure 3.1)

Has the *search objective* been agreed upon?

Have the subject area terminology and literature sources been discussed?

Are there any limits or constraints to be imposed on output (date, language, type of information item)?

C   **Search Vocabulary** (Step 4 in Figure 3.1)

Do the requester and information specialist agree on the selection and/or exclusion of search terms?

Have the options of free text and controlled term searching been discussed?

What vocabulary aids have been selected? Is there a citation known to be relevant?

D   **Search Strategy Formulation** (Steps 2, 3, and 6 in Figure 3.1)

Is there agreement on the formation of concept groups?

Have order of search statements and combinations of concept groups been discussed?

What alternate search strategies have been discussed?

Have data bases, output formats, and limits been decided?

E   **Administrative Details** (Steps 5, 7, and 8 in Figure 3.1)

Will the user be present during the search?

What are the arrangements concerning delivery of output and billing?

Has a post hoc evaluation been arranged?

Figure 3.3 Questions to check success of presearch interview

would relax the search requirement (or allow for more opportunity of matches) and permit the formulation to be satisfied by more citations. As a general principle that is independent of either data base or retrieval system, the inclusion of *or*'s increases the volume of output. On the other hand, the inclusion of *and*'s to insure that every facet is represented decreases the volume of output since every *and* condition added to a formulation tends to make the search more restrictive (or reduce opportunities of matches) and results in less output. Search objectives may affect the use of synonyms for the representation of individual facets.

It is quite possible that a given search request might be viewed by two persons as consisting of a different number of facets. This seems to depend on the expression of the information need and the interpretation of the query and indexing language by the searcher when interviewing the requester. For example, the search topic, "Audio-Visual Aids for Library Instruction of Users," has been divided into three concept groups in Formulation A and two concept groups in Formulation B:

Formulation A			Formulation B	
Audio-Visual Aids	Library Instruction	Users	Audio-Visual Aids	Instruction of Library Users
(1)	(2)	(3)	(1)	(2)

These differences in conceptualizing the query into parts will result in different online search formulations. The approaches to representing each concept or facet in a query and the combination of conceptual groups form the central core of the online search strategy process. (For more detail, see Chapter 12.)

Preparation for *Step 4, compiling the search terms to be used online,* requires some check of word lists and thesauri to insure that the search terms used will lead to useful results. Both the *controlled vocabulary* of a data base (indexing records in descriptor/identifier fields) and the *free text* (subject-conveying fields other than descriptor and identifier fields, such as title or abstract) are possible sources of such terms.

When a planned search has more than one term in it and these words occur close together alphabetically, it is fast and convenient to review the online dictionary (an alphabetic list of words in all the searchable fields of a data base). Additional terms that had not been considered previously may appear. This step is explained in more detail in Chapter 7 of this book.

If the online thesaurus is available, scanning it or the printed thesaurus may suggest to the searcher terms in the controlled vocabulary that do not appear in alphabetic proximity. (See Figure 2.6.) This tool lists the postings for each term. This data can affect the search strategy being considered.

3.4 ASPECTS OF THE PERSON-TO-PERSON CONTACT IN THE INTERVIEW

Interpersonal skills of the information specialist and the requester can make the difference in the presearch interview. The actions and expressions of either the requester or the information specialist may cause a positive or negative reaction on the part of the other. This reaction can affect the outcome of the interview.

We all take our own behavior and mannerisms as "natural" and immutable, but careful observation by a trained observer can uncover areas of improvement. The following check list developed by a researcher in interpersonal communication (Figure 3.4) may help to record the actions of both participants in the presearch interview and could help information specialists to analyze and improve their performance during the presearch interview. Either a trained observer or the information specialist could complete the check list while they listen to or view an audio or videotape of the interview after its completion.

What is listed as positive or negative on the check list is based on expert opinion and research findings. Research has shown that a *closed* question (demanding only a "yes" or "no" answer) often does not evoke a positive reaction from the answerer; competitive tone may have a negative effect; frequent interruptions and both parties talking at the same time can cause uneasiness or even annoyance.

The lack of a predominantly positive relationship during the presearch interview can cause problems. If this is what is observed, the information specialist should know what to do the next time! It may not be possible to

Behavior of Information Specialist	Behavior of Requester
Positive Occurrences	
Initially, used open questions	Freely stated information needed
*Encouraged discussion	
Answered questions in understandable way	Asked questions freely
Thoughtful pauses before answering	
Summarized or paraphrased request	Appeared confident in skill of information specialist
Listened to requester	Listened to information specialist
*Gave full attention	Gave full attention
Remained objective about subject of request	
Appeared comfortable and relaxed	Appeared comfortable and relaxed
Negative Occurrences	
Initially, used closed questions	Had to be prompted to give information
	Changed topic often
	Showed indecision about choices
*Interrupted or talked over often	*Frequently interrupted or talked over
Gave command or directives, expecting compliance	Objected to suggested strategies
Attempted to demonstrate superior knowledge	Exhibited insufficient knowledge about subject
*Placed requester on defensive	*Placed information specialist on defensive
*Gave erratic attention	
Reacted subjectively to request	
Exhibited uneasiness	Exhibited uneasiness
Appeared competitive	Appeared competitive
Appeared submissive	Appeared submissive
Ended interview prematurely	Terminated interview prematurely
Seemed annoyed	Seemed annoyed

*Assumed to be most important for successful interview.

Figure 3.4   Checklist for observing interpersonal communication during presearch interview.

quantify the overall effect as satisfactory or unsatisfactory, but with the help of an analytic review, we may be able to come closer to understanding how to control the situation and reach a positive outcome.

After the results of the online search are reviewed, this check list and the answers to the questions in Figure 3.3 may help to pinpoint why some difficulties or failures were encountered.

3.5   PRESEARCH INTERVIEW USE FOR ONLINE SEARCH—AN EXAMPLE

In Figures 3.5 and 3.6 we show how the information sheet from the requester
was completed (in part) and how this information and some clarification and
negotiation during a presearch interview resulted in a search online that was
judged successful by the requester. Several parts of the online search are
labeled in Figure 3.6 to show how the search terms were input, how

---

Item 11   Search Topic

I want to do a literature search of articles concerned with organizational aspects of library
network development. Although I am interested in organization in general, specific aspects such as:
structure, politics, financial issues, and *jurisdictional issues.*

Particular networks which are of interest are (in this order): (1) the Bio-medical Communications Network (BCN), (2) Washington (State) Library Network (WLN), (3) New York State
Interlibrary Loan (NYSILL), and (4) Ohio College Library Center (OCLC).

Articles concerned with other networks will be useful only if they are of an *evaluative* or *critical*
nature. I'm not interested in descriptions of library networks in the annual reports of county library
systems, for instance (annual reports of the 4 networks, I do want, however).

I'm only interested in material covering *1971* to the present.

Item 12   Key Words and Phrases

Words/Terms/Phrases	Synonyms Or Closely Related Terms	Meanings To BE EXCLUDED
Library networks	Library Consortia (related)	
Library cooperation	Information networks	
Intertype L.M.	Interagency cooperation	
Regional library networks	Interinstitutional coop.	
Regional cooperation		
Structure		
Model		
Objectives		
Goals/priorities		
Development		
Planning		
Jurisdiction		
Politics	Lobbying	
Administration		
Organization		
State Programs		
Financial Support		
Costs		
Cost effectiveness		
Budgeting		
Federal aid		
Grants		
(Names of networks)		

Figure 3.5 *Information sheet from requester*—excerpts from Library Network Search (item
numbers refer to Fig. 3.2).

Item 13   Sample Citations

Hacker, Harold S., "Implementing Network Plans in New York State: Jurisdictional Considerations in the Design of Library Networks," in *Interlibrary Cooperation and Information Networks.*

Minder, Thomas L., "Organizational Problems in Library Cooperation," *Library Journal,* V. 95, No. 18 (October 15, 1970), pp. 3448–50.

Item 14   Languages

   X   English   _____ any language   _____ other _____

                                                                     (specify)

Item 15   Range of Years

Most valuable   *1974, 1973, 1976, 1975, 1972, 1971*

Item 17   Scope of Search

   X   A narrower search that would yield fewer references, most of which would probably be pertinent, even if some other relevant items were missed.

Figure 3.5 *(cont.)*

preliminary output was reviewed, how the search strategies were revised, and so on. As complicated as it may all appear, this was a simple search with only two facets. The search took some 12 minutes online because of the revisions and review of output. The requester was there in person while the online search was performed. This example serves to illustrate how important the answers to certain questions can be during the presearch interview. The specification of a cutoff date turned out to be crucial for limiting output.

Decisions relating to several steps in the online search (identified as SS1, SS2, etc.) could only be made by the information specialist with the help of the information obtained on the information sheet from the requester. If the requester were not present, the form would be the only source to help make these decisions.

3.6   SUMMARY

As long as online bibliographic searching is an art form that depends on someone's knowledge of intricate features of retrieval systems, data base design, and vocabulary problems, the functions of the intermediary will be much in demand. As online searching gets streamlined and improved for naive users (first time or infrequent users), the intermediary may be by-passed, but the functions reviewed in this chapter will still have to be performed. Even if the end-user searches alone, there will still be a need to clarify and negotiate

PROG:
YOU ARE NOW CONNECTED TO THE ERIC DATABASE ←[database selection]
PROG:

SS 1 /C?
USER:
*LIBRARY NETWORKS ←[Input search terms in Facet 1]
PROG:
SS 1 PSTG (352)

SS 2 /C?
USER:
PROBLEM# OR EVAL: OR LITERATURE REVIEW ←[Input search terms in Facet 2]
PROG:
MM (EVAL:) (32)
ALL OR NONE?

USER:
ALL ←[acceptance of free and controlled terms]
PROG:
SS 2 PSTG (12266)

SS 3 /C?
USER:
1 AND 2 ←[Search logic **AND**]
PROG:
SS 3 PSTG (25)

SS 4 /C?
USER:
"PRT TI ←[preliminary review of output]
PROG:

TI - THE MULTITYPE LIBRARY NETWORK.

TI - LIBRARY INFORMATION NETWORK EXPERIMENT WITH ATS-F SATELLITE TELECOMMUNICATIONS.

TI - LONG RANGE PROGRAM FOR LIBRARY DEVELOPMENT IN OREGON WITH FIVE YEAR ACTION PLAN. <-SION OF JULY 1974.

TI - A REPORT ON LIBRARY NETWORKS.

TI - A PILOT SURVEY OF THE INDIANA LIBRARY NETWORK SYSTEM.

TI - ATTITUDES TOWARDS INTERLIBRARY COOPERATION: SUMMARY OF A STUDY.

TI - FINAL REPORT OF A LIBRARY INTER-NETWORK STUDY DEMONSTRATION AND PILOT MODEL (LIB-NAT).

TI - THE MEDICAL LIBRARY CONSULTANT - A PROPOSAL FOR INVESTIGATION AND EVALUATION.

TI - FINANCIAL FORMULAS FOR LIBRARY NETWORKS.

TI - COMPATABILITY PROBLEMS OF NETWORK INTERFACING.

Figure 3.6 Library network: search of ERIC on ORBIT

the request and to know enough about the language of the data base being searched to match the request with the basic index provided. All searchers must determine search objectives (low cost, high recall, or high precision) to effect a useful outcome to the search. As difficult as person-to-person communication can be, it may still not be easily replaceable by a direct end-user and system interface. As the old adage says, "Two heads are better than one."

TI - PRINCIPLES OF TELECOMMUNICATIONS PLANNING.

TI - A LIBRARY NETWORK FOR THE GEOSCIENCES.

TI - CENTRALIZED PROCESSING AND REGIONAL LIBRARY DEVELOPMENT: THE MIDWESTERN REGIONAL LIBRARY SYSTEM, KITCHENER, ONTARIO.

TI - THE FEDERAL LIBRARY COMMITTEE.

SS 4 /C?
USER:

"PRT FULL SKIP   11

PROG:

ED - ED057862
CH - L1003375
AU - DUNN, DONALD A.
TI - PRINCIPLES OF TELECOMMUNICATIONS PLANNING
PD - 70 ←[stopped output because date is out of scope]

SS 4/C?
USER:

1 AND 2 AND FROM 71 THRU 76 ←[revised strategy: date limit]

PROG:
SS 4 PSTG (12)

SS 5 /C?
USER:
"PRT TI 12 ←[all new output results reviewed]

PROG:

TI - THE MULTITYPE LIBRARY NETWORK.

TI - LIBRARY INFORMATION NETWORK EXPERIMENT WITH ATS-F SATELLITE TELECOMMUNICATIONS.

TI - LONG RANGE PROGRAM FOR LIBRARY DEVELOPMENT IN OREGON WITH FIVE YEAR ACTION PLAN. REVISION OF JULY 1974.

TI - A REPORT ON LIBRARY NETWORKS.

TI - A SURVEY OF THE INDIANA LIBRARY NETWORK SYSTEM AS IMPLEMENTED BY THE INDIANA STATE LIBRARY AND THE FOUR STATE UNIVERSITY LIBRARIES.

TI - A PILOT SURVEY OF THE INDIANA LIBRARY NETWORK SYSTEM.

TI - ATTITUDES TOWARDS INTERLIBRARY COOPERATION: SUMMARY OF A STUDY.

TI - FINAL REPORT OF A LIBRARY INTER-NETWORK STUDY DEMONSTRATION AND PILOT MODEL (LIB-NAT).

TI - THE MEDICAL LIBRARY CONSULTANT - A PROPOSAL FOR INVESTIGATION AND EVALUATION.

TI - A LIBRARY NETWORK FOR THE GEOSCIENCES.

TI - THE FEDERAL LIBRARY COMMITTEE.

TI - TELEFACSIMILE AT PENN STATE UNIVERSITY: A REPORT ON OPERATIONS DURING 1968-69.

SS 5 /C?
USER:
*LIBRARY NETWORKS AND FROM 71 THRU 76 ←[revised strategy: new terms for Facet 1 and date]

PROG:
SS 5 PSTG (174)

Figure 3.6 *(cont.)*

SS 6 /C?
USER:
BCN OR BIOMEDICAL COMMUNICATION NETWORK

PROG:
SS 6 PSTG (6)

SS 7 /C?
USER:
WLN OR WASHINGTON STATE LIBRARY NETWORK

PROG:
      (WASHINGTON STATE LIBRARY NETWORK)
SS 7 PSTG (2) ←[revised strategy to narrow Facet 1]

SS 8 /C?
USER:
NYSILL OR NEW YORK STATE INTERLIBRARY LOAN

PROG:
SS 8 PSTG (6)

SS 9 /C?
USER:
OCLC OR OHIO COLLEGE LIBRARY CENTER

PROG:
SS 9 PSTG (35)

SS 10 /C?
USER:
6 OR 7 OR 8 OR 9 ←[search strategy **OR**]

PROG:
SS 10 PSTG (49)

SS 11 /C?
USER:
5 AND 10 ←[narrow Facet 1 still further]

PROG:
SS 11 PSTG (19)

SS 12 /C?
USER:
*PRT TI

PROG:

TI   -   INFORMATION TRANSFER WITH THE OHIO COLLEGE LIBRARY CENTER PROGRAM AS A
           MODEL. PAPER NO. 4.

TI   -   THE FINANCING OF THE MICHIGAN LIBRARY CONSORTIUM. PAPER NO. 3.

TI   -   THE OHIO COLLEGE LIBRARY CENTER: AN OVERVIEW. REPORT NO. 1.

TI   -   NETWORKS: WHO, WHY, HOW?

TI   -   CONTEMPORARY TRENDS IN INFORMATION DELIVERY. PROGRAM FOR A WORKSHOP,
           DECEMBER 11-12, 1974, SAN FRANCISCO PUBLIC LIBRARY.

''PRT OFF-LINE ←[order output]

Figure 3.6   Library network: search of ERIC on ORBIT

Four

Terminals and Networks

4.1 COMMUNICATIONS AND THE COMPUTER

Calling up and communicating with a computer is in many ways like calling up and communicating with a person by voice telephone. The big difference, of course, is that the signals are not sounds that combine to make up words. They are letters, numerals, and other symbols that combine to make up words, numbers and codes. These basic symbols are transmitted as a stream of digital signal elements, called *bits*, much like the dots and dashes used in Morse Code telegraphy. A letter is made up of eight or nine bits (which can be zeros or ones—equivalent to dots or dashes).

Striking a key on a data communications terminal causes a stream of bits to be emitted by the terminal, out to the telephone, and eventually to the computer, as shown schematically in Figure 4.1. The computer responds with a bit stream of its own. When a string of bits reaches the terminal, a decoder recognizes the pattern and causes a particular character to be printed.

An outgoing signal from a terminal goes through a connecting device called a modem (see Section 4.1.3) to a telephone. Thence the signal can go either directly to the search service computer or to the digital communications network. Emphasis here will be on the latter mode. The telephone "talks" to a small network computer, probably located in your city. That computer may talk to one or more other computers, relaying the message from one to the other until, at the far end of the line, the message flows into the search service computer. (See Figure 4.2.)

Actually, that first computer, the one located in or near your city, may break up a message into smaller parts, called *packets*. Since neither you nor the search service computer deal with packets, but only reassembled messages, it is immaterial to you how big the packet is. As soon as a packet is received, this little computer will send it on toward its final destination, much like a telegram, over any available line. When the next packet is received, out it goes. (See

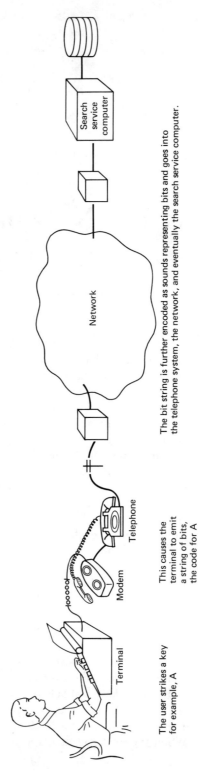

The user strikes a key for example, A

This causes the terminal to emit a string of bits, the code for A

The bit string is further encoded as sounds representing bits and goes into the telephone system, the network, and eventually the search service computer.

Figure 4.1 Transmission of a message from user to computer.

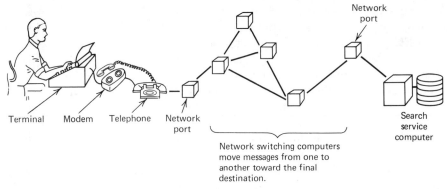

Figure 4.2   Network structure.

Figure 4.3.) It is of no consequence to the communications system or to the ultimate recipients whether the packets go over the same route as long as they are put in the right sequence before delivery to the addressee (the search computer or, coming back the other way, your terminal).

4.1.1   Data Communications Networks

A *data communications network* is the network of computers that receive messages from users, break them into packets, look for available telephone lines, transmit the packets, reassemble them near the destination, and deliver the reassembled messages to their addressee.

The network consists of a set of computers interconnected to the telephone system. It is not operated by the telephone company, however. There are

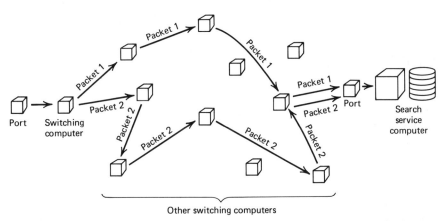

Figure 4.3   Packet switching. Packet 1 (a segment of the user's message) may go along a route through the network different from that of packet 2. The network's computer at the destination reassembles the complete message.

several independent commercial data communications networks (hereafter called, simply, *networks*). The best known in the bibliographic world are TELENET and TYMNET. The companies that operate these networks lease telephone lines and link them by computer. Thus AT&T may supply telephone services to a network, but they do not supply or operate the network's computers, nor do they directly serve the users.

In addition to transmitting packets and reassembling them, the networks provide two other critically important services. One of those services is *multiplexing* or *concentrating* a transmission, techniques whereby packets from many different sources may be sent, one immediately following the other, over a single telephone line. The network's computer finds the first open line going toward the message's destination and sends out the packet. The packet is then relayed from computer to computer, regardless of origin, as shown in Figure 4.4. In this manner the lines are kept nearly continuously busy with very high speed message traffic. When you have a voice conversation, a good bit of the time that a line is in use there is no message, only the pauses between words. This efficient use of the telephone lines by networks reduces the cost to you, the user, of telephone service. Today, it costs $3 per hour to "talk" via a data communications network between Philadelphia and Boston, and about $5 betweeen New York and Los Angeles. By comparison, an hour-long, direct-dial, weekday, full-rate call from Philadelphia to Boston would cost $19.24.

If there is no network computer in your city, you may have to pay for a long distance call to the nearest one. You pay long distance rates only for that link, not for the link between the network's *port* (entry or exit) and the search computer. Of course, as previously noted, some users are near enough to the search service to call directly, without using the network.

The other major service of a network is *error detection* and *correction*. Errors occur in digital communication—as they do in voice communication. If you are having a voice conversation and a burst of noise (static) masks out a word, you simply say, "Excuse me. Would you please repeat that?" When an error occurs in digital communication, the error must first be detected. We will not go into the methods, but there are various techniques for a computer to determine that an error has happened.[1] As soon as a network computer detects an error in an incoming message, it asks for the message to be retransmitted, in effect saying "Would you please repeat that?" This happens in a fraction of a second and is not apparent to the human user. The result is usually error-free communication, as far as you are concerned, a phenomenon noticed only when it is absent. The functioning of the network is summarized in Figure 4.5.

4.1.2   The Terminals

The word *terminal* in data communications means the same as it does in transportation. A terminal is the end of the line as in an air, rail, or bus terminal. A conventional telephone instrument is a terminal in this sense. When we talk about a terminal in terms of computers, we are usually referring

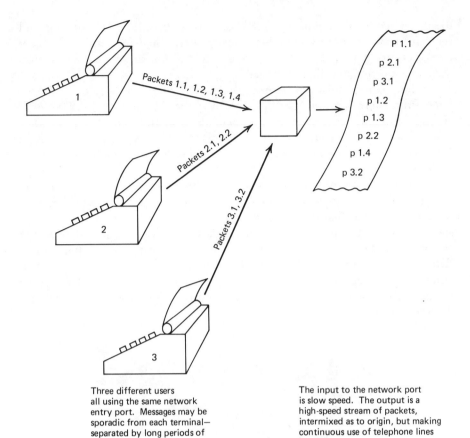

Three different users all using the same network entry port. Messages may be sporadic from each terminal—separated by long periods of no activity.

The input to the network port is slow speed. The output is a high-speed stream of packets, intermixed as to origin, but making continuous use of telephone lines possible.

Figure 4.4   Message concentration by the network.

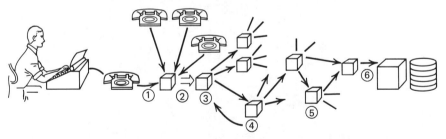

Figure 4.5   Functions of the network: 1. Receive message from user. 2. Concentrate messages from several users to improve efficiency of use of telephone lines. 3. Switch messages to whatever lines are available in appropriate direction. 4. Detect errors in transmission and call for retransmission when an error occurs, without need for user intervention or even awareness. 5. Reassemble separate packets for a single destination. 6. Transmit assembled message to destination.

to a data communications terminal—a device capable of generating and receiving codes for letters and other print symbols. The basic terminal is much like an electric typewriter. The Teletype is an old, but still used, example of a digital data communications terminal.

While one terminal type is like a typewriter, there are variations. Like a typewriter, there is a limit to the speed. A typist is limited to a maximum of around 15 characters per second. A computer can transmit at much higher speeds, so there is continual market demand for faster terminals. Rates of 30 or 120 characters per second (cps) are now common. Speeds of 480–960 cps are sometimes found.

Electronic terminals, today, use a cathode ray tube (CRT) or video display unit to display characters rather than print them on paper. The CRT is basically the same device as that used in television, but it is used to draw letters on its screen, instead of scenes. With no moving parts, a CRT can display information at a much higher rate than can an electromechanical printer, or typewriter. Rates of 30, 120, or 480 cps are common; 960 cps is available. CRT's are also quiet. Their disadvantages are they keep no paper record and have some tendency to cause eye strain after prolonged use. (A few types of terminals are illustrated in Figures 4.6 and 4.7).

Figure 4.6   A typical terminal operating in the range of 10 to 30 characters per second. This is a LA 34 Decwriter IV produced by Digital Equipment Corporation. Photo courtesy Digital Equipment Corporation.

Figure 4.7   A typical CRT or video terminal, in this case a Digital Equipment VT 100. Higher speeds are usually more possible than with print terminals. Photo courtesy Digital Equipment Corporation.

4.1.3   Modems

A small device called a *modem* connects the terminal, which is the user's means of talking to and being talked to by the computer, and the telephone lines that bring messages to and from the computer. A modem transforms a signal. Since the terminal generates sequences of *bits* and the telephone expects *sounds*, which it transforms into electrical signals, the modem converts bits into sounds and vice versa. The first conversion of the signal is called *modulation* and its retransformation back into original form is called *demodulation*. The word *modem* is made up from *mo*dulator-*dem*odulator. A typical modem is shown in Figure 4.8. The modem may be built into the terminal or bought separately. Its use is essential. Something to watch out for if you are in charge of buying equipment is that present-day modems may not handle all the transmission speeds possible. Thus if you buy a higher speed terminal, you may also need a higher speed modem.

4.2   USING THE TERMINAL

A terminal's keyboard is generally like that of a typewriter; although most terminals have similar keyboards, there are differences. Figure 4.9 shows a

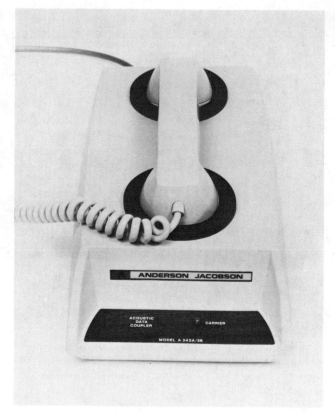

Figure 4.8 A modem converts the signals generated by a terminal into those acceptable to the telephone system, and vice versa. The illustration shows an Anderson-Jacobson Model A 242A/36 connected to the telephone system by placing the handset directly into the modem. Photo courtesy Anderson-Jacobson, Inc., San Jose, California.

typical keyboard. Among the important differences between terminals and typewriters are the following:

1 The RETURN key performs the function of returning the carriage or whatever device is used to bring the machine to the beginning of a new line. Its use will also normally cause a *line feed,* the movement of the paper up one line. So far, this is what a typewriter's RETURN key does. Unseen is another important function. The RETURN key also signals the end of a message. This key *must* be struck at the end of a message. If it is not, the network's computer just waits for such a signal and does not process the message content. There are a few exceptions to this rule, all having to do with interrupting the normal sequence of operations of the computer. The three functions of carriage return, line feed, and end of message are not necessarily packaged together in other computer systems, but in bibliographic searching such packaging is virtually universal.

Figure 4.9 The keyboard of a Decwriter showing ASCII characters on top of the keys, APL characters on the sides. Selection between them is made by the "Alt Char Set" key at the extreme left of the keyboard. Photo courtesy Digital Equipment Corporation.

2 There is a SHIFT key that puts the terminal into uppercase mode. There is also a CONTROL key which is, in effect, used to enter a third case. CONTROL is always used simultaneously with another key, for example, CONTROL-h, often abbreviated ħ, the notation we use hereafter. Use of ħ causes a different code to be generated than would be if just the letter or number key were used. That is to say, ħ generates a different outgoing pattern of bits than does h or H. The code ħ is normally interpreted as a "backspace and delete" code, erasing the previous character.

3 There is a DELETE key which may perform the functions attributed above to ħ.

4 There is a key marked ESC or ESCAPE which may have special meanings depending on the system receiving it. It is one of the keys normally used without the requirement of an end of message or RETURN key following it.

5 There is a BREAK or INTERRUPT key, often used to stop a long print out from coming from the computer. If you have ordered the computer to print-out a long list of references and then change your mind, you can stop the printing by hitting the BREAK key, even while printing goes on. It does *not* result in any character being printed, but the computer-driven typing will soon stop and the computer will indicate that it is ready for your next command. Both ESC and BREAK are attention-getting devices.

6 There is always a difference between the lower case letter l and the numeral 1.

7   There is always a difference between the letter O and the numeral 0.

8   There are a variety of special symbols, such as =, <, >, that are sometimes, but not always, found on typewriters.

9   Sometimes there is a second set of keys called *function keys*, apart from the main keyboard. These are simply packaged for convenience and given special labels, but the codes they send out are the same as some of the other keys on the regular keyboard. The function keys allow the use of so un-mnemonic a code as # to be used for the command *select*. A key would be inscribed with the word SELECT and would then be electronically wired to generate the same code as the symbol #, but it would be easier for the user to remember.

10   Some terminals have a separate bank of numeric keys, arranged in calculator or adding machine order, to simplify entry of numeric data. Again, the codes sent out are the same as for the regular keyboard's numeric keys. A set of keys such as this can be seen in Figure 4.9, on the right-hand side of the keyboard.

11   Generally, the keys on a terminal are more sensitive to touch than those of a typewriter. First-time users who are experienced typists are often surprised at the light touch and must adjust so as not to send out unwanted signals.

4.2.1   ASCII and APL Keyboards

Most terminals used for searching send out what is called the American Standard Code for Information Interchange (ASCII). This is a particular system of encoding bits into characters. A rather popular computer programming language, generally known by its initials, APL (which stand for nothing more than *A Programming Language*), uses a variety of other symbols unfamiliar to most searchers. Particularly in a university setting the keyboard may have both sets of symbols inscribed on the keys. (See the main bank of keys in the center of Figure 4.9.) There will be a switch to enable the user to select the appropriate code to go with one symbol set or the other.

When the ASCII and APL notations are mixed, the unwary user will find up to four symbols on a key, usually two in one color, two in another, or two on the top and two on the side. When you see this, be sure to determine which set you are working with and look for the selector switch if you need to change.

4.2.2   Special Functions

A terminal does more than print symbols on a page or display them electronically. It sends messages to a computer with which it is in constant communication. Therefore, more information has to be transmitted than merely the message content. There is a fair amount of *control* information as well. The principal control functions are considered next.

End of message   As mentioned earlier, striking the RETURN key denotes the end of a message. Actually, the characters are sent individually as the keys are struck, but the RETURN key says "This is the end of a message."

Backspacing   Typing errors are common and most typing errors are discovered by the typist immediately after the wrong key is struck. To move backward for correction, strike CONTROL and h simultaneously (ĥ) or DELETE. Each time you hit this combination, you back up one character and erase the computer's image of what had been there. On a print terminal, you obviously cannot erase the previously printed character, but you do erase it in the computer's memory. For example:

You type	SELECY	and recognize a typing error (the "Y").
You then type	ĥ	the symbol for CONTROL-H. This moves the carriage back one space and erases the Y in the computer's memory, but not on the printed page.
You then type	T	which has the effect of your having typed SELECT in the first place.

The sequence of characters sent is SELECYĥT, but is received as SELECT.

Cancelling a Line   The usual symbol is ESCAPE or ESC. There are variations. Use your manual and try the various codes.

Stop printing   Suppose you have asked for ten records to be printed in a long format and now you are sorry—you don't want to wait that long. Simply hit the BREAK key and printing stops. The system will then ask for your next command.

4.2.3.   Other Special Switches

Most terminals have switches as described below:

1   *Power on.* The function of this switch is, we hope obvious. It turns the machine on. If there is a separate modem, it may have its own on-off switch.
2   *Local-remote.* Terminal operations such as those we have described so far are done in *remote* mode, that is, transmitting to and receiving from a remote computer or other terminal. In *local* mode, the terminal functions more or less as a typewriter, not transmitting but printing characters generated by its own keyboard.
3   *Odd-even parity.* We made brief mention of the error detection function of a network. Extra bits, called *parity bits*, are added to each character code to assist in detection. Omitting details, there are two ways to do this, called

even parity or odd parity. You usually want even, but often it does not matter.

4   *Full-half duplex.* In a full duplex communication system, it is possible for both parties to a communication to transmit to each other at the same time. You may feel this is unnecessary, but actually every key you strike sends out a single-character message. The computer receives it and immediately sends the same message back to the terminal. The elapsed time required to do this is imperceptible to you. Thus a full duplex mode is highly desirable. A half-duplex mode means that, while two-way communication is possible, the system can operate only one way at time. If a terminal which should be operating in full duplex is inadvertently put in half-duplex, every character will print twice, like this:

SSEELLEECCTT LLIIBBRRAARRYY

and this is your clue to switch modes.

5   *Transmission speed.* Some terminals permit the operator to select from among several possible transmission speeds. The common range is 10 cps to 120, with intervening choices at 15 and 30 cps. Another measure of transmission is the *baud*. A baud is a bit per second. Characters, including their parity bits, may use 10 bits. Hence the speeds of 10, 15, 30, or 120 characters per second, expressed in baud are: 100, 150, 300, or 1200. Note: baud means bit *per second*. It is a measure of speed. We do not say baud per second. You will generally want the highest speed available, but the speed of the terminal must be consistent with the speed of the communication system. Some network ports, for example, are limited to 300 baud, or to 1200 baud.

6   *ASCII-APL.* As we noted in the preceding, some terminals offer a choice of two-character coding systems. If so, there will be a two-position switch to enable you to choose among them. For searching, use ASCII.

4.3   COMMUNICATION TROUBLES

There will be times when nothing seems to work, when your commands are obviously not being accepted and acted upon, or when you get a message saying the computer is not available, not responding, or "down." We can classify problems by origin, and there are four possible ones.

4.3.1   The Computer Is Down

If the search service computer is down (inoperative) but the network is operating, you can expect an explicit message telling you have been dropped (if you had already been connected) or that the computer is not responding or is unavailable (if you are trying to establish a connection). In the former case, there will have been a mechanical fault. In the latter, you cannot tell if the problem is a mechanical one or an overload, that is, the machine is unable to accept any new users at the time.

There is little you can do in either case. It may help to call the search service to find out exactly what the trouble is or you can just keep trying every few minutes. If you deal with more than one search service, when one is down try another one.

4.3.2   The Network Is Malfunctioning

Much less common, but still possible, is a network fault. If you have already been connected, you will find communication ceasing or becoming meaningless. If you are trying to establish communication, you will find the network not accepting your log in message. Your choices are to try again later, to call the network on a voice line to see what the trouble is, or try another network.

If the network does not respond as expected to your message, we suggest hanging up and trying again. The most surprising things can affect communication service. Many users are convinced that heavy rains cause errors in transmission.

4.3.3   Terminal Illness

Sometimes the problem will be at home. A common symptom is for a different letter to appear on the screen or page than that of the key you struck. There are many others. If you have trouble at the start of a terminal session, check first the settings of your switches:

> **Power on**
> **Remote**
> **Even parity**
> **Full duplex**
> **Usually 30 or 120 cps, or 300 or 1200 baud**
> **ASCII**

If nothing works, try another terminal, if one is available. Advice is often available from the search service when you are able to describe the exact symptoms.

4.3.4   User Errors

Not to be smug about computers, but when inexperienced users are at the keyboard, they rather than the machinery, are usually at fault. In case of troubles not recognizable by the suggestions above, check your input carefully. Look at every character. Look for missing or extraneous spaces or for the letter l instead of the numeral 1, or the letter O instead of the numeral 0. When typing passwords which do not print, a mistake is easy to make. Go slowly and carefully. Often, recovery from an erroneously entered password is difficult, even though the network or computer service asks for the password again. Starting over often helps.

Do not hesitate to call for help, in your own office, from the search service, or your library.

REFERENCES

1   FitzGerald, Jerry and Tom S. Eason, *Fundamentals of Data Communications*, New York, John Wiley & Sons, 1978.

Five

Introduction to Search Languages

5.1 COMMAND SYNTAX

In general, a command to an information retrieval system is an imperative sentence, consisting of a verb and an object of the verb, such as *begin eric*. Sometimes the object is a compound one, such as *print au, ti*. Continuing the analogy to natural language, the object could be a clause made up of one or several phrases. It is also possible to have no object, just the verb. As we shall discuss later, it is even possible for the verb to be implict and to state only the object.

Since the general form is *verb-object* we shall concentrate on that for now. A typical example is the DIALOG command *select computer*. The verb is *select*, the object *computer*. It directs the DIALOG computer to create a set consisting of all records containing the word *computer*. The verb must be present in all DIALOG commands but if the object of this particular verb is missing, the computer will treat it as a blank and will assume the command is saying *select* (nothing). It will do so and report that no citations were found.

The *select* command, or its ORBIT equivalent, *find*, can have a compound object. One may say *find computer **and** library*. The components of this sentence are quite distinct: a verb (*find*) an object (*computer **and** library*) consisting of a term (*computer*), an operator (***and***) and another term (*library*). If the operator is present, a second term *must* be present, that is, *find computer **and*** is not a valid command. If the operator were omitted, leaving *computer library*, a search system might assume this to be a search for a single, two-word term, *computer library*, and act accordingly, or, in the case of BRS, that it means *computer **or** library*.

Some commands have even more elements, such as the BRS *print*. The user must identify the set to be printed, the fields of a record to be printed, and the records of the set to be printed, all in a precisely specified order. An example is *print 1 au, ti, is /doc=1-5*. This calls for printing of *author, title,* and *issue number* from set 1. Note the last phrase. The character / is used as a *separator,* partitioning the document phrase from the others. The expression *doc=* introduces the designation of those records of the set to be printed or from which extracts are to be made for printing. The characters *1−5* tell the system to print records 1 through 5 inclusive.

Sometimes, variations are permitted in the order of listing elements. In general, though, the rule is to follow the prescribed syntax exactly. Any variation may result in the wrong interpretation or in the computer being unable to recognize and hence to execute your command.

5.2   IMPLICIT AND DEFAULT COMMANDS AND VALUES

Under strictly prescribed conditions some systems allow the user to omit certain information, either omitting an entire command or merely a portion of one. In these cases, the command or the object or portion of an object is assumed to have been given *implicity* and a *default* command or value is assigned by the system. For example, DIALOG permits you to omit to ask for a file to search. If you do not specify one, it gives you the file your organization has previously selected as the *default file,* such as NTIS, the data base of the National Technical Information Service. This means the system assumes a command selecting NTIS as the file to be searched has been implicitly given, and this assumption remains in effect until the user changes it by an explicit file selection command.

Usually, you can omit the designation of the set number from which you wish to print some records. The system *defaults* to the last set created. You may, of course, override this default assumption by specifying which set you want.

The reason for default assumptions and implicit commands is to permit an experienced searcher to go faster and, with an inexperienced searcher, to avoid continual refusal to carry out orders because they are incomplete or otherwise defective. A searcher must always be aware of the system's default assignments because otherwise search results can be incomprehensible.

5.3   SEARCH MODES

DIALOG always expects an explicit verb. ORBIT makes a default assumption—if you do not give a verb, it assumes you mean *find,* the most commonly used command verb. BRS goes one step further. A searcher gives a command to the system to enter a *mode*. Thereafter, until the mode is changed, all commands are assumed to be of a specific type corresponding to the mode. For example, once you enter search mode, until you change modes, all commands are assumed to be search commands, which are similar to ORBIT's *find*. Once in a mode, then, no verb is needed; it is always implicit. There might be this sequence of BRS commands or statements:

..search
television *and* **facsimile**

(There is more to a BRS conversation. This illustrates only the searcher's command input.) To break out of this mode, the operational meaning of which is that all subsequent commands are assumed to be verb-less search commands, the searcher must enter a new mode command. This is an example, by the way, of a case where only the object of a verb need be given.

5.4   MACHINE INTERPRETATION OF COMMANDS

When you talk to a human being from another culture it helps to know how he interprets what you say or do. Similarly, when you communicate with a computer it helps to know how the machine reacts to your messages. It is not necessary for you as a bibliographic searcher to know all the programming details of how the computer interprets your input, but it is helpful to have some idea so that you can interpret the machine's reaction when it interprets your message to it.

If you send the computer a totally unintelligible message it responds with an error message. Each search service has its own standard error messages. Typically, it will respond one way if it cannot tell what command you sent and another way if it knows what the command (verb) was but cannot decipher the object. Maddeningly, some of the most common errors searchers make cannot be detected as errors by the machine, so searchers must be alert to unexpected responses.

For example, DIALOG permits you to use a command name or a one- or two-character abbreviation for the command name. (There is also a one-character code, generally involving punctuation symbols that we do not treat in this book). The abbreviation for the command *select* is *s*, for *print* it is *pr*. DIALOG looks first for the full command name and, if it does not find one, then looks for a valid command abbreviation. If it does not find *that*, it sends an error message.

Thus if you say

select book,	it searches for *book*
slect book	it searches for *lect book*
zelect book	it responds *invalid command code*

How does DIALOG make its decision? Starting at the beginning (left-hand end) of your message (your command) it takes one letter, then another, then another, and so on, checking for the existence of a command name. Finding a blank stops the process. If it matches your command with one in the list of legal commands, then it assumes that was the command you intended. The computer then proceeds to check the objects of the verb, looking for the specific format it expects to be associated with the command it found. If no legal command name is found, the machine starts again at the beginning of the message you sent looking for a legal abbreviation. If there is one, everything to the right of it, except leading blanks, are assumed to be part of the object.

By these rules, *select* followed by a blank results in selecting a blank descriptor, *s elect* results in selection of the term *elect*, because the space following *s*, in DIALOG's "eyes," ends the command and begins the object, although it could simply have been a typing error. The command *se lect* would be interpreted as a command to select (abbreviation *s*) the compound term *e lect*.

The other search services do similar things. ORBIT assumes you are sending a *find* command unless you make it explicitly clear to the contrary. In ORBIT if you say *find book*, it will search for *book*. If you say *fnid book*, it will search for *fnid book*, treating the entire statement as an object of an understood verb because the first word is not a legal command name. Similarly, *rpint ti, au 5*, which was intended to ask for printing of the title and author of record 5, of the most recently created set, will result in a response from ORBIT telling you there are no postings. Because of the typing error, it assumed the entire expression was an object of *find* and so looked up *rpint ti, au 5* in the dictionary rather than acting on it as a command.

You may well ask why the machine is programmed to be so contrarily literal. These errors we have illustrated seem so obvious, why cannot a computer detect them and rectify them? The answer is that it is one thing to detect the probable existence of an error and quite another to know exactly what the nature of the error was. For example, one might well use *print* as a search term. If that were the case, then a message consisting just of the word *print* could be either an incomplete *print* command or a complete *find print* command. How can the machine possibly tell which one is meant? Or, you might have entered *1 and 2 and* meaning, in ORBIT, to combine sets 1 and 2 and . . . . The *and* at the end has no meaning. Does it signify that another set number should be added or that the user simply got in the habit of typing *and* after a set number? It is impossible for a machine to tell. If no sets other than 1 and 2 had been defined, then it could only mean the latter, but if more sets are in existence, only the user can tell what is meant.

Since numerals can be found as terms in a data base, it is also possible for confusion to arise between a number as a search term and as a set number. In both ORBIT and BRS one *could* say *1 and 21* and one *could mean* combine set number 1 with a new set based on the "word" *21*. Other possible meanings are obvious. If a set bearing any number used in this way has been defined, both systems will assume that is what you meant, rather than using the numerals as descriptors. By the way, BRS has a usage to help you avoid this problem—

when you don't mean a set number, put the number in quotes, as *1 and '21'* means set 1, but term *'21'*.

Our point in this section has been that all searchers make errors sometimes, but that recovering from an error depends on the searcher's understanding of how the computer reacts to it. Even more important, errors sometimes come out as syntactically legitimate commands, although not the ones we intended. What the machine does in response to one of these may seem silly if you do not understand what causes that behavior.

Six

The Data Bases

6.1 RANGE OF DATA BASES AVAILABLE

Perhaps the most vivid point that can be made about the data bases or files available for searching through online systems is that the list is too long and too rapidly growing to be completely contained in a book such as this. Williams[1] gives a picture of the historical growth of the number of files available, and there are several compendia regularly published.[2-4]

The major commercial vendors, BRS, Lockheed, and SDC, offer about 25 to 100 files each, with some overlap among their lists. Our purpose here is to indicate the range of what is available, present a few samples, and then refer the reader to appropriate reference works for more complete and up-to-date information.

Data bases can be classified by subject, of course, but for our purposes it might be more meaningful to consider them in terms of the nature of the supplier and the type of material contained. The data base suppliers are publishers; they acquire information, edit it, reproduce it, and disseminate it widely for fee. In most cases the publisher supplied essentially the same kind of information in print form before online systems appeared on the scene, and most continue to do so. Generally, the data base supplier is *not* the search service supplier but in two major cases, those of the National Library of Medicine (MEDLINE) and the New York Times (The Information Bank), the data base supplier also vends the search service. Some suppliers, such as ERIC and NTIS, are government agencies using this as a means of fulfilling their statutory obligation to disseminate information. Some are nonprofit professional societies, such as the American Institute of Physics, and some are profit seeking organizations such as Predicasts. Data bases are not only produced in the United States. The British Institute of Electrical Engineers produces

INSPEC, and Excerpta Medica of the Netherlands produces a data base of the same name.

Below are some very brief descriptions of a few commonly used data bases. Appendix C contains an example of the Inform data base descriptions found in the users' manuals of DIALOG, ORBIT, and BRS as well as a directory to search aids for all the data bases on DIALOG, no matter where produced.

6.1.1 Government Data Bases

Among the most commonly used data bases through the commercial search services are ERIC, NTIS, and AGRICOLA. MEDLINE is offered through a search service provided by the National Library of Medicine.

1 ERIC maintains two main files, one containing bibliographic records from the report literature and called *Resources in Education (RIE)*. The other, *Current Index to Journals in Education* (CIJE) covers more than 700 publications in many aspects of the educational profession. A controlled list of descriptors is maintained and published as the *ERIC Thesaurus*. The files cover the period 1966 to date. They are updated monthly and currently contain about 339,000 citations.

2 NTIS is produced by the National Technical Information Service, an agency of the U.S. Department of Commerce. Its primary function is to disseminate report literature for all U.S. agencies not restricted by military security. Thus the NTIS file contains information on reports produced by or for such agencies as the National Aeronautics and Space Administration, the Department of Energy, and the National Science Foundation. Unlike ERIC, there is no single thesaurus of descriptors for NTIS because it spans so many subject fields. Hence there is no single indexing language used to describe its many and diverse documents. NTIS went online in 1964 and now has about 725,000 records in its files.

3 AGRICOLA is produced by the National Agricultural Library (NAL). It contains citations to journal articles, government reports, monographs and other materials acquired by NAL. It was begun in 1970 and now contains about 1,265,000 records.

6.1.2 Professional Society Data Bases

The first available data bases for general use were government produced. Then came those produced by professional societies; for a time, those made up the fastest growing segment of the data base market. By now, almost every discipline has an online data base to cover its literature. A few examples of this type are:

1   CA CONDENSATES/CASIS is produced by Chemical Abstracts Service of the American Chemical Society. It covers journal articles, patent specifications, reviews, technical reports, monographs, conference proceedings, and the like. Begun in 1970, it and some closely interrelated data bases now contain over four million records.

2   COMPENDEX is produced by the Engineering Index, Inc. and covers engineering journals and conference proceedings world-wide. It is available from 1970 and contains about 766,000 records.

3   PSYCHOLOGICAL ABSTRACTS covers over 900 periodicals as well as books and technical reports. Its coverage began in 1967. It is produced by the American Psychological Association and now contains 300,000 records.

6.1.3   Commercial Data Bases

By now, the fastest growing segment of the online data base market is that of commercially sponsored data bases. The following are a representative few:

1   Among the earliest to appear was Predicasts' FORECAST ABSTRACTS. This file contains abstracts of published forecasts from a wide variety of sources such as newspapers and government reports. In addition to subject descriptors, it contains actual numerical data reported in the articles abstracted. Thus a user can retrieve not only a reference to an article giving, say, a forecast of the market for computer terminals, but the actual data reported as well. Furthermore, through the Predicasts Terminal System, offered through DIALOG, a user can perform various statistical processes on the data contained in the abstracts without recourse to the original documents. This seems a clear harbinger of the future for online information systems.

2   CIS INDEX is produced by Congressional Information Service (a private corporation) and covers "significant publications" of the U.S. Congress. Like Predicasts' FORECAST ABSTRACTS, the CIS INDEX can be used for bibliographic retrieval as well as for direct retrieval of some factual data, such as who testified on a certain bill. It covers the period beginning 1970 and contains 121,000 citations.

3   MAGAZINE INDEX indexes over 370 popular American magazines. It is aimed not solely at the technical searcher, but at the general public as well. Its indexing permits direct identification of product names, which gives it a commercial value beyond that of general library use. It is produced by Information Access Corporation, began in 1976, and contains 227,000 records.

Descriptions of these and other files are available in the search services' users' manuals and, often, in separate documentation sold by the publisher (see

Appendix C for an example of these). Because there are some differences in search service capabilities, the descriptions of the same data base by different search services may differ.

6.2 RECORD STRUCTURE

Unfortunately, but inevitably, the structures of online files are not all alike. This means we have to learn to expect that files will differ in terms of the data elements contained, which elements can be used as the basis of a search, and how the data elements are coded. Just as we cannot expect every textbook to have the same chapter organization, number and placement of examples, or vocabulary, we must expect that data bases created for different reasons will be different. We can make so few generalizations about what will be found in any given data base that the best generalization is the rule, "Look it up in a users' manual before beginning a search!"

A *record* in our terminology, is a collection of data about a single entity within a file or data base. In the context of bibliographic files a record typically consists of the complete bibliographic citation, subject indexing terms, and, often, an abstract or extract. All the information in a given file about a given work can usually be found within a single record. This record is analogous to a card in a library's card catalog, but almost always has much more information.

Within a record are *data elements*, or *fields*, examples of which are *title*, *author*, *abstract* (long, but still just another data element), *corporate source* and *pagination*. Computers usually attempt exact, character-by-character matches of input terms with data elements. Hence it is necessary for the searcher to know just how data elements are organized or coded. A well-known and often vexing example is the author element. Any librarian or experienced library user knows the many variations possible in listing an author's name, aside from pseudonyms. A name can be

> **John Quincy Adams**
> **John Q. Adams**
> **J.Q. Adams**
> **Adams, J.Q.**
> **and so on**

Even the commas and periods and the number of spaces between names or initials can be important, for a computer sees Adams, J.Q. as different from Adams, J Q or from Adams, J. Q. (note spacing) unless it is specifically programmed to ignore punctuation and spacing. Rarely will a computer be programmed to equate Adams, J Q with John Q. Adams; it is nearly always up to the searcher to think about the possible variations and to enter all that may be necessary.

In the NTIS file, dealing as it does with technical reports, *corporate source* is an important data element. Because of problems similar to those of authors' names, a numeric coding system was developed. Hence one does not query the NTIS file for *General Electric Company*; one has to get the code number. Unfortunately, these are not listed in search services' users' manuals, the code list being rather extensive. For example, there are some 200 listings under *General Electric Company* in NTIS's source listing, and these are separable from each other by location of a facility or organizational component.

In Appendix C, Part 6, we have included a DIALOG Bibliographic Verification Aid which was prepared to show how five data elements (year, author, journal, corporate source and title) in more than 100 data bases can be accessed. Variations in the first three data elements are the most pronounced.

An important variation in data base structure is the presence or absence of a thesaurus. If present online, the thesaurus constitutes a second file within the data base. It contains information about the relationships among terms in an indexing language. A typical example is the sample page from the ERIC Thesaurus (old and new editions) shown in Figure 6.1. All entries are in boldface type. Valid terms are in all capital letters; entries in lower case are not to be used. The symbols used to show interrelationships among terms are

BT: Broader term—the term following the symbol is broader than the entry.

NT: Narrower term—the term following the symbol is narrower than the entry.

RT: Related term—the nature of the relationship depends on context; the user must decide at search time and in his own context whether he considers any two terms related.

UF: Used for—the term to the right is not a valid descriptor; use the entry in boldface instead.

U: Use—the term to the right should be used instead of the entry; the converse of UF.

SN: Scope note—information about the descriptor.

The thesaurus may be converted to machine readable form and made available for online search. Of the three major search services, only DIALOG offers an online thesaurus at this time, and even DIALOG does not do this for every data base because not every data base has a thesaurus. A sample of a DIALOG print-out from the ERIC thesaurus is shown in Figure 6.2. Searching a DIALOG thesaurus is described in Chapter 7. Note that the online thesaurus is not identical to the printed one. The online version does not contain *use* references, scope notes are truncated, and date of inclusion is omitted. Occasionally, as in 1980, there may be a time when there is a totally revised ERIC thesaurus *in print* and the online thesaurus will be of an older version.

COMPUTATIONAL LINGUISTICS Jul. 1966
CIJE: 70   RIE: 268
NT   MACHINE TRANSLATION
BT   LINGUISTICS
RT   AUTOMATIC INDEXING
     INFORMATION PROCESSING
     INFORMATION RETRIEVAL
     LINGUISTIC THEORY
     MATHEMATICAL LINGUISTICS
     MATHEMATICAL LOGIC
     PROGRAMING LANGUAGES
     SEMANTICS
     STATISTICS
     WORD FREQUENCY

Computer Aided Instruction
USE   **COMPUTER ASSISTED INSTRUCTION**

Computer Assisted Indexing
USE   **AUTOMATIC INDEXING**

COMPUTER ASSISTED INSTRUCTION Jul. 1966
CIJE: 1,244   RIE: 1,985
UF   Cai
     Computer Aided Instruction
     Computer Based Instruction
BT   Programed Instruction
RT   Autoinstructional Aids
     Autoinstructional Methods
     Branching
     Computer Graphics
     Computer Oriented Programs
     Computers
     Dial Access Information Systems

Educational Technology
Instructional Media
Man Machine Systems
Programed Materials
Programing
Teaching Machines
Time Sharing

Computer Based Instruction
USE   **COMPUTER ASSISTED INSTRUCTION**

COMPUTER BASED LABORATORIES Jul. 1966
CIJE: 48   RIE: 83
BT   Laboratories
RT   Computers

COMPUTER GRAPHICS Feb. 1970
CIJE: 72   RIE: 142
SN   Computer techniques for the display of
     graphic information on output devices.
RT   Computer Assisted Instruction
     Graphic Arts
     Photocomposition
     Reprography

Computer Languages
USE   **PROGRAMING LANGUAGES**

Figure 6.1. (*a*)   An excerpt from *ERIC Thesaurus of Descriptors*, 7th ed. Copyright © 1977 by Macmillan Information, a division of Macmillan Publishing Co., Inc.

Eventually the online thesaurus is updated too. Figure 6.1 shows both the old and new printed versions of the ERIC thesaurus. Online, when a descriptor is a single word, the number of occurrences shown is for occurrence in all fields, for example, *title* or *abstract* as well as *descriptor*.

A thesaurus is not a static thing as Figure 6.1 clearly shows. Like a natural language, an indexing language is a living one that changes with the times. In the printed ERIC thesaurus each entry carries with it the date of its appearance in the file. As new terms are added and old ones dropped and others inevitably change their meaning, the searcher must be aware of these changes and must not use, for example, a descriptor added in 1978 to search records prepared in 1975. Review of several editions of a thesaurus may sometimes be necessary if the history of vocabulary changes is not recorded in the latest edition.

COMPUTATIONAL LINGUISTICS Jul. 1966
CIJE: 90   RIE: 309
SN   Branch of linguistics concerned with the
       use of computers for the analysis and
       synthesis of language data—for example,
       in machine translation, word frequency
       counts, and speech recognition and syn-
       thesis
NT   MACHINE TRANSLATION
BT   LINGUISTICS
RT   AUTOMATIC INDEXING
       COMPUTER SCIENCE
       LANGUAGE PROCESSING
       LINGUISTIC THEORY
       MATHEMATICAL LINGUISTICS
       MATHEMATICAL LOGIC
       PROGRAMING LANGUAGES
       SEMANTICS
       STATISTICS
       STRUCTURAL ANALYSIS (LINGUISTICS)
       WORD FREQUENCY

Computer Adaptive Testing
USE   **COMPUTER ASSISTED TESTING**

Computer Aided Instruction
USE   **COMPUTER ASSISTED INSTRUCTION**

Computer Aided Instructional Management
USE   **COMPUTER MANAGED INSTRUCTION**

Computer Applications
USE   **COMPUTER ORIENTED PROGRAMS**

Computer Assisted Indexing
USE   **AUTOMATIC INDEXING**

COMPUTER ASSISTED INSTRUCTION Jul. 1966
CIJE: 1,745   RIE: 2,709
SN   Interactive instructional technique in which
       a computer is used to present instructional
       material, monitor learning, and select addi-
       tional instructional material in accordance
       with individual learner needs
UF   Cai
       Computer Aided Instruction
       Computer Based Instruction
       Computer Based Laboratories (1967 1980)
       #
BT   Programed Instruction
RT   Autoinstructional Aids
       Computer Managed Instruction
       Computer Oriented Programs
       Computers
       Educational Media
       Educational Technology
       Feedback
       Individualized Instruction
       Intermode Differences
       Man Machine Systems
       Programed Instructional Materials

Figure 6.1. (*b*) An excerpt from *Thesaurus of ERIC Descriptors*, completely revised edition. Copyright © 1980 by Oryx Press, Phoenix, Arizona.

6.3   ORGANIZATION OF FILES

In computer science there is a concept called *data independence*. This refers to an arrangement whereby users can think about and write commands about data in terms of structures that are meaningful to themselves, while being unconcerned with the actual physical layout of the data. For example, a user might, for his own purposes, want to think of a bibliographic file as containing only titles and corporate sources, with the file entries being in order according to the corporate source entry. If the information system had true data independence, the user could visualize the file this way and ignore all other information or order of data.

6.3.1   Types of Files

In this section, we will deal with file structures as they *appear* to the user, not necessarily as they are physically implemented in the computer. All the major

Programed Tutoring
Teaching Machines

COMPUTER ASSISTED TESTING Mar. 1980
CIJE: 20   RIE: 33
SN   Use of computers in test administration or
       construction
UF   Computer Adaptive Testing
       Computer Tailored Testing
BT   Testing
RT   Computer Oriented Programs
       Computer Science
       Item Banks
       Test Construction
       Test Items
       Tests

Computer Based Instruction
USE **COMPUTER ASSISTED INSTRUCTION**

Computer Based Instructional Management
USE **COMPUTER MANAGED INSTRUCTION**

Computer Based Laboratories (1967 1980)
USE **COMPUTER ASSISTED INSTRUCTION;
       LABORATORIES**

Computer Based Reference Services
USE **ONLINE SYSTEMS; REFERENCE SERVICES**

Computer Conferencing
USE **TELECONFERENCING**

COMPUTER GRAPHICS Feb. 1970
CIJE: 109   RIE: 198
SN   Techniques for graphic or pictorial repre-
       sentation of information in a computer—
       representations may be in hardcopy or on
       display screens
BT   Graphic Arts
RT   Computers
       Display Systems
       Input Output Devices
       Photocomposition

Computer Languages
USE **PROGRAMING LANGUAGES**

Figure 6.1 (*b*)   (*cont.*)

systems have, by whatever name, a *dictionary, index,* or *inverted file* as well as a *main,* or *citation file.* The citation file (Figure 6.3) contains the bibliographic records and is most commonly in order by date of entry of records into the file, with newest records first. This is almost always the order in which records are printed out, unless the user specifically requests a different order. (See Section 7.5.) The citation file resembles volumes of an abstract journal on a library shelf, although the former usually contains far more information about each item.

6.3.2   Types of Data Elements

Just as with manual searching of an abstract journal in a library, it would be quite tedious, even for a computer, to have to search through each citation file record looking for a record concerning a particular author. Think about doing this manually with the card catalog if the search term were, say, a publisher. For this reason, computers use an inverted file that corresponds to a combined author-title-subject card catalog. Using such a file, the computer can quickly locate the record for a particular author and retrieve from that record a reference to all entries in the citation file for that author. Since a given name can occur as an author, title, or subject, the elements of a record are sometimes

? EXPAND COMPUTER ASSISTED INSTRUCTION

Ref	Index-term	Type	Items	RT
E1	COMPUTER ASSISTED DIAL ACCESS VIDEO RETRIE -----------------------		1	
E2	COMPUTER ASSISTED DISTRIBUTION AND ASSIGNM ----------------------		1	
E3	COMPUTER ASSISTED GUIDANCE --		1	
E4	COMPUTER ASSISTED INDEXING ---			1
E5	COMPUTER ASSISTED INSTRUCTIO --		1	
E6	COMPUTER ASSISTED INSTRUCTION -------------------------------------		3640	18
E7	COMPUTER ASSISTED INSTRUCTION CENTER ------------------------------		1	
E8	COMPUTER ASSISTED INSTRUCTION DIVISION ----------------------------		1	
E9	COMPUTER ASSISTED INSTRUCTION LABORATORY ------------------------		2	
E10	COMPUTER ASSISTED INSTRUCTION STUDY MANAGE ---------------------		1	

-more-

? EXPAND E6

Ref	Index-term	Type	Items	RT
R1	COMPUTER ASSISTED INSTRUCTION ---------------------------------------		3640	18
R2	CAI --U		765	1
R3	COMPUTER AIDED INSTRUCTION ---------------------------------------U			1
R4	COMPUTER BASED INSTRUCTION ---------------------------------------U		4	1
R5	PROGRAMED INSTRUCTION--B		3074	28
R6	AUTOINSTRUCTIONAL AIDS--R		1067	13
R7	AUTOINSTRUCTIONAL METHODS ---R		274	2
R8	BRANCHING ---R		241	5
R9	COMPUTER GRAPHICS---R		252	4
R10	COMPUTER ORIENTED PROGRAMS-------------------------------------R		2082	9
R11	COMPUTERS --R		3588	31
R12	DIAL ACCESS INFORMATION SYSTEMS-------------------------------------R		129	17
R13	EDUCATIONAL TECHNOLOGY --R		2075	12
R14	INSTRUCTIONAL MEDIA--R		3101	19

-more-

Figure 6.2. A portion of the ERIC thesaurus as stored by DIALOG and intermixed with an inverted index. The upper portion shows the terms in the alphabetical neighborhood of a search term, *computer assisted instruction*. The lower portion shows some of the terms defined by the thesaurus to be related to *computer assisted instruction*.

tagged as to their meaning. In the DIALOG version of ERIC, an author is designated by the prefix AU=, an index term (descriptor) by the suffix /DE. Thus, AU= ADAMS, J. Q. denotes an author entry. ADAMS /DE would indicate Adams as a word in a descriptor field.

6.3.3   The Dictionary File

A record of the dictionary file contains a tag, if used, the value of a term (name, title, etc.), and the numbers of the records in the main file that contain this term. It may have the appearance of

$$AU=ADAMS, J. Q. \quad 123$$
$$456$$
$$789$$
$$\cdot$$
$$\cdot$$
$$\cdot$$

Main or Citation File	Inverted File or Dictionary	
TITLE: CHEMISTRY BASICS	AU=BUNSEN, B.	101
AUTHOR: BUNSEN, B.	AU=DARWIN, C.	102
SUBJ: REACTIONS	AU=NEWTON, I.	103
DOC NO: 101	AU=SECANT, C.	105
	AU=SMITH, A.	104
TITLE: BIOLOGY	BASICS/TI	101
AUTHOR: DARWIN, C.	BIOLOGY/TI	102
SUBJ: EVOLUTION	CHEMISTRY/TI	101
DOC NO: 102	ECONOMICS/TI	104
	EVOLUTION/DE	102
TITLE: INTRODUCTION TO PHYSICS	GEOMETRY/DE	105
AUTHOR: NEWTON, I.	GRAVITY/DE	103
SUBJ: GRAVITY	INTRODUCTION/TI	103
DOC NO: 103	MATHEMATICS/TI	105
	MONEY/DE	104
TITLE: ECONOMICS	PHYSICS/TI	103
AUTHOR: SMITH, A.	REACTIONS/DE	101
SUBJ: MONEY		
DOC NO: 104	.	
	.	
TITLE: MATHEMATICS	.	
AUTHOR: SECANT, C.		
SUBJ: GEOMETRY		
DOC NO: 105		
.		
.		
.		

Figure 6.3. A citation file, shown on the left in highly abbreviated form, contains the bibliographic record. The inverted file, or dictionary, is an index to the citation file.

The numbers indicate identification numbers of records in the main file which contain ADAMS, J. Q. tagged as an author entry. The numbers, 123, 456 . . . may have no meaning outside the computer, and the user never sees them. You are told how many records there are in the citation file, not which ones, when you search the dictionary. When there is a thesaurus as well as a dictionary, the functions of the two files can be combined and together they can tell searchers how many records contain a given search term as well as how many other terms are related to it, as shown in Figure 6.2.

6.3.4   Using the Files Together

In summary, a typical data base has at least two files: a citation file containing the complete bibliographic records in date sequence and a dictionary file containing a list of all searchable terms occurring within the citation file, in alphabetical order. For each such term, there is a list of the citation file records containing that term. Searching is done first in the dictionary file to quickly locate the term desired and its list of containing records, as shown in Figure 6.4. Then, if requested by the user, the citation file records can be retrieved and displayed. Thesaurus information may be integrated with the dictionary data. Multiple word descriptors, as well as single words, may be put into the basic index or dictionary file.

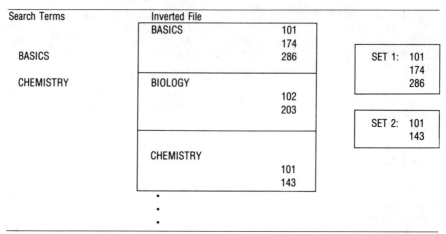

Figure 6.4. In searching, a term is looked up in the inverted file and record numbers are retrieved. Each group of record numbers for a search term constitutes a set. If the search was for *basics* **and** *chemistry* a third set would be created containing only the record numbered 101.

6.4   MAINTENANCE OF FILES

How does a bibliographic file get started? As we have noted, only rarely is the organization providing the search service also the one that provides the data base. The data base publisher typically produces a file in printed form for some time before deciding to offer it through a computer search service. In some cases a data base publisher may use computer processing at some stage in the production of his published material and, having the information already in a form that could be read by a computer (computer readable form), make the decision to move to a computer search service so much easier. If not in computer readable form, the data would have to be put in that form in order for it to be entered into a search service computer. The decision by the data base supplier to begin use of a search service must involve consideration of both the economics of supplying data in the appropriate form and the impact on sales of printed documents.

The exact format of the bibliographic records must be known to the search service whose computer is to read the data. For example, the service needs to know the order of occurrence of data elements, (e.g., *accession number, title, author,* and so on). The service must know exactly how many character positions each element or field will occupy and whether any elements, such as subject descriptors, can occur more than once in a record. Since each data base can be expected to be different from others to some extent, the search service's programmer will usually have to write a special computer program to convert the data from its original format to one their computer is able to deal with. This program then reads the specific data base and turns the information over to other programs that file away the data in the computer and create inverted files as needed. Creation of these latter files is time-consuming and expensive and is a hidden cost in the price of searching.

Periodically (exactly how often being the joint choice of the data base publisher and the search service) new information is added to the existing file. Changing files by adding to them or by modifying or deleting records is called *file maintenance.* In bibliographic systems, it is the former operation, adding records, that receives most of the attention. After whatever period is chosen—a month, three months, or whatever—the data base vendor sends a computer tape to the search service containing the new records for that period. These are entered into the computer, probably at night or on weekends when the machine is not being used for searching. Then, the next day, the newly updated file is ready for use. The frequency of updating should be noted in search service documentation of the individual file. The date of the most recent update may be a term in the citation records.

Records can be deleted from files, but most bibliographic data bases seem to grow indefinitely. Computer memories tend to improve in storage capacity and to decrease in cost at a rate faster than that at which the files grow, so there always seems to be room for new material. How long this will continue, we cannot forsee. The National Library of Medicine has attacked the problem by moving older records periodically into separate files containing two or three years' of data each. The searcher, then, may search only the most recent records or, at his own choice, may go back in time as far as NLM's data permit. Having large numbers of old records in a data base is not necessarily of benefit to users—it adds to the cost and to the difficulty of isolating the few records wanted. However, sometimes it is valuable.

If these files contained the personnel records of a large institution, a bank's depositor account records, or the inventory records of a company, we would expect their content to change often, as people were promoted, deposits were made, or goods sold. Bibliographic records, on the other hand, do not change much. They *might* change as, with time, new significance is discovered, authors' names change, or a new data element is added or a new thesaurus is used. However, the cost of changing is high and so it is rarely done. Thus if it is discovered that a document has been misclassified or an author's name misspelled, the error will probably not be corrected and searchers must learn to be aware of and cope with this situation.

6.5 USING VENDORS' FILE DESCRIPTIONS

Because of the large number of files and search services, each having its own version of documentation, it is difficult to provide any but the most general description of what vendors' documentation offers.

Every search service will provide a users' manual for its service, a book on how to use the search service (commands available, how to log in, telephone numbers to call in case of trouble, etc.). Usually these manuals will also contain at least a brief description of each file the service offers. The minimum information that should be present is:

- Scope of the file: what kind of source documents does the file refer to (report literature, journal articles, etc.), date that coverage began.
- Frequency of update.
- Structure of the records: what data elements are present, what fields are searchable.
- Special codes and abbreviations used: for example, how is the author field designated or a subject descriptor indicated.
- Special features, depending on the data base and search service: for example, since DIALOG uses fixed output formats, it must tell users which ones are available with each file.

The data base vendors sometimes publish their own documentation of their files. If available, this can be expected to be much more thorough in explaining anything related to content. Because computer search programs are different, it is still necessary to use search service documentation to verify some of the mechanical aspects of searching: the codes and abbreviations the search services use, output formats, and so on.

Search service documentation, in particular, changes often. It is *necessary*, in addition to having the service's original documentation, to receive its periodic newsletters, which will tell about the occasional changes in search commands, file availability, and other matters.

We have included in Appendix C an example of the documentation provided for a data base by the data base vendor and the search services.

Finally, there may be a thesaurus used in connection with a given file. It may be separately published or included in other file documentation. It may also be computer stored and computer searchable, but a computer search for a simple thesaurus term is much slower than looking it up manually in a handy book. Searching a file without having all documentation available to the searcher can be hazardous in terms of both effectiveness of the search and its cost.

REFERENCES (see also Appendix B and C)

1 Williams, Martha E. and Laurence Lammon, "Data Bases On-Line in 1979," *Bulletin of the American Society for Information Science,* **6,** 2 (December 1979)) 22–31.

2 *Directory of Online Information Resources,* 5th ed., Rockville, Md., CSG Press, 1980.

3 Landau, Ruth N., Judith Wanger, and Mary C. Berger (Compilers and Editors), *Directory of Online Databases,* Fall 1979, Santa Monica, Calif., Cuadra Associates, 1979, Vol. 1, p. 1.

4 Williams, Martha E. (Ed.), *Computer-Readable Data Bases: A Directory and Data Sourcebook,* 1979 Ed., White Plains, N.Y., Knowledge Industry Publications, 1979.

Seven

Basic Commands

7.1 THE FUNCTIONS OF THE BASIC COMMANDS

There is an indication from research studies[1] that most of the commands used in interactive searches are drawn from only a relative few of the total number of command types available for use. We call these the *basic commands*. What the research studies seem to be saying is that it is possible to do meaningful searching with just this basic command set and that is what is done most of the time. These are the commands we shall discuss in this chapter. Besides these, there are some other commands necessary to beginning and terminating a search and these are discussed in Chapter 9. The intervening chapter will cover some of the advanced commands. All these commands for several systems are shown in Appendix A.

We shall discuss four classes of commands here:

1 Commands for choosing terms and for initial set formation.
2 Commands for combining sets.
3 Commands for limiting the contents of already-formed sets.
4 Commands for displaying the contents of sets.

All these commands are used after the file to be searched has been chosen. That function is among those discussed in Chapter 9.

7.2 TERM SELECTION COMMANDS

The term selection commands are those that enable a user to look up a term in a dictionary or thesaurus or to create a set based on a single term. Both dictionary search and term selection commands are alike in that they provide the searcher with information about a single term, its number of occurrences, or the other terms related to it. They differ in that the dictionary and thesaurus look-up commands yield information only; the set-forming commands can take action as well as provide information.

7.2.1   Dictionary and Thesaurus Search

Whether or not there is a thesaurus associated with a given data base is a function of the particular data base supplier and the search service. Not all data bases include thesaurus information about related terms. However, there is always a dictionary file, or basic index, whose entries are searchable terms, with a count of the number of records that contain each term. Occurrence counts are usually maintained by field type, for example, how many times a term occurs in titles or abstracts. The dictionary *may* contain information about the number of semantically related terms and if it does, it is also functioning as a thesaurus. By its very alphabetic organization a dictionary can be readily searched for those terms that are, or appear to be, related by virtue of their spelling. In other words, *chemotherapy* will be found near *chemotropism* in the dictionary and the relatedness of both terms can easily be judged by the knowledgable searcher. But *pharmacology* will not be near either of those terms in the alphabetic array. Thus unless there is a file entry that draws a searcher's attention to this term, it would be easy to overlook it in searching for appropriate alternatives. That suggestive capability is the main value of a thesaurus.

A typical first step in a search is to look up a term in the dictionary file to see if it is in the dictionary, how often it occurs, and what other terms are nearby. A term is entered as the object of a dictionary search command or as an *argument* of a search. The result is that the computer displays several terms, in alphabetical order. All major search services require a separate step in order to form a set based on the entered term or any others displayed.

In DIALOG the command is *expand* <term>. (This notation means that the command, *expand,* is followed by the entry of a term. The brackets mean use any term.) The statement *expand computer assisted instruction* will result in the display shown in Figure 6.2. On this display can be seen a column of line numbers (E1-E10), a list of terms in alphabetic order, the number of citations, or "items" for each term, and in some files, including the one used here, the number of related terms. Related term information is available only in a few data bases.

In ORBIT, you say *nbr computer* (*nbr* means *neighbor,* but only the abbreviation is used as a command.) and get the five-line listing shown in Figure 7.1. ORBIT then asks you if you want to see any more terms in this array and lets you "go" up or down the list, as many terms at a time as you want. You could, for example, say *up 10* and this will give you the ten terms preceding the top one on your first list in alphabetical order. ORBIT gives only alphabetically related terms—it has no thesaurus capability.

BRS is slightly different. Here, you enter *root* <term>, when doing a search. Thus *root retriev* will give a list of all terms (up to 100) that begin with this root, as shown in Figure 7.2. To go up or down, enter a new root.

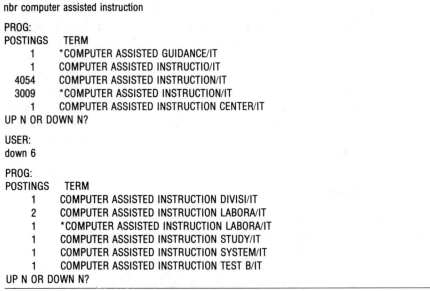

USER:
nbr computer assisted instruction

PROG:
POSTINGS   TERM
    1   *COMPUTER ASSISTED GUIDANCE/IT
    1   COMPUTER ASSISTED INSTRUCTIO/IT
 4054   COMPUTER ASSISTED INSTRUCTION/IT
 3009   *COMPUTER ASSISTED INSTRUCTION/IT
    1   COMPUTER ASSISTED INSTRUCTION CENTER/IT
UP N OR DOWN N?

USER:
down 6

PROG:
POSTINGS   TERM
    1   COMPUTER ASSISTED INSTRUCTION DIVISI/IT
    2   COMPUTER ASSISTED INSTRUCTION LABORA/IT
    1   *COMPUTER ASSISTED INSTRUCTION LABORA/IT
    1   COMPUTER ASSISTED INSTRUCTION STUDY/IT
    1   COMPUTER ASSISTED INSTRUCTION SYSTEM/IT
    1   COMPUTER ASSISTED INSTRUCTION TEST B/IT
UP N OR DOWN N?

Figure 7.1.   Use of the ORBIT *nbr* command.

Back to DIALOG, which has a more complicated set of options for what to do next, after an *expand*. You can go the equivalent of down, by using the command *page*, and the system responds by giving you the next "page" of the dictionary (terms alphabetically following the last term of the current display). You can always enter another *expand*, using any term you want. Or, you can say *expand* [line number] and that is interpreted as a request for display of the terms related to the term on the line specified, as *expand e6* will result in a display of the terms related to the term on line 6. (Note: Beware—if you haven't just completed an *expand*, or if there aren't any terms related to the one on the

BRS — SEARCH MODE — ENTER QUERY
   1__;   root retriev
        RETRIEV$

R1	RETRIEVABILITY	11 DOCUMENTS
R2	RETRIEVABLE	23 DOCUMENTS
R3	RETRIEVAL	3579 DOCUMENTS
R4	RETRIEVALS	8 DOCUMENTS
R5	RETRIEVE	141 DOCUMENTS
R6	RETRIEVED	129 DOCUMENTS
R7	RETRIEVEL	1 DOCUMENT
R8	RETRIEVER	17 DOCUMENTS
R9	RETRIEVERS	1 DOCUMENT
R10	RETRIEVES	6 DOCUMENTS
R11	RETRIEVING	129 DOCUMENTS

Figure 7.2.   Dictionary searching in BRS. By using the modifier *root* while in search mode, the user can ask for any terms that begin with the same root term entered, in this case *retriev*.

designated line, what you get is a dictionary page based on the "term" *e6*. See Figure 7.3.)

To form a set in DIALOG and BRS you can use line numbers or retype the terms. In ORBIT you must reenter the term if you wish to form a set—there is no line number option.

The more experienced you are with a given data base, the less you may need these commands. If you know what terms are used in the bibliographic records or if you use the printed thesaurus, you can search faster. But, for the latest frequency counts or a check on word variants, dictionary look-up can save a great deal of time. Its purpose, remember, is to help you use the appropriate terms in a search.

7.2.2 Set Formation

Once you have settled on the terms you would like to use in a search, the next step is to form sets. Recall that a set literally consists of a set of record numbers, but that we treat it as if it contained the records themselves. All three major search services number the sets for you in the order in which you create them. Creating a set is a necessary step before you can later do any browsing among the records.

The most direct way to create a set is to use a set-forming command followed by the term you are interested in. The commands are:

? e e6

Ref	Index-term	Type Items RT
E1	E3 ---	4
E2	E30r ---	1
E3	E31r ---	1
E4	E4r --	2
E5	E585r --	1
E6	E6r --	2
E7	E783r --	1
E8	E800r --	1
E9	E9r --	2
E10	FR ---	2282
E11	F NR INDEXR --	1
E12	F OLSEN LTDR ---	1
E13	F RATIOR--	2
E14	F SCALER ---	1
E15	F TESTR --	6
E16	F TESTSR ---	2
E17	F.AR--	5
E18	F.A.U.LR ---	1
E19	F.BR--	2
E20	F.B.C---	1

-more-

Figure 7.3. Result of expanding on a line number containing no related terms.

select lasers	(DIALOG)
*find lasers or lasers**	(ORBIT)
..search lasers†	(BRS)
lasers	

All accomplish the same thing—the computer will search for all records containing the term *lasers* in a searchable field and create a set containing the numbers of records in which it is found. It is only necessary that a field contain the word *lasers*, not that *lasers* be the entire content of the field. These commands will, for example, retrieve a document with the title *Gallium Arsenide Lasers*, as well as one with the descriptor *lasers*.

Following any of these commands the search system will respond with a message containing the set number and a count of set membership, that is, how many records contain the requested term. It is important to read and understand this message, for it may affect the way you should conduct the remainder of your search. For example, is the set size so small (or even zero, a *null set*) that you have clearly gotten the wrong term? Is it so large that you will clearly have to modify your search to get a useful volume of output? Beginning searchers often, inexplicably, do not read this message, and merrily go about continuing the search after having gotten a null set or retrieved 30,000 records, without any thought to what either of these outcomes implies.

7.2.3 Variations on Set-Forming Commands

There are many variations on the basic set-forming commands. While the online services are alike in the set-forming commands, the variations may differ widely. Some are so important as to require a considerable amount of attention later in this chapter and the next one.

Qualification.   You can specify in what data element or field the search term is to be found, for example in the title, descriptor or author field. This is generally done by annexing what DIALOG calls a *suffix* to the term. For example,

select school

calls for a record that has *school* in any of the fields of the *basic index*. The basic index is a list of mainly subject related terms, defined for each data base. The command

select school/ab

---

*The verb *find* can be omitted. If not present, ORBIT assumes this was the verb intended. We shall omit it henceforth.

†The command *..search* can be omitted once issued, that is, once BRS has been put into search mode. We shall omit it henceforth in our examples, but bear in mind that the command cannot be totally omitted in an actual search.

calls for only records having the word *school* in the abstract (*ab*) field. DIALOG also uses prefixes, which designate bibliographic fields (reserving the subject descriptive fields for the suffixes). These fields include *author, publication date,* and so on. An example of the use of a prefixed field is

select au = smith, a.b.

The prefix *au* indicates *author* and the equal sign is required, just as the / is with DIALOG suffixes.

Truncation.   You can truncate the search term, thereby asking for retrieval of all records containing a word that begins with the root you supply. As described here, all the search services' truncation capabilities work the same way, but their symbols are different. There are variations which are treated later. If you are searching for anything to do with computers or computation, you might search on the root *comput,* using these commands

select comput?	(DIALOG)
comput:	(ORBIT)
comput$	(BRS)

In this context, $, : and ? all have the same meaning, which is to permit any number of letters to occur in their place, including zero. That is, the term *comput,* followed by the appropriate truncation symbol, would retrieve records containing *comput, computer, computing, computation,* and so on. Note that these are set-forming commands; if you want to know what variants are to be found in the files, use the dictionary look-up commands.

Line Number Designation.   This is something DIALOG and BRS allow. If you have done an *expand lasers* or *root laser* and seen, in part, the following

DIALOG	BRS
E1 LASE	R1 LASER
E2 LASER	R2 LASER-APPLICATIONS
E3 LASER APPLICATIONS	R3 LASER-MEMORY
E4 LASER MEMORY	R4 LASER-OPTICS
E5 LASER OPTICS	R5 LASERS
E6 LASERS	I
I	I
I	I
I	

you can form a set based on *laser memory* by the command *select e4* or *search r3,* using the line number instead of the term. Should you want to select only the terms *laser* or *lasers,* you can use *select e2, e6* or *r1, r5.*

Logical Combination.   Many times you want to search for combinations of terms, such as for records containing both the words *laser* and *memory.* All the major search services allow this to be done in a single command. These options are covered in Section 7.3.

Term Context.   One of the most logically powerful capabilities available is that of being able to specify not only what other terms should appear in the same record but just how words will appear in context with each other. This is called *natural language* or *text searching* and is covered in Chapter 8.

7.3 SET COMBINATION

The kinds of commands most familiar to beginning searchers are the set combination commands, probably because, to those unfamiliar with computers, this type of command is almost intuitive. The reason for having set combinations is that it is rarely enough to define a set in terms of a single term, even if the term is a descriptor assigned by an indexer. Usually you will find that there are several terms with similar meanings, all of which you would like to use in a search, and there may be unrelated terms that you want to find together in selected records.

7.3.1 Basic Ways to Combine Sets

The major search services allow you to form set combinations using the same command that was used for initial set formation. (DIALOG has a command used only for combination, not for original creation. The dual-purpose command indicates that the latter is preferable.) For example, if your interest is lasers used in computer memories, you can directly ask for:

select laser and memory	(DIALOG)
laser and memory	(ORBIT)
laser and memory	(BRS)

An alternative is first to form the individual sets and then to combine them. DIALOG's single-purpose command works this way:

select laser	(forming set 1)
select memory	(forming set 2)
combine 1 and 2	(forming set 3)

Or, you can use the *select* command, in the third step, in the same way:

select s1 and s2	(forming set 3)

Another notational variation, using ORBIT to illustrate it, is:

memory	(forming set 1)
laser and 1	(forming set 2, the equivalent of set 3 in the previous examples.)

DIALOG has an additional variation which gives intermediate results. If you use the command

select steps laser and memory

you would be ordering the computer to form a set for *laser*, form a set for *memory*, and then form a set for the combination, printing out to you the set numbers and sizes as they were formed. The value of this is that you can later refer to each component of your ultimate set if you wish to revise the search later. In an actual use of the command, *select steps laser and memory*, applied to the NTIS data base, yielded the following results:

Set Number	Number of Citations	Set Definition
1	17724	LASER
2	7393	MEMORY
3	132	1 and 2

7.3.2   Set Combining Logic

If we want selected records to be in both sets 1 and 2, we define a new set which is the *intersection* of 1 and 2. (Figure 7.4) Verbally, the operation of intersection is described using the word **and.** We say the new set, 3, is made up of 1 *and* 2.

As a rule of thumb, intersecting two sets produces a new set that is smaller than either of the original ones, because we want to take from 1 only those that are also in 2, and from 2 only those in 1. Thus, 1 **and** 2 cannot be bigger, in number of records, than the smaller of 1 and 2. It can be, and usually is, smaller.

If we want to create a set of those records that are either in 1 or 2 or both, as shown in Figure 7.5a, we call this the *union* of the sets, and represent it by *1 or 2*. The *exclusive or,* meaning 1 or 2 but not both, is available in BRS, using the notation *1 xor 2* (Figure 7.5b).

1 or 2 gives a larger set than 1 or than 2, usually. It consists of records that are in 1 and, in addition, any that are in 2, but not 1. *1 or 2* cannot be smaller than the larger of 1 and 2.

Sometimes we want to exclude certain records, such as those representing works of a certain author or published in a certain journal. The reasons may be that we know these works quite well, rather than that we are uninterested in them. In this case, we might want to create a set of records that are in set 1 **and** in 2 but not in set 3. Thus a set of records containing the term *computer* and the term *library*, but not the term *circulation* can be represented as *computer **and** library **not** circulation*. The **not** operator is illustrated in Figure 7.6.

When you have in mind possible synonyms for some term, the thing to do is to form their union, or, in the jargon of searching, *"or"* them together, as *computer **or** data processor **or** automation*. The terms need not be synonymous in all contexts, just in the one you have in mind. The terms *computer* and

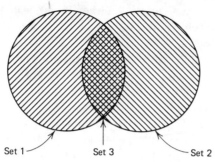

Figure 7.4. The *and* operator. Set 3 consists of those elements which are in set 1 and are also in set 2.

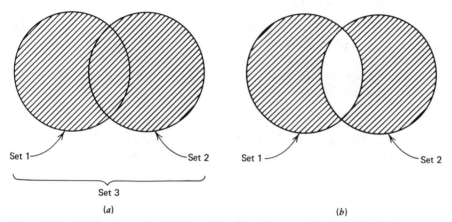

(a)   (b)

Figure 7.5. (*a*) The *or* operator. Set 3 consists of those elements which are in either set 1 or set 2 or both. (*b*) The *xor* operator does not result in inclusion of the intersection, the unshaded area.

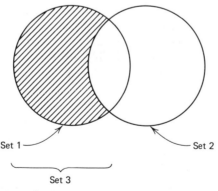

Figure 7.6. The *not* operator. Set 3 consists of those parts of set 1 which are not also part of set 2.

automation are not synonyms, but either might lead to documents on the automation of library circulation systems, because a computer is usually at the heart of such a system.

When you have different concepts and want material that is about all of them, use *and.* For example, *computer and library* combines two dissimilar terms. In this case we are using one term to modify another, rather than treating them as synonyms.

The term *strategy* is sometimes applied to a *set combination expression,* such as *1 and 2 or 3.* We feel this is a misnomer. Our ideas on strategy are found in Chapter 12. We think the proper word to describe a combination is *expression,* which is used in mathematics and in computer programming to describe exactly this concept.

7.3.3   DIALOG and BRS Variations

We mentioned earlier that DIALOG and BRS permit you to select a term by using the line number of a term in an *expand* display. Refer to the example in Section 7.2.3. Assume you wanted to form a single set from *laser, laser applications, laser memory,* and *lasers,* but did not want to include *laser optics.* You could use the expressions

$$e2-e4,e6 \text{ or } r1-r3, r5$$

which means select terms on all lines from E2 (R1) through E4 (R3) and also the term on line E6 (R5). This expression gives results identical to

$$laser \text{ or } laser \text{ } applications \text{ or } laser \text{ } memory \text{ or } lasers$$

7.3.4   Notes on Using Combining Operators

Just about any search service offers the same basic operations. We can intersect or join (form the union of) sets, or we can negate a set. The following are some examples of the use of these operations.

Europe or Africa and not Ireland includes any country in Europe or in Africa, but excludes any record that has Ireland as a term. (Figure 7.7)

Europe and Africa requires that both the terms *Europe* and *Africa* must be present in any record selected. If we are interested in wine-making in this region of the world, we would, with this expression, retrieve only records mentioning both continents; we would fail to select one that discussed only the Algerian wine industry if it does not name the continent.

To insure retrieval of any record mentioning Europe or any country in it, we might have to resort to: *Europe or Italy or France or Spain or.* . . . (see Figure 7.8). Unless there is a code for location that was so composed that it included both an indication of country and continent, we cannot be sure that an article on European energy use is necessarily going to mention Italy, or vice versa. Such a search is obviously tedious and indicates why special geographic

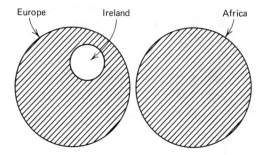

Figure 7.7. A schematic representation of the geographic concept *Europe or Africa but not Ireland.*

codes that give the hierarchical relationship between country and continent are still of value, even in mechanized systems.

If you use **not** logic, you have to be very careful. A request, as illustrated above, for *Europe **not** Ireland,* say in conjunction with a search on wool production, is going to *exclude* a paper on European wool production in general, including Ireland, because you said you wanted to exclude any record mentioning Ireland. (See Figure 7.9.) This usage is occasionally found when the searcher means to exclude all records mentioned *only* Ireland and, instead, excludes all records mentioning Ireland whether or not they mention other countries. There is no way, in most retrieval system languages, that you can express the former limitation, that is, that a record must mention one and only one country, subject, or author.

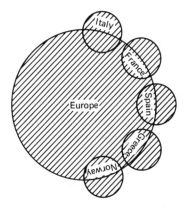

Figure 7.8. Geographically, *Europe* includes the individual countries, but bibliographically, a mention of *Europe* or of *Italy* does not imply that the other term was mentioned. Hence to retrieve *everything* about Europe, it is necessary to create the union of sets defined by *Europe, Italy, France,* and so on.

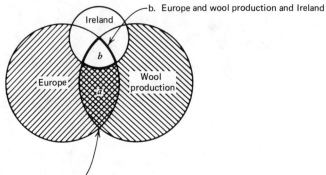

a. Europe and wool production not Ireland

Figure 7.9. *(a)* Europe and wool production not Ireland. *(b)* Europe and wool production and Ireland. Set *a* is the set actually requested by the expression *Europe* **and** *wool production* **not** *Ireland.* Set *b* shows a subject area including both parts of *Europe* and *wool production* and which mentions Ireland but is not exclusively about Ireland; it could include information about other countries as well which the search expression unintentionally deleted.

7.3.5   Concept Groups or Facets

Often, you have several terms or descriptors that are synonyms or near synonyms for each other. All these terms represent different ways of expressing a single concept and, together, they are called a *concept group* or a *facet.* A common search tactic is to create an individual set for each term of a concept group and then combine them into a single set, linking all the terms in an expression by the *or* operator. An example is *defense, national defense, security, or military preparedness* as individual terms all related to the concept of a nation's military strength or readiness. By creating a set for each of these terms and then combining them into a single set as the union of the individual sets, you can create a set expressing that single concept or that facet of a search topic.

7.3.6   Combining Concept Sets

A search usually involves more than one concept set. For example, you may be interested in military preparedness and its relationship to the national economy. To perform this search you could create a concept set based on military preparedness and another based on the concept of national economy. Then, intersect the two concept sets and hope thereby to hit exactly what you were looking for. (See Figure 7.10.) This would involve a possibly long string of combine-type commands, forming the first concept set, then the second, and then the intersection of the two.

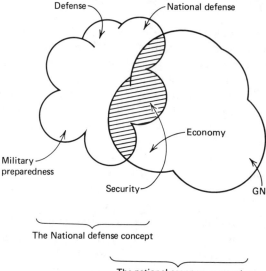

Defense   National defense

Military
preparedness

Economy

Security   GNP

The National defense concept

The national economy concept

Figure 7.10. The intersection of two concept sets. When the intersection is formed we do not which individual terms in one concept are co-occurring with terms in the other, and we do not need to know.

7.3.7 Set Sizes

When using combining commands it is well to bear in mind that *or* is an operator that tends to create a new set larger than any of its constituents. The union of sets 1 *or* 2 *or* 3 cannot be smaller than the largest of these and may be larger than all of them. When using *and,* the resulting set tends to be smaller than the constituent sets. The intersection of sets 4 and 5 and 6 can be no larger than the smallest of them and may be smaller yet. (See Figure 7.11.)

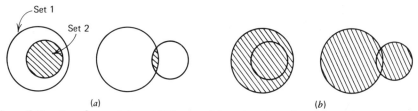

Set 1

Set 2

(a)   (b)

Figure 7.11. Bounds on set sizes. (a) The size of the intersection of two sets can be no larger than the smaller of the intersecting sets. (b) The size of the union of a group of sets can be no smaller than the largest of the joined sets.

7.4 SET LIMITATION

One way to interpret an expression such as *gun and butter* is that it directs the computer to find all records containing *gun* and then to delete from that set all except those that also contain *butter*. While each search service has different computer programs, and it may be that some actually perform the search that way, conventionally the set for *gun* would be formed and then the set for *butter* and then the intersection would be found by comparing record or accession numbers of the elements of the sets and selecting for the new set only those in both original sets. (See Figure 7.12.)

There are times, though, when what we actually want to do is to reduce the records in a set by removing all those not having some stated qualification. Probably the most common basis for doing this is *date*. You might well want to take a set with whose contents you are otherwise satisfied and eliminate from it all records dated before some given year. Or, you might want to eliminate all records about documents that are not journal articles, eliminating report literature that may be harder to find in a library. All three search services offer some form of limiting, other than by use of the *and* or *not* operator. Exactly how you can limit is a function of the service and of the data base and, therefore, once again we must refer you to the manual for the service you plan to use. Here, though, are examples from each of the major languages, showing one way in which the function can be used.

In ORBIT, *4 and from 74 thru 76* reduces a previously formed set, assuming its number was 4, by limiting it to documents dated from 1974 to 1976, inclusive. A new set will be created and numbered after this command.

In DIALOG, *limit 4/ej* is a way for ERIC searchers to limit a previously defined set number 4 to the journal literature subfile, EJ being a code for the *Combined Index to Journals in Education* portion of the ERIC file.

For BRS users, there is a wider range of options, an example of which is

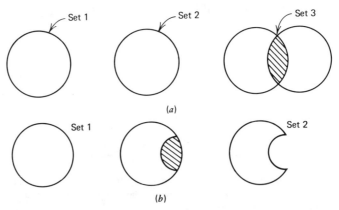

Figure 7.12.   Set intersection contrasted with limitation. *(a)* Set intersection: form set *1*, form set *2*, intersect the two to form set *3*. *(b)* Set limitation: form set *1*, remove part of it to form set *2*.

..limit/4 yr gt 67 which means to limit set number 4, again assumed to have been previously defined, to those records for which the year is greater than 1967. Each combination of search service and data base has its own defined set limitation rules.

7.5   DISPLAY AND BROWSING

Dictionary search, set formation, and set combination commands all provide some kinds of feedback to the searcher, but this is generally restricted to lists of terms that may be used and numeric data about the terms or about sets formed by their use. One can go just so far in using set sizes alone to guide further searching. Eventually you want to see some of the records you are retrieving. Search services provide two kinds of commands to enable you to see the contents of records they retrieve. One covers the online display, or printing, records at the searcher's terminal. The second covers offline printing of records on a high-speed printer located at the service's computer center, records that are then mailed to the user, as shown in Figure 7.13.

Basically, these commands, which can look quite different among the services, must in one way or another convey the same information from searcher to computer: (1) what set is to be printed or displayed; (2) what records of that set are to be displayed; (3) what portions of those records (i.e., what data elements) are to be displayed; (4) in what format will elements be printed; and (5) where the records will be printed (on the terminal or high-speed printer).

BRS and ORBIT provide the most flexibility in browsing and display commands, but to take advantage of the flexibility, the user must expend more effort. DIALOG is particularly limited in display format; they offer only eight predetermined formats to choose from but, to compensate, choice of a format is easy. BRS and ORBIT expect the user to enter abbreviations for all data

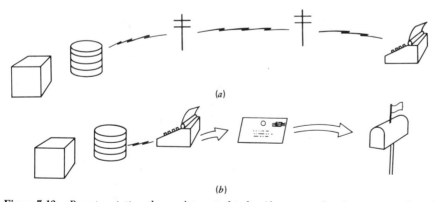

(a)

(b)

Figure 7.13.   Remote printing: the user's terminal is directly connected to the computer through the telephone system. *(b)* Offline printing: information is printed at the computer center and mailed to the user.

elements or fields to be printed, although default sets of elements exist for use when the user does not specify them, and a few codes for standard formats are available.

The following are examples of online print commands in use by the three services. Suppose, in each case, you have searched ERIC, are interested in set number 3, know it contains more than 15 records and want to look at records 6–15. You decide that the only fields you are interested in are *title, author,* and *accession number.*

DIALOG does not have a predetermined format exactly matching this requirement. You must choose between their format 6, which has title and accession number only, or format 3, which provides *accession number, title, author, source,* a list of *descriptors,* and a few other items. Furthermore, assume you are working with a print terminal. Then the command is *type 3/3/6-15.*

In ORBIT, you can select the specific fields of the record that you want. The command is *print ti, au, an, 10 skip 5.* The abbreviations *ti, au,* and *an* represent the title, author, and document accession number fields. The 10 tells how many records are wanted. ORBIT starts with the first record in the set unless you tell it to skip some, in this case to skip 5, and then start counting, so you end up with records 6–15.

To print offline, on the high-speed printer, the command structures are about the same. DIALOG calls for a different verb with the same command structure; that is, you would use *print 3/3/6-15.* ORBIT asks you to add the phrase *off line* following *skip 5.* BRS would have you say

> *..printoff 3 ti, an, au/doc= 6-15/ id= Smith, Jane, c/o Bio Dept*

The results are identified by searcher (Jane Smith) and the library that receives the print-out can then send it to her (at the Biology Department).

7.6   THREE SAMPLE SEARCHES

In this section we show three simple but more or less complete searches, in the three different languages. Each has the same objective. They are directed toward similar, but not identical data bases, Compendex and INSPEC. Annotations to the right of the commands explain each command's function within the overall search. We have omitted certain housekeeping commands whose functions we have not yet described.

The subject of the searches is the use of heat pumps in residential buildings. The objective is to find a modest number of papers or reports that are not too highly technical in nature. The concept sets are *heat pumps* and *residences.* Either concept may be expressed in more than one way. We use slightly different strategies in each search, to show some of the many variations available. These are intended to resemble typical searches done by relatively inexperienced searchers, not by experts.

7.6.1 DIALOG Search

The searcher selects file 8 (Compendex) and receives information about costs incurred prior to this *begin* command (a). Then, confirmation is given as to what file is being searched (b). The first actual search command is *expand heat pumps* (c). The user sees several terms of interest and selects *heat pump?*, using the truncation symbol ? to include any ending on the word *pump*. The word *residential* is then used (d) to search the dictionary file and the searcher decides to select *residence or residential* (e). He then combines the first two sets (f) and requests that some of the retrieved records from set 3 be typed on his terminal (g).

The format selected for typing is 6, which gives little more than title and identification number, but gives a quick look at many records. We have highlighted the terms in the retrieved records (h) that match the search terms, but remember that other terms in the record might have contributed to selection, but were not printed in this format. These are not bad, but are not quite what was wanted.

To see some more detail, the user types out a single record in the more expansive format 5, and, again, we highlight the terms which led to selection of the record (i). Then, he decides to become more stringent and require that the word *residential* appear in the title (j). The results (k) look more appealing for the casual searcher, and the searcher decides to stop (l).

(a.)? begin8

4jan80 10:11:28 User7001
$3.80 0.253 Hrs File8 6 Descriptors

(b.)File8:COMPENDEX 70-79/NOV
  (Copr. Engineering Index Inc.)

Set Items Description (+ =OR; * =AND; − =NOT)

(c.)? expand heat pumps

Ref	Index-term	Type Items RT
E1	HEAT PUMP HEATING SYSTEMS	1
E2	HEAT PUMP PERFORMANCE	2
E3	HEAT PUMP PROCESS	1
E4	HEAT PUMP STATIONS	2
E5	HEAT PUMP SYSTEMS	556
E6	HEAT PUMPS	6
E7	HEAT RADIATION	3
E8	HEAT TRANSFER	4
E9	HEAT RATE	1
E10	HEAT RATE TEST	1
E11	HEAT RECLAIM	1
E12	HEAT RECOVERY	47
E13	HEAT RECOVERY BOILERS	3
E14	HEAT RECOVERY EQUIPMENT	3
E15	HEAT RECOVERY EXCHANGER	1
E16	HEAT RECOVERY EXCHANGERS	1
E17	HEAT RECOVERY INCINERATION SYSTEMS	1
E18	HEAT RECOVERY METHODS	2

? selectheat pump?

        1   561 HEAT PUMP?

(d.)? e residential

Ref	Index-term	Type Items RT
E1	RESIDENT ENGINEER	1
E2	RESIDENT SYSTEMS	1
E3	RESIDENT-DEPENDENT EFFECTS	1
E4	RESIDENT'S	3
E5	RESIDENTAL	1
E6	RESIDENTIAL	1248
E7	RESIDENTIAL ALARM SYSTEMS	1
E8	RESIDENTIAL AREAS	4
E9	RESIDENTIAL BUILDINGS	6
E10	RESIDENTIAL DENSITY	1
E11	RESIDENTIAL ELECTRICITY DEMAND	1
E12	RESIDENTIAL ENERGY USE	3
E13	RESIDENTIAL HEATING	1
E14	RESIDENTIAL HOUSES	1
E15	RESIDENTIAL HOUSING	2
E16	RESIDENTIAL LOCATION	2
E17	RESIDENTIAL SECTOR	2

(e.)? s residence or residential

        1135 RESIDENCE
        1248 RESIDENTIAL
    2 2354   RESIDENCE OR RESIDENTIAL

(f.) ? combine 1 and 2
        3   65   1 AND 2

(g.)? type 3/6/1-5

(h.)3/6/1
  ID NO.—EI791187122   987122
    METHANOL-BASED **HEAT PUMPS** FOR STORAGE OF SOLAR THERMAL ENERGY.
    Energy Technol: Proc of Therm Energy Storage Contract Inf Exch Meet, 3rd Annu, Springfield, Va, Dec 5-6 1978 Organized by Sandia Lab, Livermore Calif for DOE (CONF-781231), Washington, DC, 1978. Available from NTIS, Springfield, Va p 425-432

  3/6/2
  ID NO.—EI791187120   987120
    HEAT PUMPS. VOLUME 2. 1978-JANUARY, 1979 (CITATIONS FROM THE ENGINEERING INDEX DATA BASE).
    NTISearch NTIS/PS-79/0234/9EES, Search period covered: 1978-Jan 1979. Publ by NTIS, Springfield, Va, Apr 1979. Available from NTIS 113 p

  3/6/3
  ID NO.—EI791187119   987119
    HEAT PUMPS. VOLUME 1, 1970-1977 (CITATIONS FROM THE ENGINEERING INDEX DATA BASE).
    NTISearch NTIS/PS-79/0233/1EES, Search period covered: 1970-1977. Publ by NTIS, Springfield, Va, Apr 1979. Available from NTIS 242 p

  3/6/4
  ID NO.—EI791187118   987118

HEAT PUMPS (CITATIONS FROM THE NTIS DATA BASE).
NTISearch NTIS/PS-79/0232/3ENS, Search period covered: 1964-Jan 1979. Publ by NTIS, Springfield, Va, Apr 1979. Available from NTIS 175 p

3/6/5
ID NO.—EI791078791   978791
SOLAR-ASSISTED **HEAT PUMP** FOR **RESIDENTIAL** HOUSING.
Pap ASAE for Winter Meet, Chicago, Ill, Dec 18-20 1978. Publ by ASAE, St. Joseph, Mich, 1978 Pap 78-4533, 18 p

(i.) ? type 3/5/1
3/5/1
ID NO.—EI791187122   987122
METHANOL-BASED **HEAT PUMPS** FOR STORAGE OF SOLAR THERMAL ENERGY.
Anon
EIC Corp, Newton, Mass
Energy Technol: Proc of Therm Energy Storage Contract Inf Exch Meet, 3rd Annu, Springfield, Va, Dec 5-6 1978 Organized by Sandia Lab, Livermore Calif for DOE (CONF-781231), Washington, DC, 1978. Available from NTIS, Springfield, Va p 425-432
The basis of the **heat pump** storage system is a chemical reaction that proceeds in one direction at high temperature and in the opposite direction at low temperatures. A gas-solid reaction maximizes storage energy density and provides ready separation of the chemical products. Methanol is particularly suited as the vapor due to its low freezing point, high entropy vaporization, and relative freedom from hazards. Twenty inorganic salts were screened in a specially designed thermogravimetric analyzer (TGA) employing fixed $CH//3OH$ vapor pressure and slowly varying temperatures. Appreciable reaction was thermodynamic and kinetic behavior approximately suitable for use in a **heat pump**: $MgCl//2$, $FeBr//2$, $CoBr//2$, and $CaCl//2$. The use of the reaction between $CaCl//2$ and $CH//3OH$ vapor in a thermally activated **heat pump** for solar storage, heating and cooling appears promising for **residential** use. 2 refs.
DESCRIPTORS: (***HEAT PUMP** SYSTEMS, *Design), (SALTS, Energy Storage), (HEATING, Solar), CARD ALERT: 643, 505, 901

(j.) ? select s3 and residential/ti
                              365 RESIDENTIAL/TI
              4   25   S3 AND RESIDENTIAL/TI

(k.)? type 4/6/1-5
4/6/1
ID NO.—EI791078791   978791
SOLAR-ASSISTED HEAT PUMP FOR RESIDENTIAL HOUSING.
Pap ASAE for Winter Meet, Chicago, Ill, Dec 18-20 1978. Publ by ASAE, St. Joseph, Mich, 1978 Pap 78-4533, 18 p

4/6/2
ID NO.—EI790970233   970233
PERFORMANCE OF SOLAR ASSISTED HEAT PUMP HEATING SYSTEMS FOR RESIDENTIAL USE.
ASME Pap n 79-HT-12 for Meet Aug 6-8 1979 11 p

4/6/3
ID NO.—EI790861677   961677
WAERMEVERTEILUNG, WAERMEDAEMMUNG UND WARMWASSERBEREITUNG IN VERBINDUNG MIT WAERMEPUMPEN ZUR BEHEIZUNG VON WOHNGEBAEUDEN. $left bracket$ Heat Distribution, Heat Insulation and Water Heating in Conjunction with Heat Pumps Used for Residential Space-Heating.
Elektrowaerme Int Ed A v 36 n A2 Mar 1978 p A113-A118

4/6/4
ID NO.—EI790752652   952652

COMPUTER SIMULATION FOR RESIDENTIAL HEATING ENERGY REQUIREMENTS USING SOLAR SUPPLEMENTED HEAT PUMPS.
Proc Summer Comput Simul Conf Newport Beach, Calif, Jul 24-26 1978. Sponsored by Soc for Comput Simul (SCS), La Jolla, Calif, 1978. Available from AFIPS Press, Montvale, NJ p 760-765

4/6/5
ID NO.—EI790643225   943225
WAERMEPUMPEN-VERSUCHSANLAGE MIT LATENTSPEICHER ZUR WOHNHAUSBEHEIZUN-G. $left bracket$ Heat Pump Pilot Instllation with Latent Store for Residential Heating $right bracket$.
Elektrowaerme Int Ed A v 36 n 6 Nov 1978 p A319-A324

(l.) ? logoff
4jan80 10:22:51 User7001
$2.87 0.191 Hrs File8 4 Descriptors

LOGOFF 10:22:54

tc>   dropped by host system

7.6.2   ORBIT Search

This time the user, having already chosen Compendex, directly searches on the terms *heat* and *pump,* again using a truncation symbol (:) to indicate that any suffix on *pump* will be acceptable (a). There are 100 references to pump in various contexts, and the user asks for all of them (b). Set 1 is then formed (c). Set 2 is formed of terms indicating residential buildings (d). The two sets are combined (e) and a sample ordered to be printed (f). The resulting titles (g) are not the same as in the DIALOG search, but are of the same type, appearing rather technical. Again, the search is modified to require one of the residence terms to appear in the title of a document (h) and the result (i) is nearly the same as in the other search. The searcher then logs off (j).

PROG:

(a.)SS 1 /C?
USER:
heat and pump:

PROG:
MM (PUMP:) (100)
ALL OR NONE?

(b.)USER:
all

(c.)PROG:
SS 1 PSTG (1505)

(d.)SS 2 /C?
USER:
residential or residence or home

PROG:
SS 2 PSTG (3275)

(e.)SS 3 /C?
USER:
1 and 2

PROG:
SS 3 PSTG (118)

(f.) SS 4 /C?
USER:
print ti 5

PROG:

(g.)-1-
TI — EVERYDAY OPERATIONAL ASPECTS OF AN ELECTROCOATING SYSTEM.

-2-
TI — METHANOL-BASED HEAT PUMPS FOR STORAGE OF SOLAR THERMAL ENERGY.

-3-
TI — LOW-TEMPERATURE THERMAL ENERGY STORAGE PROGRAM OVERVIEW.

-4-
TI — COGENERATION SYSTEMS FOR RESIDENTIAL/COMMERCIAL APPLICATIONS.

-5-
TI — ENERGY CALCULATION PROCEDURES FOR RESIDENCES WITH FIELD VALIDATION.

(h.)SS 4 /C?
USER:
residential/ti or residence/ti or home/ti

PROG:
SS 4 PSTG (725)

SS 5 /C?
USER:
1 and 4

PROG:
SS 5 PSTG (39)

SS 6 /C?
USER:
print ti 5

PROG:

(i.) -1-
TI — COGENERATION SYSTEMS FOR RESIDENTIAL/COMMERCIAL APPLICATIONS.

-2-
TI — SOLAR-ASSISTED HEAT PUMP FOR RESIDENTIAL HOUSING.

-3-
TI — PERFORMANCE OF SOLAR ASSISTED HEAT PUMP HEATING SYSTEMS FOR RESIDENTIAL USE.

-4-
TI — WAERMEVERTEILUNG WAERMEDAEMMUNG UND WARMWASSERBEREITUNG IN VERBIN-
DUNG MIT WAERMEPUMPEN ZUR BEHEIZUNG VON WOHNGEBAEUDEN [Heat Distribution
Heat Insulation and Water Heating in Conjunction with Heat Pumps Used for Residential
Space-Heating.

-5-
TI — COMPUTER SIMULATION FOR RESIDENTIAL HEATING ENERGY REQUIREMENTS USING SOLAR SUPPLEMENTED HEAT PUMPS.

(j.) USER:
stop

PROG:
DONE? (Y/N)

USER:
Y

PROG:
TERMINAL SESSION FINISHED 01/04/80 7:59 A.M. (PACIFIC TIME)
ELAPSED TIME ON COMPX: 0.40 HRS.
TOTAL ELAPSED TIME: 0.51 HRS.
PLEASE HANG UP YOUR TELEPHONE NOW. GOOD-BYE!

7.6.3   BRS Search

In this example, the INSPEC data base is used, since Compendex is not available through BRS. The searcher tries for a direct statement of the entire search objective in one expression (a). There are 11 cited documents. A print command (b) is given, calling for the titles of the first five documents. As with the others, the titles seem relevant but too technical. Again, the technique used is to require that the key words appear in the title. Note in the command (c) that the suffix *ti* applies to all terms within the parentheses, following normal algebraic usage. Another print command is issued (d), and the resulting titles (e) seem what was wanted.

BRS/INSP/1977-NOV79

(a)   BRS — SEARCH MODE — ENTER QUERY
　　　1__: heat and pumps and (residence or residential)
　　　RESULT   11

(b)   　2__;   .. print 1 ti/doc=1−5
　　　　1
　　　TI INSTALLATION OF HEAT PUMPS IN HOUSING.

　　　　2
　　　TI HEAT RECOVERY FROM SEWAGE FOR ST. LAWRENCE PHASE B OF THE CITY OF TORONTO.

　　　　3
　　　TI ELECTRONIC CONTROLLER FOR RESIDENTIAL HEAT-PUMP AIR CONDITIONERS.

　　　　4
　　　TI COMPUTER SIMULATION FOR RESIDENTIAL HEATING ENERGY REQUIREMENTS USING SOLAR SUPPLEMENTED HEAT PUMPS.

　　　　5
　　　TI FORECASTING NATIONAL GAS DEMAND BY MODELLING FUEL PURCHASING DECISIONS FOR END-USE CUSTOMER GROUPS.

　　　　　　　　　END OF DOCUMENTS

```
        . . SEARCH
(c)  BRS — SEARCH MODE — ENTER QUERY
        2__:   heat.ti, and pumps.ti. and (residence or residential or housing).ti.
        RESULT     4

(d)     3__;  . . PRINT 2 TI/DOC=1−4
        1

TI  INSTALLATION OF HEAT PUMPS IN HOUSING.

        2
TI  COMPUTER SIMULATION FOR RESIDENTIAL HEATING ENERGY REQUIREMENTS USING SOLAR
    SUPPLEMENTED HEAT PUMPS.

        3
TI  HEAT PUMPS FOR RESIDENTIAL HEATING USING UNDERGROUND HEAT.

        4
TI  USING AIR-AIR HEAT PUMPS FOR RESIDENTIAL HEATING IN FRANCE.

R0601 * END OF DOCUMENTS IN LIST
```

REFERENCE (See also Appendix A)

1   Standera, Oldrich, "On-Line Retrieval Systems: Some Observations on the User/System Interface," *Proceedings of the 38th ASIS Annual Meeting*, Boston, October 26−30, 1975, Washington, D.C., American Society for Information Science, 1975, 38−40.

Eight

Text Searching

8.1 ORIGINS OF TEXT SEARCHING

When information retrieval systems were first developed in the early 1960's, the records in the files (the citation records) did not generally contain abstracts. It was expensive to convert these to machine readable form and too expensive to store them in the computer. Users, not expecting them, did not demand them. The basic commands we now use with online search systems were developed around the idea that dictionary files made from specific searchable fields would contain a word or short phrase that would be matched with a search term.

As computer memory became cheaper, it became ever more common to include an abstract in the machine-stored record and to invert every word* in the abstract and list it in the dictionary file. Now it is the conventional thing to do. Even before this changeover was completed, there arose interest in searching for individual words within a title or even a single word within a multiword descriptor. Thus came about the ability to search *within* a field, be it by descriptor, title, or abstract and to expand the dictionary file beyond the descriptors assigned by indexers or by the words in the title. There are several ways of searching within a *field,* as we shall describe below. Before doing so, for those not familiar with the concepts, we shall review the difference between *controlled* and *uncontrolled* vocabularies in document indexing. Those already familiar with these concepts may skip Section 8.

---

*In natural language processing, we *almost always* omit the articles, prepositions, and so on, in making up dictionary files and unless we say to the contrary, assume we mean to omit these words in this and other discussions of the subject.

8.2   CONTROLLED AND UNCONTROLLED VOCABULARIES

If we go back to the earliest experiments with computers used for information retrieval, we will find that a record consisted, as noted previously, of a series of short fields containing such data elements as *title, author, date of publication,* and *descriptors.* Descriptors assigned from a controlled vocabulary represent an intellectual effort to describe what an item is about using only a predetermined set of words or terms or codes. Descriptors can be any of a combination of traditional classification codes (as in the Library of Congress or Dewey Decimal systems), subject headings, or key words and phrases. Typically, a key word is a single word or short phrase whose use in an index, combined with other key words, could be more descriptive of subject content than a hierarchical classification code or several subject headings. The key word combinations gave the indexer more freedom to use basic language building blocks to construct highly specific document descriptions and to be able to describe subject concepts unforeseen in the development of the controlled language.

One way to use key words is first to construct a list of acceptable ones. While such a list can be changed, at any moment an indexer or searcher is expected to limit his search or descriptive vocabulary to those terms. Thus the vocabulary is *controlled.* Sometimes, these become hierarchical, as relationships among terms are added to the lexicon and the word lists become thesauri. The important relationships are expressed as broader, narrower, and closely related. Synonymous terms may be linked with a note to *use* one *for* the other. See the example from the ERIC thesaurus in Figure 6.1.

The indexers in some data base systems can also use *free key words,* that is, words and phrases chosen at the moment of use. The choice of free key words (sometimes also known as *identifiers*) depends on what is needed to describe a particular document, not what is in a thesaurus. Free key words look like controlled ones, but they lack an authority for their use. In some systems, they may be used especially for names of projects, places, equipment, facilities, and so on. Setting aside a field in a record for free key words made indexing easier, especially when indexing documents with new, fast-changing subjects. Unfortunately, in the past, the searcher has had few clues as to how the indexer may have elected to handle some given subject with the use of free key words.

In addition to these kinds of terms, it is now common for the computer to create an inverted file of all words in specified fields that are designated as a *searchable fields* in a record. The dictionary or inverted file can be viewed as a file of computer-selected terms, although it also contains all those assigned by the human indexers. Figure 8.1 shows a small sample of an inverted file and illustrates the difference between what the inverted file would be like if it contained only indexer-chosen words and what it looks like if it contains all words in all searchable fields. The inverted file contains all of the words used in

Citation File

Record No.: 1
Title: Abstracting Theory
Author: Smith
Descriptors:
  Abstracting
  Documentation
  Information Retrieval

Record No.: 2
Title: Searching
Author: Miller
Descriptors:
  Online Searching
  Library Automation

Record No.: 3
Title: Theory of Information Retrieval
Author: Baker
Descriptors:
  Information Retrieval
  Library Automation

Inverted File A

Entry	Record No.
AU=BAKER	3
AU=MILLER	2
AU=SMITH	1
DE=ABSTRACTING	1
DE=DOCUMENTATION	1
DE=INFORMATION RE-TRIEVAL	1, 3
DE=LIBRARY AUTOMATION	2, 3
DE=ONLINE SEARCHING	2

Inverted File B

Entry	Record No.
AU=BAKER	3
AU=MILLER	2
AU=SMITH	1
ABSTRACTING/DE	1
ABSTRACTING/TI	1
AUTOMATION/DE	2, 3
DE=DOCUMENTATION	1
DE=INFORMATION RETRIEVAL	1, 3
DE=LIBRARY AUTOMATION	2, 3
DE=ONLINE SEARCHING	2
DOCUMENTATION/DE	1
INFORMATION/DE	1, 3
INFORMATION/TI	3
LIBRARY/DE	2, 3
ONLINE/DE	2
RETRIEVAL/DE	1, 3
RETRIEVAL/TI	3
SEARCHING/DE	2
SEARCHING/TI	2
THEORY/TI	1, 3
TI=ABSTRACTING THEORY	1
TI=SEARCHING	2
TI=THEORY OF INFORMATION RETRIEVAL	3

Figure 8.1. Dictionary, or inverted file. Inverted File A is composed only of indexer-selected authors (AU) and descriptors (DE). Thus, these are the searchable terms under this arrangement. Inverted file B also includes *titles* (TI) and individual words that appeared in a title or descriptor, except for common words (e.g., *of*). In file B individual words are tagged with suffixes to show the field from which they were taken. Thus searching is possible on a complete term, such as *information retrieval*, or a single word, such as *retrieval*. The complete contents of a field are denoted by a prefix. This figure is intended to approximate, but not exactly describe, any particular system.

the search fields *except* the so-called common words which are said to contain no information. These are words like *of, and, it, to,* and *the.* Services desiring to remove these words from the dictionary create a list of them, often called a *stop list* and use this stop list to exclude words from being put into the dictionary. By doing so, as much as 50 percent of the total words in the text of a document (or title or abstract of one) may be excluded with little or no loss of information. For all practical purposes, an inverted file is a concordance of the full text of all the fields designated as searchable. The BRS stop list is shown in Figure 8.2.

In summary, we may have controlled and uncontrolled terms assigned to a record by an indexer, and we may have additional terms that are "selected" by the computer merely because they were present in a field designated as searchable. Both sets of terms are typically found intermingled in the inverted file. Multiword descriptors used in indexing, such as *laser memory*, will appear in the inverted file once for the complete term and once for each constituent word. In this case, three entries might be generated, for example, *laser, laser memory*, and *memory*.

A	IF	THAN
ABOUT	IN	THAT
AMONG	INTO	THE
ALL	IS	THEIR
AN	IT	THESE
AND	ITS	THEY
ARE	***	THIS
AS	MADE	THOSE
AT	MAKE	THROUGH
***	MANY	TO
BE	MAY	TOWARD
BEEN	MORE	***
BETWEEN	MOST	UPON
BOTH	MUST	USED
BUT	***	USING
BY	NO	***
***	NOT	WAS
DO	***	WERE
DURING	OF	WHAT
***	ON	WHICH
EACH	OR	WHILE
EITHER	***	WHO
***	SAME	WILL
FOR	SEVERAL	WITH
FOUND	SOME	WITHIN
FROM	SUCH	WOULD
FURTHER	***	***
***		
HAS		
HAVE		
HOWEVER		
***		

Figure 8.2.   The BRS stop word list.

8.3 THE USE OF TEXT SEARCHING

The classical way to search any library's collection, whether manually or by machine, is to use one or more classification codes, subject headings, or controlled vocabulary descriptors. When doing this, the searcher is placed in the position of trying to guess or deduce what terms the cataloger or indexer would have used. This is one reason that it is usually desirable to have the assistance of a professional librarian, because such a person can usually do a better job of matching a user's requirements with a cataloger's or indexer's decisions than can a subject matter expert without library training.

Computers add to the searcher's arsenal another weapon, the ability to search for *any* word in the bibliographic record, or in most fields of it. This means that a searcher can, in effect, skip the process of guessing about descriptors and instead use the words he knows or hopes an author or abstractor would have used to describe a subject. If searcher and author are in the same discipline, this can be far easier than anticipating indexers' actions. This capability is valuable in two particular situations. When a new word comes into the professional language or jargon, there is necessarily a delay before it can enter the controlled vocabularies. Thus a searcher working in a fast-developing science such as high-energy physics, may find the field far ahead of the bibliographers. The second major value of being able to search for individual, uncontrolled words is when a searcher is having difficulty finding anything on a subject in a given file or needs to fine-tune a search which provided too much output. Then, he can augment the controlled language with a few uncontrolled terms that make for a finer degree of subject description than otherwise. This degree of freedom for the searcher to look for words anywhere within a text leads to the mode of searching sometimes called *free text searching*.

However, the needs of searchers are never fully satisfied. If a searcher can look for the words *toxicity* and *testing*, he cannot be assured that their co-occurrence in a citation implies the subject *toxicity testing* is being discussed. To be certain, he needs either a subject heading or classification code or the ability to search for that very phrase rather than its component words individually. *Text searching* is the term given to this mode of searching in which it is possible to specify not only what words must occur, but in what sequence or how closely together they should occur within a text.

8.4 SEARCHING ON WORD FRAGMENTS

As we hope you will have realized by now, when you do a *select, find,* or *search* with a single word as object of one of these verbs, you are searchirg for that word to be found *within* a descriptor, title, abstract, or other field. You are not necessarily requiring that your word *be* the entire field you are searching. What this means is that you have the choice of searching for descriptors and titles in their entirety or for individual words within them. Thus even if you restrict yourself to controlled vocabulary descriptors, you can search for one word used within a multiword descriptor, or you can search for that one word occurring anywhere within an abstract.

As soon as you back off from searching for an exact match with a controlled term, you run into problems of spelling variations. If, for example, you are interested in computers as a subject and you happen to be searching in ERIC, you find from the thesaurus that the approved way to spell that word is the plural form: *computers*. That, then, is the controlled descriptor, and it is the only spelling that need be used in doing a search with controlled vocabulary. Suppose you have used *computers*, did not find enough material and suspect more is available. One option is to begin looking for the word *computers* or any of its near-synonyms as part of another descriptor (e.g., *analog computers*) or as part of a title or abstract. If the word had occurred as a descriptor, that meant, of course, that an indexer decided that *computers* was an important topic of the document represented.

The fact that the word might appear once within the body of an abstract does not necessarily imply that the concept is important to that document. You must decide whether you want to find these additional appearances of a concept and risk what are called "false drops"—retrieval of records that satisfy your formal request but are not actually on the desired subject. For example, an abstract may refer to a tax computation and, in a later sentence, to a library of tax law. This document could be retrieved in a search for *computer* or its variants or in a search for *library* or its variants. If so, it would represent a false drop, for it is not on the subject of computers in libraries. The word *computers* is not going to be used every time the author of a title or abstract decides to refer to the concept. Instead, he will sometimes use *computer*, *compute*, *computation*, *computational*, or *computing*, all of which have essentially the same meaning in terms of the subject denoted. Rather than expect you to enter all these possible synonyms, linked by *or*, all the retrieval systems give you the alternative of entering a root word and indicating by a special symbol that you will accept any characters at all as part of a word beginning with your root. In the case just illustrated, you might enter

select comput?	(DIALOG)
comput:	(ORBIT)
comput$	(BRS)

In this case, the three symbols ?, :, and $ all mean the same thing. They each specify that the searcher will accept any word that begins with the root and has any number of additional letters (including zero). In other words, all of the variants on *computer* listed above would be retrieved by any of these commands.

There are limits to what you should try with this technique. For example, *select com?* is a legal command, but not particularly meaningful, because too many words begin with this root, having nothing more in common than an old Latin prefix.

Each search service has its own variations on this basic capability. For example, it is possible to specify only one character in a position designated by a special character. If you are searching for variations on the word *woman*, you can use a truncation symbol at the end to catch the possessive form, and you can use a similar symbol within the word to allow for singular and plural forms. In ORBIT, you would say *wom#n:* to indicate that you will accept any *one letter* in the position shown by #, and *any number* of letters in the position shown by the colon. Also, in ORBIT, *woman:* will retrieve *womanlike*, but *woman#* will not. In DIALOG, *wom?n?* will accept any *one letter* in the fourth position and *any number of letters* following the *n*, The term *wom?n? ?* will accept only a single letter following *n*. The final ?, set off by a space, indicates that ?s preceding the space are to be treated as indicating a single character each. BRS permits the usage *woman$4* to mean up to four letters following *woman*.

8.5   SEARCHING STRINGS OF WORDS

Searching on individual words, even with the various forms of truncation, still does not allow for the specificity sometimes needed. Earlier, we used the phrase *toxicity testing*. A particular type of toxicity testing is *in vitro toxicity testing*. A searcher, knowing that this phrase is almost certain to be used in the title or abstract of a document concerned with the subject, might want to use the entire phrase in a search, to be sure to get exactly this phrase and not other possible combinations of the words. Similarly, *computer graphics* has a particular meaning within computer science, not necessarily implied by the co-occurrence of the words *computer* and *graphics* within the same title or abstract. All the services provide a facility for specifying such phrases as these or, say, *solar energy collectors* to be found within a descriptor, title, or abstract field. How the searcher does this brings out more differences among the services than any other search action.

ORBIT permits direct specification of the phrase sought once you have built a set. If you want *solar energy collectors*, you say just that. The command, however, is a new one, called *string*. (The string is the sequence of letters and spaces and possibly other symbols that makes up the specification.) A string command must follow at least one set-forming command, that is, *it operates only on the results of a previous set*. In a sense, *string* is a limiting command, used only to reduce a previously defined set. In the example here, you might create a set for a broader term, such as *energy*, and then seek the specific string of interest.

DIALOG and BRS are alike in that the searcher specifies which words he is interested in and how he expects to find these words linked. For example, in DIALOG the command *select solar (w) energy*

tells the system to find the word *energy* with (in this case adjacent to) *solar* in some field of the record. You can put a coefficient (numeric prefix) before the *w* and specify a longer interval between words.

select information (2w) retrieval

would find either the phrase *information retrieval* or *information storage and retrieval*, the *and* being ignored. The requirement is that no more than two words (or whatever is the coefficient) intervene between *information* and *retrieval*.

This notation is called an *infix*. A DIALOG infix of *f* [e.g., *information (f) retrieval*] means the searcher wants the two words to be found anywhere in the same field. An infix of *c* means find them anywhere within the same citation. The command

select information (c) retrieval

gives results identical to either the sequence

select information   or *select information **and** retrieval*
select retrieval
*combine 1 **and** 2*

BRS uses the equivalent of infixes, the special words *adj* (for adjacent), *with*, and *same*. The first of these means the same as DIALOG's (w). Then, *with* calls for words to be in the same sentence, say of an abstract, and *same* the same paragraph or field. A BRS command might be

*solar **adj** energy **adj** collectors*

which asks for retrieval of any record containing the phrase *solar energy collectors*. If the linkage were *with*, the system would find any record with these three words in the same sentence, and if it were *same* the system would find records with these in the same field or paragraph. BRS's notation can become quite elaborate. For example, the expression *(solar thermal)* **adj** *energy **with** residen$4* can mean *solar energy* with *residence* or *residential* or other variants in the same sentence, or *thermal energy* with any word beginning with *residen*.

Truncation symbols can be used within a search command, so that you could say

wom#n: athlet:
or
select wom?n? (1w) athlet?
or
(woman$ women$) adj athlet$3

and retrieve with either such phrases as women's athletics, women in athletics, woman athlete, and so on.

Finally, a word about common words. All the systems maintain a "stop list" of words deemed to have no informational content. These words *may* be ignored in text searching. For example, in the illustration above, the *in* in *woman in athletics* is not counted by ORBIT in determing word adjacency.

Figures 8.3−8.5 show some examples of the various text search commands and the results they might obtain.

8.6   WHEN TO USE TEXT SEARCHING

A few points have been made about when it is appropriate to use text searching. Let us repeat these and then project ahead some unknown number of years and see how some possible new technological developments might combine with expanded text searching capabilities to change our entire approach to literature searching.

Today, almost all abstracting and indexing services use some form of controlled language—classification, subject headings, descriptors, or a combination of these techniques—to describe the subject content of documents. A successful search requires a decision on which of these to use. Whenever there is a reason to believe that the searcher can do a good job of selecting the appropriate controlled search terms, then term searching seems to be the most effective way to do it.

When refinements are needed, for example, a level of discrimination among like subjects beyond the capacity of the controlled language, then text searching becomes more valuable. This is also true when the searcher, for whatever reason, does not know how to select appropriate controlled terms, for example, when new words are entering a discipline's vocabulary. In fact, a highly useful technique is to use free text searching to find a few good citations, then find within these the most appropriate controlled descriptors and use them to reformulate the search to find even more relevant material.

Text searching is also valuable when searching for relatively obscure material, such as when a document touches only lightly on a subject and the searcher believes indexers are likely to have ignored the concept. Obviously, text searching is useful when, for whatever reason, a concept is not represented in the controlled language.

Bibliographic Record
Title: Online Literature Searching

Abstract: This work discusses the automation of reference searching through various systems for storage and retrieval of document surrogates using online, mechanized search systems, such as DIALOG, BRS, ORBIT, or MEDLINE. These are described, as are some research projects involving automatic indexing and abstracting of documents by computer. Published in a special library binding.

BRS Search Expressions	Result:
	Record Retrieved
1. *literature **adj** search$3*	Words appear together, in the specified order in the title
2 *dialog **with** medline*	Both words occur in same sentence.
3 *searching **with** online*	Both words occur in same sentence, order is not considered.
4 *library **same** automation*	Both words occur in the abstract, even if not in the same sentence.
	Record not Retrieved
5 *online **adj** searching*	Words do not occur adjacent to each other.
6 *library **with** automation*	Words do not occur in same sentence.
7 *literature **with** automation*	Words do not occur in same paragraph.

Figure 8.3. BRS text searching. In the left-hand column are several possible search expressions that might be used in a BRS command. In the right-hand column is a statement about whether or not the given expression would retrieve the bibliographic record shown at top.

DIALOG Search Expression	Result:
	Record Retrieved
1 *online (2w) search??? ?*	Retrieved through either title or abstract.
2 *online (f) searching*	Retrieved through title or abstract.
3 *library (f) automation*	Both terms occur in abstract
4 *literature (c) search*	*literature* found in title, *search* in abstract, both in same citation.
	Record Not Retrieved
5 *online (w) searching*	Terms not adjacent.
6 *literature (w) search*	Terms not adjacent.
7 *literature (f) search*	Terms not in same field.

Figure 8.4. DIALOG text searching. Portions of DIALOG text search commands are shown in the left-hand column. In the right-hand column are comments on the results of applying the expressions to the record in Figure 8.3.

ORBIT Search Expression (A set containing the abstract in Figure 8.3 will have been established.)

		Result:
		Record Retrieved
1	*search:*	Found in both title and abstract.
2	*search system#*	String found in abstract.
3	*abstracting documents*	The phrase *abstracting of documents* occurs in abstract; the *of* is not counted.
4	*abstract: document:*	A broader expression than that above.
		Record not Retrieved
5	*search system*	*search systems* occurs, but not the given expression.
6	*abstract# document#*	Since # represents only a single letter, this expression does not occur in the record.
7	*orbit dialog brs*	The terms occur, but not in the order stated.

Figure 8.5. ORBIT text searching. Portions of ORBIT string search commands are shown in the left-hand column. Comments about the result of applying these expressions to the record in Figure 8.3 are in the right-hand column.

Throughout the history of libraries, it has always been true that without some form of subject organization it is impossible to find a work on any given subject except by memorization, an unlikely option for a large library. Modern computers, however, are bringing us to the day when it will be both convenient and economical to enter the entire text of a document into a computer and to omit entirely any subject cataloging or indexing. Instead, searchers would rely on advanced methods of text searching. Experiments performed over a number of years by Gerard Salton at Cornell University[1] indicate that this style of searching need not be any less effective than using controlled language indexing.

8.7   FULL TEXT ONLINE—A NEW EXPERIMENT

Recently, BRS announced a new experiment placing the entire text of a journal article, rather than a citation and abstract, in its online files. The announcement, appearing in *BRS Bulletin* for April 1980 is reproduced below.

"BRS, in cooperation with the American Chemical Society, Washington, D.C., has created a private test database of the full text of approximately 1000 articles from the *Journal of Medicinal Chemistry* (1976−78). The file includes citations, titles, abstracts, and the *full text* of the articles, all of which are directly searchable. The purpose of the project is to determine the technical feasibility of establishing a primary journal file and to have a panel of users evaluate the file's utility.

"This online retrieval from complete text is made possible as a result of a new feature of the BRS software called full text *"in-context"* searching.

When a search is performed on a full text database such as the ACS test file, the system provides not only the standard result indicating the number of articles containing the entry term but also an in-context result display indicating the exact location (paragraph, sentence, and word numbers) of the term within the article. The searcher can then browse within the text, requesting only those paragraphs that contained the search term.

"A sample search of the *Journal of Medicinal Chemistry* text file, illustrating this new in-context feature, is shown below.

"Because of the searchability of the entire article, which is divided into sections, searchers can compare methods, results and facts which occur in the bodies of articles. Similarly, researchers will be able to locate replications and fine points of articles easily because it is possible to browse through and print key paragraphs of the article, such as the first and the last, which usually contain the purposes and conclusions. The full text file allows more in-depth and refined searching, and a greater assurance that a project or experiment is not a duplication of effort.

"As a result of this joint project with the American Chemical Society, BRS has given a new meaning to the concept of "full text" searching. It no longer refers only to free-text searching as an alternative to controlled vocabulary index terms, but to an even more exciting alternative method for the future—the possibility of rapidly searching and browsing the full text of documents online."

Here is a sample search using the new technique.

Command and Response	**Comment**
1__: *melting adj point$1*	This expression will retrieve *melting point* or *melting points*.
RESULT 88	There are 88 documents satisfying the request.
2__: .. *print 1 oc/doc=1*	
	The user requests the *in-context* result, or the location of the occurrence.
1	
OC PARAGRAPH SENTENCE WORD	This is the exact location: paragraph, sentence, and word number.
TX(8) 3 7	
tx(8)	The user asks to see the text of paragraph 8.
1	

TX PARAGRAPH 8 OF 20. EXPERIMENTAL SECTION. MELTING POINTS WERE TAKEN ON A THOMAS-HOOVER CAPILLARY MELTING POINT APPARATUS AND ARE CORRECTED. WHERE ANALYSES ARE INDICATED ONLY BY THE SYMBOLS OF THE ELEMENTS, ANALYTICAL RESULTS WERE OBTAINED FOR THESE ELEMENTS WERE WITHIN +−0.4% FOR ALL COMPOUNDS AND WERE FOUND TO BE CONSISTENT WITH THE ASSIGNED STRUCTURES.

The full text of original documents is also used in certain legal data base systems, for example, LEXIS, offered by Mead Data Central. Is this the way that scholarly journals will be *published* as well as searched in the future?

REFERENCE

1. Salton, Gerard, (comp.), *The SMART Retrieval System; Experiments in Automatic Document Processing*, Englewood Cliffs, N.J., Prentice-Hall, 1971.

Nine

Beginning and
Ending a Search

We have now described the essence of how to search. However, except for a general description of the computer and communications systems involved, we have not yet described how you get started on a search. The process is not unlike making a long distance telephone call to a person in a large organization. You have to go through a certain ritual of the telephone system (dial tone, dialing area code and telephone number, ringing) to get a connection with the office you are calling. Then, you have to negotiate with the switchboard operator to find the individual you want ("Hello." "Is *X* in?" "Yes, Who is calling?" "This is *Y*.", etc.) Only after this can you begin the substance of your call.

Once you have established telephone contact with the search computer, the steps in beginning a search are: (1) link your terminal with the search service's computer, (2) go through a logging in (or logging *on*) procedure by which you identify yourself to and are are accepted by the search service, (3) possibly receive recent news of the search service that might affect your search, and (4) select a file to search. There is a shorter ritual at the end by which you tell the computer you are done, get a summary of time used, and ask the computer to disconnect you from it. This is called *logging out* or *off*.

9.1 LINKING TO THE COMPUTER

For all search services and communications networks (we are assuming dial-up service here) there is a similar set of steps involved in linking your terminal with the search service computer. These are:

1 Link your voice telephone to the network.

2   Couple your terminal to the telephone.

3   Identify your terminal type.

4   Identify your destination computer—the search service computer.

5   The network links itself to the destination computer.

6   You identify yourself to the destination computer, by use of a password or user number.

Figure 9.1 shows these steps graphically.

At the end of this process you begin your conversation with the search service's computer. The procedures described in this section are not peculiar to search services or searching; they are used for computers involved in other kinds of applications as well.

9.1.1   Linking to the Network

Using a regular voice telephone, you call the nearest entry point, or *port*, into the network. In larger cities this is usually a local call. Elsewhere, it may require a toll call. The network's port computer answers the call and emits a high pitched monotone to verify that it has done so. This is your signal that connections have been established.

9.1.2   Coupling to the Terminal

The telephone handset is placed into an acoustic coupler or modem that is either an integral part of the terminal or is wired to it. The role of the coupler is to convert digital codes emitted by the terminal into sounds that can be transmitted by telephone (like those sent out by a Touch-Tone telephone). A similar coupler will transform the tones back into digital signals at the other end. Couplers have a cup each for the mouthpiece and earpiece of the telephone. One cup is marked "cord." The mouthpiece (the cord goes in through the mouthpiece) goes into this cup. Another kind of modem, particularly those produced by the Bell System, is connected by wire to the telephone and terminal, and it is only necessary to press a button when a connection is made, not to physically link the telephone and modem at that time.

9.1.3   Identify Terminal Type

There are many types of terminals. The network computer must know some physical characteristics of the terminal it is to communicate with, such as speed (characters per second). A simple message of as little as one character can tell it. The computer-to-network link may be able to operate at speeds as high as 480 or even 960 characters per second, or as low as 10 cps. The computer must adjust its speed to the terminal's speed. For example, the character A identifies a terminal to TYMNET as a 30 cps cathode ray tube (CRT) device. B denotes a Model 37 Teletype, operating at 15 cps.

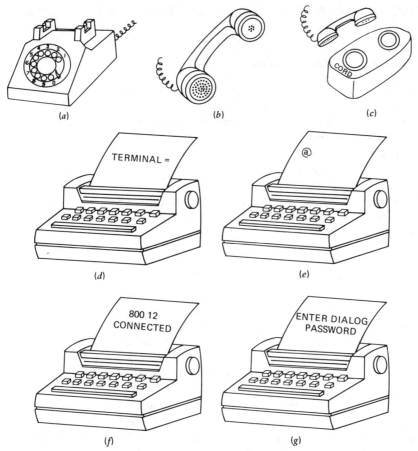

Figure 9.1. Steps in linking the user's terminal to the search service computer. (*a*) Dial the network. (*b*) Verify connection by monotone signal. (*c*) Place phone handset in acoustic coupler or modem. (Press button on a Bell modem.). (*d*) Network asks for identification of terminal type. (*e*) Network asks you to identify your destination computer. (*f*) Network confirms connection to the destination computer. (*g*) Search system asks for a password whose entry completes the linkages.

9.1.4 Identify Destination Computer

The network does not exist to serve a single computer. Each network services a great many of them, therefore you must specify which one you want. The code for doing so is always part of the instructions you get from the search service. BRS, for example, is identified as *C 315 20 br* on TELENET.

9.1.5 Link Network to Search Service

Now, the network sets up a path from its entry port in or near your city, to its exit port in or near the search service's computer. Then, there must be another telephone link to the destination computer, called, in network terminology, the "host" computer. This link may include several other network computers, each receiving messages and relaying them to the next computer in line.

9.1.6   User Identification

Your first interaction with the host computer will consist of it requesting the password from you. Only when this formality is successfully completed will you get the sometimes cheery greeting reserved for paying customers, for example, HELLO FROM ORBIT or SIGN ON IS COMPLETE (BRS).

Passwords, we must stress, are codes issued by the search services when you make an agreement with them for the service. The host computer identification you must give the network is not secret. It is a number devised by the network to identify its customers. Knowing this number does not get you "into" the host computer, only to its entry point, where the password is demanded.

9.2   PASSWORDS

The log in process begins when you have connected your terminal to the search service's computer. Its first message to you will be to ask for a password. When the password is given to the computer and found valid, it is treated as authorization for the search service to bill your account number for the computer time about to be used. It is analogous to giving an operator your telephone company credit card number or asking to have a call billed to a different number from that at which you are calling. Many organizations find it expedient to change passwords now and then to protect their accounts from unauthorized use. By using different passwords for different user groups within an organization, some additional security can be achieved.

Usually, the computer is programmed to protect your password even from being seen by a person near by. This is done by not displaying it as you type it (on a CRT terminal) or by typing a series of x's before you type your password, so no one can read the characters as you type. Figure 9.2 shows examples of the initial log in conversation.

If the password is accepted, the program goes on to the next step. If it is not accepted, whatever the reason, most systems will ask several times for it. Then, if it can't understand you, or your password is invalid (e.g., you haven't paid your bill), it will disconnect you.

9.3   NEWS

Some services will begin to function, once you have logged in, by sending you some news—messages concerning recent or near-future changes that might affect you. Typical examples might tell that a certain data base is not available now, that the computer is going to close down early tonight, or that a new data base has just been put online.

In addition to this news, which is forced on you, there may be more, optional news. The searcher can read it if he wants. To get to these news files, use the command:

explain news*   (DIALOG)

news   (ORBIT)

In BRS, you ask for news in response to a question

ENTER DATA BASE NAME   (BRS)

You reply with the word *news* and are shown the following table of contents.

TABLE OF CONTENTS	DOCUMENT NUMBER
SYSTEM NEWS	2
DATABASES ONLINE	3
DATABASES OFFLINE	4
CURRENT MONTH	5
DATABASE ROYALTIES	6
DATABASE NEWS	7
TRAINING SCHEDULE	8

PLEASE ENTER DOC=N WHERE N IS THE DESIRED DOCUMENT NUMBER. (PRESSING RETURN WILL CAUSE THE NEXT DOCUMENT TO BE DISPLAYED.)

As a casual user of someone else's terminal and password, you would probably not use the news commands much. If it is *your* system and your password or funds are involved, then periodically reading the news is a sound practice.

9.4 CHOOSING A DATA BASE

The next step is the important one of selecting the data base you are going to search. None of the search services permits searching more than one at a time. If there is more than one that seems pertinent to your search, you will have to search them sequentially. Thus you must select a file initially, and then you may have to change files during the search. Some services may permit merging of the results of separate searches into a single output file.

DIALOG and ORBIT expect an explicit command to choose a file,

---

*There is a single character abbreviation for the *explain* command, as there is for every DIALOG command. For *explain*, you can use ?. This is the only of these nonalphabetic codes that is commonly used. For consistency, we shall not use it, but will use the full command name.

a.   please type your terminal identifier
     -1032-052-
     please log in: αrs

     password:
     tc>   host is online

     ENTER YOUR DIALOG PASSWORD
     ████████
     LOGON File1 Tue 27may80 9:58:50 Port041

     EXCERPTA MEDICA SPLIT INTO 3 FILES,
         SEE ?NEWS
         SURF COAT ABS (FILE 115) NOW AVAILABLE.
         SEE ?NEWS

b.   TELENET
     215 8M

     TERMINAL=

     @c 213 33

     213 33E CONNECTED
     /login libudrx1
     YOU ARE ON LINE LF3

     HELLO FROM SDC/ORBIT IV. (01/04/80 7:28 A.M. PACIFIC TIME)
     YOU ARE NOW CONNECTED TO THE ORBIT DATABASE.
     FOR A TUTORIAL, ENTER A QUESTION MARK. OTHERWISE, ENTER A COMMAND.

c.   TELENET
     215 19B

     TERMINAL=

     @c 315 20BR

     315 20B CONNECTED

     ENTER BRS PASSWORD
     ████████
     ENTER YES IF BROADCAST MSG IS DESIRED ____: Y

     INFORM HAS BEEN RELOADED AND NOW INCLUDES A SEARCHABLE YR FIELD (79. YR.) AND
         JOURNAL CODEN FIELD (CD-XXXX). ***** FEDEX IS NOW ONLINE. FILE LABEL IS FEDE. ****
         DATABASE GUIDES FOR INFORM AND FEDEX ARE ENCLOSED WITH THE APRIL BULLETIN.

Figure 9.2.   The log in conversation. Illustrated are logging into DIALOG using TYMNET (*a*), ORBIT using TELENET (*b*), and BRS (*c*) using TELENET.

although both will "put you in" some file if you do not specify one when you log in. That is called the *default* file. With DIALOG, you make an agreement with the service when you sign a contract with them, for the default file for your installation. ORBIT puts you into a file called the ORBIT DATABASE, which has no meaningful records in it, but can serve as an administrative convenience. The charge for search time is a function of the data base you are working with.

The DIALOG AND ORBIT commands are similar. Normally, start off a DIALOG search with *begin*<**n**>   (DIALOG)

ORBIT's command is

file<**file name**>   (ORBIT)

where <file name> means the name or abbreviation of the file that is recognized by ORBIT.

In BRS, the computer will initiate the action by asking you what file you want to search

ENTER DATA BASE NAME   (BRS)

and you reply with a four-character code for the data base. To change data bases, you can say *..change* which elicits the message above from BRS, or you can say ..change <file> to complete the conversation in one statement.

Where do you get these codes, or how do you find what files are available? All the services have a means for you to ask for a display of the list of files available, which will also show you the codes or abbreviations to use. These will result in a list of data bases:

explain files   (DIALOG)
files?   (ORBIT)

In BRS, you get the same results by responding to the data base name question with one of the paragraphs of the NEWS data base, that is,

ENTER DATA BASE NAME
data bases

ORBIT has a data base that contains descriptive information about the other data bases. If you have no idea which file you want to search, you can select the Data Base Index (DBI). Then search that file, in the normal way, until you have retrieved enough information to tell which data base to switch to. Figure 9.3 shows an excerpt from DBI.

File lists can be long and therefore expensive to print out. They do not change often. A good idea is to post a copy near the terminal to assist users, but to avoid having each of them type out the list at the start of each search. This list should be regenerated once a month. Search services also issue printed directories of data bases available and make frequent announcements of changes in their lists.

9.5 BEGINNING AGAIN

A search is not synonymous with a session on the computer. Often, a person will want to do more than one search during one continuous session. These searches might be done for different people, for example. It would be useful to

---

USER:
file dbi

PROG:
ELAPSED TIME ON ORBIT: 0.01 HRS.
YOU ARE NOW CONNECTED TO THE DATA BASE INDEX DATABASE. THIS IS THE MASTER INDEX TO ALL
SEARCH SERVICE DATABASES.

SS 1 /C?
USER:
online and search; prt 2

PROG:
SS 1: (23) DATABASES

-1-
DN — INSP6976

-2-
DN — INSPEC

Figure 9.3. ORBIT's Data Base Index. Shown here is a brief search in the ORBIT Data Base Index. The user searches for data bases containing information on *online* and *search*. There are 23 data bases that include these words in their descriptions. The user asks for two members of the set to be printed (*prt 2*, a stacked command) and is given the names of two data bases. INSP6976 is the INSPEC file for the years 1969–76 and INSPEC, as a file contains all INSPEC records since 1977.

know how much each search cost, convenient to start set numbering over again so that each search begins with set number 1, and generally helpful to make the system behave as if the searcher were just beginning.

The services vary somewhat in how this can be accomplished. It is possible merely to set back the set numbers or to go all the way back to the point immediately following the entry of the user's password.

In DIALOG, *begin* <n> selects a new file (or the default file if none is specified) and causes the set numbers to be reset to 1. When a *begin* is issued, the time at which the change is made is reported, as well as the cost of searching in the file *from which you are changing.*

ORBIT uses the command *eraseall* to reset the set numbers. (That is, you erase the record of the sets.) *restart* puts you all the way back at the initial message following the password. The difference is slight and concerns only special commands not covered in this book. You can also erase selectively, by stating which sets you want to erase.

BRS uses *purge* to reset set numbers. Both BRS and ORBIT enable you to use *erase* or *purge* to delete some, but not all, of the sets you have created.

9.6   ORDERING DOCUMENTS

A relatively new innovation with most commercial search services permits you to order documents whose citations you have retrieved. To do so, you would have to identify the documents wanted and the vendor (the search services themselves usually do not sell the documents, but merely pass your orders along to someone who does). The commands are different enough that we refer you to users' manuals.

9.7   TIME AND COST

As mentioned previously, searchers need data about their searches, to keep track of their own efforts, to account for computer time used, or to provide the basis for an invoice to clients.

All services provide some kind of summary of time, cost, or both. There is something of a controversy among searchers about whether the actual cost should be displayed. Some feel it would frighten away clients not used to spending anything for library services, some feel that the number is misleading because the library must add an overhead cost on top of it, and others feel the online cost is necessary in spite of all drawbacks.

DIALOG and ORBIT automatically give time and cost whenever you change files or end a search. BRS gives you an option, by agreement, to receive time or cost information. The services have changed in the past and may change again. Watch what your service actually does.

The results of a DIALOG *begin* and *end* are illustrated in Figure 9.4. Figure 9.5 shows the corresponding ORBIT messages, and Figure 9.6 the analogous BRS messages.

9.8   LOGGING OFF

As we noted above, ending a search does not necessarily mean ending your stay at the terminal. However, when you are ready to leave, there is a command for you to tell the computer. Whatever the particular service's command is, it tells the computer the following: (1) to add up your bill, (2) to accept no more commands from you unless reauthorized by you, and (3) to disconnect your telephone line from the search computer but not the network. There is always at least a summary of time used, and possibly of cost as well, after a logging off command.

The specific commands are:

$$
\begin{array}{ll}
\textit{logoff} & \text{(DIALOG)} \\
\textit{stop} & \text{(ORBIT)} \\
\textit{..off} & \text{(BRS)}
\end{array}
$$

ORBIT asks "ALL DONE? (YES/NO)" after a STOP command. If you do not really want to stop at this point, just answer *no*. It may be surprising how often you decide to quit, then realize after giving the command that you have a

```
? begin 8
          27may80 9:59:57 User7001
   $0.30   0.020 Hrs   File1*
File8:COMPENDEX 70-80/MAY
(Copr. Engineering Index Inc.)
                    Set Items Description (+=OR: *=AND; −=NOT)
   --------------------------------------------------------------------------------------------------
? select computer?
                          1 75811 COMPUTER?
                                    •
                                    •
                                    •
? end
          27may80   10:04:25   User7001
   $1.14   0.076 Hrs   File8   4 Descriptors
```

Figure 9.4. The DIALOG commands for changing files and ending a search. *begin*, whether it comes at the start of a search or later, results in the display of time and cost information for the previous file in use (if there was one). The *end* command provides essentially the same information.

```
SS 1 /C?
USER:
file compx

PROG:
ELAPSED TIME ON ORBIT: 0.03 HRS.
YOU ARE NOW CONNECTED TO THE COMPENDEX DATABASE. COVERS FROM 1970 THRU DEC 1979
(7912)
```

Figure 9.5. The ORBIT command for changing file and time summary

```
   1____:  .. CHANGE/INSP
  CONNECT TIME   0:03 HH:MM****

EST CROS COST:  CHRS . . . $.64   DB-ROY . . . $.00   COMM . . . $.26   TOTAL . . . $.90

BRS/INSP/1977-NOV79

BRS — SEARCH MODE — ENTER QUERY
   1____:  HEAT ADJ PUMP$
```

Figure 9.6. The BRS *change* command. Here, a change is made from data base CROS to INSP (the INSPEC data base). Changes are shown for connect hours, data base royalties and communication, and the total cost of the use of the previous file. The new file is then verified and the searcher is automatically put into search mode.

116

few more things to do and you don't want to have to type in the entire search again.

In all systems, if you simply hang up the telephone, you end your search and you are not further charged. There is a way to get back on again, if this was accidental, and the services keep your search data for a few minutes. Hanging up without a proper logoff is not a good practice. Not only do you miss getting useful time and cost information, but you are increasing the cost of the search service providing your service and this, if abused, will soon be reflected in the price to everyone.

We have now covered the basic search commands and the procedures for beginning and ending a search. If you have mastered them, you are ready to begin doing meaningful searches. What follows is intended to make you a better searcher.

Ten

Storing
Searches and SDI

10.1 STORING A SEARCH

So far, all the searching we have described involves composing a search as it is executed, retrieving what is hoped will be the desired set at the end, and then logging off. However, there are times when you can create a search with the intent to use it later, storing the list of commands in the computer until you are ready to use them. There may be any of several reasons for doing this:

1 You are going to search more than one file and do not want to have to reenter the search each time you change files.
2 You want to search a file periodically, whenever it is updated, to check for new records that satisfy your search.
3 Your stored search is only a partial one, to be used as a portion of more than one future search.
4 You may want to log off, ponder your results, and then come back to the terminal and try your search again, perhaps with some small changes.

The second of these points briefly summarizes *selective dissemination of information* (SDI). SDI is a procedure for scanning new arrivals for information that matches a "profile" or interest statement of various users, and it is not restricted to online search services. Incoming information is sorted according to user interest categories and each user is informed only of those new arrivals of interest. SDI services are sometimes operated entirely on a manual basis, but they can also be operated by storing online searches and using them to search only the new records added to a file. How often this might be done depends on how often the files are updated or on how often you want to be updated.

To store a search is a relatively simple process, consisting of several steps:

1   Generally, you must identify a search as one to be saved *before you enter it.* In effect, you must put brackets around the commands of the search to be saved and then direct that everything in the brackets be stored.

2   If a search is going to be saved and later recalled, there must be a way to identify the search—a name or number not unlike a set number.

3   There must be a command for recalling a search. If you think about it a bit, you will realize that there are two reasons for recalling a search—to run it or to review it with an eye to possible change. There must be a way to tell which you intend to do.

4   There must be a way to discard unwanted but previously saved searches.

5   While it would seem that there should be a way to modify a stored search, this is not always possible.

Leaving out SDI for the time being, we will illustrate how these steps can be performed. As usual, the search services differ in the commands used and, to some extent, in what can be done, but the general concept is about the same.

10.1.1   DIALOG

The beginning "bracket," or first step, is a *begin* command and the ending bracket is the command *end/save*. On receipt of *end/save*, DIALOG gives you a four digit search number (step 2) that you can subsequently use to retrieve the search. All commands between the most recent *begin* and the *end/save* will be stored under this number.

To recall and execute a search (Step 3), use *.execute<n>*, where n is the search number. This causes the entire search to be executed. You are given the number of records in any sets formed along the way, but only the final set is numbered. The command *.execute steps<n>* causes each command to be executed and the results printed just as if you were typing in the commands as you go. It does form and number intermediate sets. You can execute part of a stored search by specifying *.execute<n>/<C_1>-<C_2>* where C_1 denotes a command number within the search at which you want to begin and C_2 denotes the command at which you want to stop.

To recall a search (Step 4) just to review it, or to prepare to release it (remove if from storage) the command is *.recall<n>*. To release it, follow this with *.release*. You must *recall* before you *release*. You can only add to a stored search; otherwise you cannot change it. To make a change you must release it and start all over again. The following is an example

? *begin 1*	
? *select television*	
? *select radio*	
? *combine 1* **and** *2*	
? *end/save*	This is the end bracket of a saved search. Retroactively, the *begin* becomes the beginning bracket.
SERIAL 1234	DIALOG gives you the serial number of the search.
.	You proceed with other searching
.	
.	
? *.execute 1234*	You later call up the saved search by number.
593 TELEVISION	Intermediate results (but no set numbers) are typed out or displayed.
248 RADIO	
1 12 1 and 2	The result of the search is displayed as set number 1.
? *type 1/6/1-5*	You ask for typing from the resultant set.
.	You are satisfied and feel you no longer need the stored search.
.	
.	
? *.recall 1234*	You recall the search.
SELECT TELEVISION	The search is typed out.
SELECT RADIO	
COMBINE 1 AND 2	You release the search. It is no longer retained in memory, and the serial number can be used with a different search.
? *.release*	

Figure 10.1.   DIALOG search being saved, recalled, executed and released.

10.1.2 ORBIT

The beginning bracket for an ORBIT search is the command *save<s>*, where *s* is the search name *you* assign. The end bracket is the command *finished*.

To recall, as in DIALOG, you use *recall<s>*, but in ORBIT this command executes the search as well as prints it.

delete<s> removes a search from storage and permits reuse of the name. Again, there is no way to revise a stored search. ORBIT has a number of variations on these commands that we will not illustrate. The following is an example.

SS 6/C?	You have been searching for some time, and reach search statement 6.
USER:	You tell ORBIT to begin saving your search, calling it MEDIA. This is the beginning bracket.
save media	
PROG:	ORBIT reminds you this is a saved search (*SVS*) and resets the set number, or search statement number, to 1.
SVS SS1/C?	
USER:	
*television **and** radio*	
PROG:	
SS 1 PSTG (12)	Your search is executed as you type it.
SVS SS/C?	
USER:	
print ti	You put a print command into your search.
PROG:	
SVS SS 3/C?	
USER:	
finished	You declare the saved search to be finished, by using the end bracket.
PROG:	
SAVE COMPLETED	The program verifies the completion.
SS 7/C?	The program now resumes the sequence of search statement numbers interrupted earlier by the *save* command.
SS 9/C?	
USER:	
recall media	Later, you decide to use the saved search.
PROG:	You get the results of the search.
SS 1 PSTG (12)	
USER:	You then can continue your overall search.

Figure 10.2. ORBIT search saved and recalled.

10.1.3 BRS

To save a search, use the command *..save*. There is no beginning bracket. *save* refers to all commands that have been issued but have not been deleted or purged during this search. *The save command is the end bracket.*

Step 2 is performed by the user who supplies a four-character label, or name, for the search, to be used in recalling it.

To recall the search, the command is *..exec<1>*, where *1* is the label. The search is recalled and executed.

For Step 4, the command *..purge* erases a saved search. For example:

ENTER COMMAND:

__: *..search*

BRS SEARCH MODE. ENTER QUERY

1__: *television **and** radio*

RESULT 12

2__: *..print 1, ti/doc =all*

__: *..save medi*

   QUERIES HAVE BEEN SAVED,
RETURN TO CONTINUE

__: *..change/ntis*

   .
   .
   .

__: *..exec medi*

BRS - SEARCH MODE

00001   TELEVISION AND RADIO

RESULT   12

EXECUTION ENDED

__: *..edit*

ENTER Q NUMBER

qmedi

ENTER EDIT REQUEST

c 2

ENTER QUERY

1 and children and reading

Enter search mode. There is no beginning bracket for a BRS saved search.

You supply the search name—up to four characters. BRS verifies the save.

After saving the search you go on doing something else. Then, you want to execute your saved search.

The saved search puts you in search mode

The results of your commands are printed. 00001 is a line number.

You decide to change the search.

You identify the search to be changed.

c calls for changing an existing statement, number 2.

You enter the new version of this statement

Figure 10.3.   BRS search saved, executed, edited and purged.

ENTER EDIT REQUEST

save   You order the revised search to be saved.

SAVED

ENTER EDIT REQUEST

end   You are done with the changes.

BRS - SEARCH MODE - ENTER QUERY

..exec medi   You now ask for the new version to be executed.

.
.
.

EXECUTION ENDED   The search is executed.

__: *.purge medi*   You erase the search.

Figure 10.3 (*continued*)

10.2 SELECTIVE DISSEMINATION OF INFORMATION

The saved searches illustrated above are recalled by the searcher and used to search an entire file just as nonsaved searches are. In SDI searching, a search is run against only those records added to a data base since the last SDI search, that is, the new acquisitions. Thus it is necessary to specify that only *new* records are to be searched unless you are sure the system's computer would know this by the nature of the saved search.

10.2.1 DIALOG

Instead of *end/save* use *end/sdi*. This causes all commands since the last *begin* (1) to be saved (you will be given a search number) and (2) to be run automatically against all subsequent updates to a file. *end/sdi* is *not* available with all DIALOG files, so it's best to check.

There is also a field in some data bases that indicates the date the record was added to the file—the date of update. This field can be used with a *limit* or *select* command to retrieve only the records that have the desired dates, such as those of the most recent update of the file.

A saved search should contain a *print* command, to be sure you get your results, which, of course, you will receive by mail. *.recall<n>* and *.release* will recall for viewing search *n* and delete it from storage, respectively.

10.2.2 ORBIT

This search service also uses a data element for the date of update in an SDI search. The *update code* indicates the year, month, week, or issue in which an update is made. Which of the latter terms depends on the data base. The best information on update status is found by using the ORBIT command *updates*.

For example, to search for *television **and** radio,* assuming you have been doing some searching prior to deciding to do an SDI search:

.
.
.

SS 4/C?

USER:

updates
PROG:

UPDATES 12/20/79
  ITEMS WITH * ARE UPDATES FOR WEEK OF DEC 20—
*ACCT: 2ND QTR 1979 (7902)
AGRICOLA: DEC (7812). UPDATES DELAYED DUE TO TAPE FORMAT CHANGE.
APILIT: NOV (7911)

USER:

*television **and** radio*

SS 4 PSTG (12)

SS 5/C?

USER:

*4 **and** 8001 (up)*   You ask for a set that is the intersection of set 4 and those records containing an update code (UP) of 8001, meaning month 1 of year 1980.

Figure 10.4. ORBIT search updated.

10.2.3 BRS

To complete an SDI search, first put yourself in search mode, enter the expression or profile and follow this with the command *..sdi.* The system assigns a search number and runs the search automatically against every new batch of records entering the selected data base after entry of the search. This is similar to DIALOG's procedure. For example:

..search

BRS SEARCH MODE. ENTER QUERY

*1__: television **and** radio*

RESULT 12

2__: ..sdi ti/id=p. atherton

Figure 10.5. BRS SDI search.

ti indicates the title is to be printed; *id* the name of the requester.

10.3 CROSS-FILE SEARCHING

One of the vexing problems of searching when multiple files are available is to be able to search more than one of them without having to repeat a search completely. Of course, that is one of the major applications of the save search feature—that a user can plan and execute a search against one data base and then use it again, without reentering it, to search another data base. However, the problem of deciding which data base to search remains. In Chapter 9 (Figure 9.3) we illustrated the ORBIT data base index, which enables you to do a conventional search in order to retrieve the names of files that match your selection criteria.

However, sometimes you would like more information; you would like to know what you are likely to find in a given data base. DIALOG publishes a file called DIALIST that lists the occurrence rates of terms across a number of frequently used data bases. This file is published in microfiche form and can be used to determine quickly with what frequency a term occurs in each of the files and hence what the likelihood of retrieval is using the term. DIALOG has recently introduced online a more advanced feature of this. It is called DIALINDEX.

BRS/CROS/			
1 ALL		2 LIFE SCIENCES	
3 PHYSICAL SCIENCES		4 BUSINESS	
5 SOCIAL SCIENCES		6 USER OPTION____: 1	
(a)		(b)	
BRS — SEARCH MODE — ENTER QUERY		BRS — SEARCH MODE — ENTER QUERY	
1____: *retrieve*		1____: *retrieve and (computer or computers)*	
BIOL	2	BIOL	0
BOOK	0	BOOK	0
CAIN	2	CAIN	0
CHEM	1	CHEM	0
DISS	2	DISS	0
DRUG	1	DRUG	0
ECER	19	ECER	1
ERIC	141	ERIC	49
INFO	110	INFO	59
INSP	147	INSP	44
MDOC	0	MDOC	0
MESH	34	MESH	9
MGMT	6	MGMT	2
NCMH	171	NCMH	15
NIMI	16	NIMI	0
NTIS	166	NTIS	62
PAIS	2	PAIS	0
PSYC	147	PSYC	10
SMIE	110	SMIE	48
SSCI	3	SSCI	0

Figure 10.6. The BRS CROS file. The user selects a subject term (*a*), and is given a list of frequencies of occurrence in each file. The input expression can be a term or a logical combination (*b*).

BRS has an online file called CROS that performs much the same function. The file is selected as is any other BRS file. You are given a choice, illustrated in Figure 10.1, of which broad subject areas you wish to search. Each represents several data bases. You enter a search expression and are given a list of frequencies of occurrence of that expression in each individual data base within the selected subject area.

10.4 SUMMARY

Saving searches saves the time it would take to reenter the searches each time they are used, and it reduces the chance of error inherent in doing so. Searches are saved when it appears that they are going to be used over again, typically either to try a search developed for one data base against another or, in SDI fashion, against newly arriving records. Considerably less time is used to execute a saved search than to type anew and execute as you type.

Eleven

Assistance

We hope our text and the search services' users' manuals have not sounded too much like the advertisements for those assemble-it-yourself children's toys that say "Just follow the simple instructions." Sometimes, however hard you try, those "simple" instructions just cannot be followed, and rarely are they simple. What can you do? Fortunately, search services, unlike toy manufacturers, generally provide a variety of special services for the perplexed user.

11.1 REVIEWING SEARCH SETS

One of the easiest ways to become befuddled is to forget what sets have been created in a search, or their exact definitions or sizes. This is especially true when working at a CRT terminal, with no printed record that enables you to check back easily. After creating and browsing through ten sets or so, it is quite easy to forget what has been done or how some particular set was defined. The three major services each provide a command that recapitulates what sets have been created and the definitions given in the commands that generated them. This command can be used at any time. Its use is a good idea when things seem not to be going well and it is time for some reflective reviewing.

The commands used are:

display sets	(DIALOG)
history	(ORBIT)
..display	(BRS)

Figures 11.1–11.3 show the results of using these commands.

The command *display sets* in DIALOG always gives you the complete history of your search since the last *begin*. If you often do several searches at a sitting and are inclined to use this command, it represents another reason for

```
? select steps laser and memory
    1   17724 LASER
    1    7393 MEMORY
    3     132 1 AND 2
? select computers and memory
         20309 COMPUTERS
          7393 MEMORY
    4    1624 COMPUTERS AND MEMORY
? select laser and computer
         17724 LASER
         60557 COMPUTER
    5     575   LASER AND COMPUTER
? ds
SET ITEMS DESCRIPTION
    1   17724 LASER
    2    7393 MEMORY
    3     132   1 AND 2
    4    1624   COMPUTERS AND MEMORY
    5     575   LASER AND COMPUTER
```

Figure 11.1 The DIALOG *display sets* command. The commands used to create five sets are shown, followed by the summary of them.

```
SS 6 /C?
USER:
history

PROG:
SS  1:   HEAT AND PUMP: (1505)
SS  2:   RESIDENTIAL OR RESIDENCE OR HOME (3275)
SS  3:   1 AND 2 (118)
SS  4:   RESIDENTIAL/TI OR RESIDENCE/TI OR HOME/TI (725)
SS  5:   1 AND 4 (39)

SS  6   /C?
```

Figure 11.2 The ORBIT *history* command.

```
3____:   ...display all
  1 HEAT AND PUMPS AND (RESIDENCE OR RESIDENTIAL)
RESULT     11

  2 HEAT. TI. AND PUMPS. TI. AND (RESIDENCE OR RESIDENTIAL OR HOUSING). TI.
RESULT      4

        ****    END OF DISPLAY    ****
```

Figure 11.3 The BRS *display* command.

using *begin* to re-initialize set numbers, so that you do not get annoyingly long print-outs here.

The command *history*, in ORBIT, if used alone, gives the complete history, as does *display sets*. However, you can, if you wish, specify which sets or search statements you want to review. *history 5* gives you the history of statement 5. *history 1-5* gives the first five statements and their results. You can also say *history 1, 3-5* which gives you sets numbered 1, 3, 4, and 5.

The command *display* in BRS has almost the same options as *history*. Used alone, it gives *only the previous statement*. *display all* gives the entire search history, and *display 1,3* gives you sets 1, 2, and 3.

11.2 ASKING THE COMPUTER QUESTIONS

Perhaps the next most likely form of trouble a searcher gets into is forgetting some detail about how to use a command. For this, too, there is usually a command.

DIALOG has the command *explain*, which can be abbreviated by a question mark. To query on the use of a command, say *explain* <command> or ?<command>, that is, the command *explain* or ? followed by the name of the command you want information about. Examples of *explain* and its variations are:

? combine leads to an explanation of the *combine* command.

explain news leads to the news (See Section 9.3)

? file <n> leads to a description of file number *n*.

explain fields <n> leads to a description of the fields contained in file number *n*.

? limit gives the rules applicable to the *limit* command for the particular data base you are using.

? update <n> leads to the update status (date of latest revision) of file *n*.

explain explain gives you a list of what can be explained by *explain*. (You may wonder, if you were unsure how to use *explain explain*, whether you should enter *explain explain explain*. If you are wondering this, go back to Chapter 5 and then try to decide for yourself what would happen. Try it on the terminal.)

ORBIT also uses *explain*, a rare coincidence of terms. You can ask for an explanation of a command, of a message you received from the computer, or some miscellaneous points. The following are some examples:

> *explain find* (or *help, nbr, news, print,* etc.)
> *explain no postings* (or *up n* or *down n,* etc.)
> *explain and* (or *or, default mode, schedule,* etc.)

ORBIT also has a command called *help* by which you can convey specific problems to ORBIT for advice on how to proceed. At present, *help* gets you the message from ORBIT shown in Figure 11.4.

ORBIT gives you a chance to do more than ask a standard set of questions. A command *comment* permits you to send any message you want to the SDC Search Service, including any question you may want to ask. If you identify yourself you will get an answer online, by telephone, or by mail, depending on length of reply or the search service's interpretation of urgency. As the name implies, the command can also be used to send comments not requiring an answer. Figure 11.5 shows a use of the *comment* command.

BRS does not have a command corresponding to *explain* or *help*. They do have a way to send messages from your terminal to that of a person at BRS who will try to answer your question. BRS also has a rather extensive list of error messages, explained in their users' manual, so they can be precise in identifying an error without tying up too much time printing. Many inexperienced users, however, prefer being told what is wrong, rather than being given a code to look up in a book.

11.3   TELEPHONE AND OTHER ASSISTANCE

The *explain* and *help* commands are limited in what they can do for you. As often happens with computer systems, they were designed under the assumption that a user basically knows what he is doing and that the problems he gets into are going to be readily identifiable and relatively resolvable.

Life, however, is not so kind to us. You can find yourself hopelessly bogged down in a search due to a fundamental problem, such as not knowing how to work your terminal. Or, you might see that your search is not working and have no idea what has gone wrong or what to do about it. There are still constructive options.

Most bibliographic searching is done in a library, usually by a librarian on behalf of clients. That person may have a special title such as data systems librarian or technical information specialist and will be the best resource to go to first, with a problem. If no such person is available (or, if you are that person!) and if there has been some forethought given to the possibility of a severe problem, you can go (by telephone) to a nearby library whose search specialists have arranged with yours to help out on an exchange basis. A telephone explanation of the situation is often enough. This kind of interlibrary cooperation does not cost anything, and most libraries are willing to agree to have their specialists cover for each other's absences.

Another possibility is to call the search service. Most have a toll-free telephone number leading to a person whose job it is to help with any aspect of the use of the service. Yet another possibility is to call the marketing representative who handles your area or the data base supplier (often also toll-free) if you suspect your troubles may be related to understanding or

USER:
help

PROG:
    BRIEF REVIEW OF OPERATING FEATURES:

1.   TO CORRECT TYPING ERRORS ON MOST TERMINALS, USE THE CONTROL AND H KEYS TO ERASE BACK ONE CHARACTER AT A TIME, OR USE THE DOLLAR SIGN AND CARRIAGE RETURN TO DELETE AN ENTIRE LINE.

2.   TO COMBINE SEARCH TERMS AND/OR SEARCH STATEMENT NUMBERS, USE THE LOGICAL OPERATORS (AND, OR, AND NOT).

3.   TO SPECIFY THE FIELD TO BE SEARCHED, ENTER THE TERM FOLLOWED BY A FORWARD SLASH AND THE FIELD NAME ABBREVIATION, E.G. DEATH/TI.

4.   TO PRINT SEARCH RESULTS ONLINE, USE ANY OF THE STANDARD PRINT COMMANDS (PRINT FULL, PRINT, PRINT TRIAL). TO REQUEST AN OFFLINE PRINT TO BE MAILED TO YOU, ENTER PRINT FULL OFFLINE.

5.   TO VERIFY THE CORRECT FORM OF ENTRY FOR A SEARCH TERM, USE THE NEIGHBOR COMMAND WITH THE TERM, E.G., NEIGHBOR FISHERIES.

6.   TO TRUNCATE FOR A SINGLE VARIABLE CHARACTER, USE THE HASH MARK (#). TO TRUNCATE FOR MULTIPLE CHARACTERS, USE THE COLON (:).

7.   FOR A COMPLETE LIST OF ONLINE EXPLANATIONS, ENTER EXPLAIN EXPLAIN. FOR A LIST OF COMMAND NAMES AND ABBREVIATIONS, ENTER EXPLAIN COMMANDS. FOR A DESCRIPTION OF ORBIT IV SEARCHING TECHNIQUES, ENTER EXPLAIN ORBIT IV. FOR A DESCRIPTION OF A DATABASE, ENTER THE EXPLAIN COMMAND WITH THE DATABASE NAME, E.G., EXPLAIN SSCI.

USER:
explain neighbor

PROG:
THE NEIGHBOR COMMAND, ABBREVIATED NBR, SEARCHES THE INDEX OF YOUR DATABASE AND FINDS YOUR TERM (OR THAT CLOSEST TO IT) AND DISPLAYS TERMS ON EITHER SIDE OF IT.
    THE NBR COMMAND IS MOST OFTEN USED TO DETERMINE THE CORRECT FORM OF ENTRY AND TO VERIFY THE PRESENCE OF A TERM IN A DATABASE.

NBR BANKING   (DISPLAYS 5 TERMS ALPHABETICALLY-RELATED TO BANKING WITH BANKING NEAR THE CENTER DISPLAY.)

USER:
explain eric

PROG:
ERIC COVERS REPORT LITERATURE (RIE) AND JOURNAL LITERATURE (CIJE) IN MANY EDUCATION AND EDUCATION-RELATED AREAS: CAREER EDUCATION: COUNSELING AND PERSONNEL SERVICES: EARLY CHILDHOOD EDUCATION: EDUCATIONAL MANAGEMENT: EXCEPTIONAL CHILDREN: INFORMATION RESOURCES: LANGUAGES AND LINGUISTICS: READING . . .

USER:
explain explain

PROG:
THE FOLLOWING ITEMS MAY BE EXPLAINED ONLINE BY ENTERING THE EXPLAIN COMMAND WITH THE NAME OF THE ITEM TO BE EXPLAINED, E.G., EXPLAIN COMMANDS; EXPLAIN FILE.

1.   COMMANDS
FILE, FIND, HISTORY, NEIGHBOR, PRINT, STOP, BACKUP, ERASEALL, KEEP, RESTART, SENSEARCH, STRINGSEARCH, SUBHEADINGS, SAVE-SEARCH, STORE, STOREOLD . . .

Figure 11.4 The ORBIT *help* command. At the top, the response to *help* is shown. This is followed by examples of the use of *explain <command name>*, *explain <data base name>*, and *explain explain*. The complete messages are not shown.

```
SS 2 /C?
USER:
comment

PROG:
ENTER MESSAGE OR TYPE DONE.

USER:
this search is done as an example

PROG:
ENTER MESSAGE OR TYPE DONE.

USER:
done

PROG:

SS 2 /C?
```

Figure 11.5   The ORBIT *comment* command.

misunderstanding the data base. Finally, there are always users' manuals, which should be kept handy whenever you are searching. Simply hanging up the telephone is always possible. Although we will not go into the details here, there are ways to temporarily store the search you have developed so far, and even the sets you have created, for a short time. This gives you a chance to think or research a question without the pressure of hourly charges.

The key point is that even a relative novice, working in his own office at night, need not feel alone or reluctant to call for help. If you are a customer of a search service, you are paying for that service and they are happy to have you use it. Similarly, the librarians in whose domain you may be working are usually glad to help users. Often, they will have enough background in your subject field to converse at a technical level. If not, they will try to find someone who can. It is a terrible feeling to be working at a computer terminal, realize you are unable to do some basic task, and be unable to get any help. With online bibliographic search services, you can always get help. Use it.

Twelve

Search Strategy

12.1 WHAT IS A SEARCH STRATEGY?

Search strategy is a concept that encompasses several steps and levels of work in online bibliographic retrieval. Not every writer on the subject agrees on the scope of the term. Some writers have suggested that this subject should properly be called search *tactics* instead of search *strategy*, but we will continue to use the commonly accepted term.

For us, *search strategy* encompasses at least *three critical decision points* which are reached by the online searcher *before* going online and one or two decision points reached *while* online (see Figure 12.1). Search strategy is part of the effort that comes *after* clarifying the information need, *after* negotiating the search request, and *after* establishing search objectives. It does *not* include the choice of data bases to search. Reference to Chapter 3 would help here, but certain information provided there will be repeated here for the ease of the reader.

Steps 1 and 2 in an online search (See Figure 12.2) are very important data gathering steps that will greatly affect the critical decision points in a search strategy.

Developing a good search strategy will involve use of all the knowledge one can gain about online searching systems and all one can learn about indexing vocabularies and the conventions practiced in bibliographic data base construction. For the intermediary who is searching online for someone else, it requires a full understanding of the information needed as expressed clearly in a *search request*. It also requires ascertaining *search objectives*. It must be clear to the online searcher whether *all relevant* items should be sought after or *only relevant* items. If the former is the search objective, then a *high recall* search strategy will have to be planned and all avenues will have to be exhausted before signing off. If, on the other hand, the search objective is to retrieve *some* relevant items at the lowest possible expense, then the online searcher must

Before Online

1 Which *concept* or facet in the search request is to be searched online first? Which second? etc.

2 What *terms,* in what form, are to be searched online to represent each concept groups in the search request?

3 What features of the retrieval system are to be used to satisfy search objectives?

While Online

4 How to *react* to unfavorable preliminary results, e.g., too many or no postings for terms or concepts searched?

5 How to *revise search logic* to reach search objectives via a way different from previously planned (e.g., expand search terms or limit search output, etc.)?

Figure 12.1 Critical decision points in search strategy.

Steps (not in Fixed Order)

1 **Clarifying and Negotiating the Information-Need and Search Objective**

   Interviewing the information requestor clarifies the narrative form of the *request* and determines *search objectives*:
   (a) retrieve *all* relevant items (high recall);
   (b) retrieve *only* relevant items (high precision);
   (c) retrieve *some* relevant items (brief search).

2 **Identifying Relevant Data Bases**

   Determining which online data base to use first, which next, and so on.

3 **Formulating Basic Search Logic   Planning Search Strategies**

   Analyzing the search topic into parts called facets or concept groups.
   Planning approaches to search strategy for combining concepts of the topic.

4 **Compiling the Search Terms**

   Choosing indexing terms from the data base's thesaurus or other printed word lists.
   Selecting terms for free text searching of the subject-conveying fields (title, abstract, etc.).
   Deciding to use thesaurus and alphabetic word lists online.

5 **Making Choices**

   Limiting and printing output (offline and online).
   Selecting an approach to search strategy which best satisfies the search objectives expressed by the requestor.

6 **Conceptualizing the Search as Input to the Retrieval System**

   Arranging the search terms into concepts or facets for search strategies using features of the retrieval system, for example, truncation, word proximity.
   Noting most important and less important concept groups and deciding on sequence input to access these concept groups efficiently.
   Restricting or limiting output based on search objectives.

7 **Evaluating Preliminary Results**

   Reviewing search results, step by step.
   Considering alternative search strategies to meet search objectives (recycling Steps 1–6).

8 **Evaluating Final Results**

   Determining requestor's satisfaction with search results.

Figure 12.2 Steps in the presearch interview and the online search (see Figure 3.1).

develop a *brief search* to satisfy this goal, using shortcuts for combining concept groups in the search request and ordering output expeditiously.

A *high recall* search* is formulated when the information seeker needs to find *everything* on the stated topic (i.e., *all* relevant items). In this case, the search strategy would include a way to search all word variants and synonyms for each concept represented in the search logic formulation (see Step 3 in Figure 12.2).

Oftentimes a certain volume of non-relevant or marginally relevant output would have to be examined to ascertain that high recall had been obtained.

A *high precision† search* retrieves much relevant material, but with fewer nonrelevant items in the output (i.e., *only* relevant items). To reach this objective, the search strategy would usually be to search only specific descriptors or terms representing concepts in the search with no generic or synonym term searching.

The *brief search* is done if there is a need to retrieve a few items either to lessen expenses or to perform a rapid survey of the file before a more comprehensive and lengthy search. The *brief search* is necessarily a low recall search, performed in such a way that maximum results can be achieved with little online time. Choice of priority concepts is a factor in designing a brief-search. A glance back at Chapter 3 might be helpful at this point.

From Figure 12.1, it is clear that the first critical decision point in developing a search strategy comes in Step 3 of Figure 12.2.

All the forms described in Chapter 3 will be of help in formulating a search strategy. How the search topic will be analyzed into parts or concept groups is very critical. As we indicated in Chapter 3, if the search topic is "Audiovisual Aids for Library Instruction," and one searcher divides it into two concept groups and another into three, they will get different results. Assuming there is agreement about the number of concept groups in a search topic, a decision still must be made about which concept to search first, (Decision Point 1), how to represent it in words or phrases (Decision Point 2) and what features of the retrieval system to use (Decision Point 3) to combine terms in a concept group and how to combine concept groups. Earlier chapters in this book have shown how to use certain searching commands (truncation, word proximity, field delimiters, etc.). We will not repeat all that again, but the following discussion will include examples of the choices available at these critical decision points.

12.2 STRATEGIES FOR SEARCHING CONCEPT GROUPS AND TERMS

It is not easy to make the first decision about which concept or facet of the search to represent first or second. There are several possibilities—the most specific facet or concept group or the one with the fewest postings. Some will

---

*Recall is defined as the percentage of relevant items in a file that are retrieved by the search.
†Precision is defined as the percentage of retrieved items that are relevant to the search topic.

say, decide to search the most *important* concept first, but that is usually difficult to define. Others may say it doesn't matter because all concept groups will have to be input eventually. That is not necessarily true, as we shall show below. Regardless of which criterion is used, remember that when that decision is made, you have passed the first decision point and your search strategy has begun. What is decided at that point will affect each subsequent step in the search formulation (the choice of terms, choice of features, revision of search strategy, etc.). For this reason, we would like to dwell a little longer on this decision point and explain the various alternatives. We have used the catchy names devised by Charles Bourne, Barbara Anderson, and Jo Robinson, and we have inserted illustrations to help you remember the choices that must be made. Each approach can affect the whole search process.

12.2.1   Most Specific Facet First

If the choice is made to start a multifaceted search formulation with the *most specific* or most familiar aspect of the query *and* the postings are sufficiently low after scanning the results, the searcher usually chooses not to impose the remaining conditions to the search. They are options and only need to be input if high precision performance is a search objective. (See Figure 12.3.)

If the topic were "4-H Clubs: their members and activities," the search formulation could be one that first used all the variant spellings of the club as this represents the most specific facet. If enough citations are retrieved, the search is terminated without applying the "members" or "activities" aspect of the search.

If there are too many citations after searching the most specific facet, then the *next* most specific facet should be searched and combined in an **and** relationship with the results obtained with the first facet. The resulting intermediate result may then be small enough that there is no need to impose the rest of the search conditions. This approach can be very efficient.

Underlying the use of this strategy is another necessary decision as to whether the concept will be represented by the controlled index vocabulary of the data base (e.g., descriptors in a thesaurus) or by free text terms (Decision Point 2). Both decisions relate to search objectives.

12.2.2   Lowest Postings Facet First

Another approach is to start a multifaceted search with the facet that is estimated (e.g., from the term frequency search aids and online files mentioned in Chapters 3 and 10) to have the smallest number of postings. See Figure 12.4. If the postings are sufficiently low there may be no reason to continue searching additional facets. For example, a searcher may safely assume that the facet *girl scouts of america* derived from a topic on "Success rates in higher education of students who were members of the Girl Scouts" has fewer postings than the facet *higher education* in the ERIC data base. In actual fact, the facet *girl scouts*

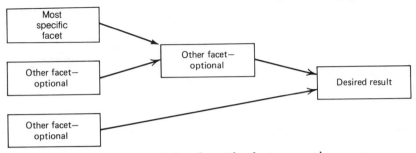

Figure 12.3.   Most specific facet first. Other facets may not be necessary.

results has less than 20 ERIC citations; this being the case, the searcher is able to terminate the search before applying the second facet *higher education* to the formulation.

12.2.3 Building Block

In the building block approach, the topic is broken down into several concept groups, but a decision is made to search all three groups online. See Figure 12.5. For the search topic, "Identification of the artistically gifted," the three concept groups or facets would be: *gifted, identification,* and *artistic.* In the table below are listed the three facets accompanied by search terms in various forms chosen to represent the facets in the search formulation (Decision Points 1 and 2):

Artistic	Gifted	Identification
Art	Gifted	Identify
Arts	Talent	Identified
Artistic	Talents	Identifying
Artistically	Talented	Identification
Esthetic -ally		Identifies
Esthetics		
Aesthetic -ally		
Aesthetics		

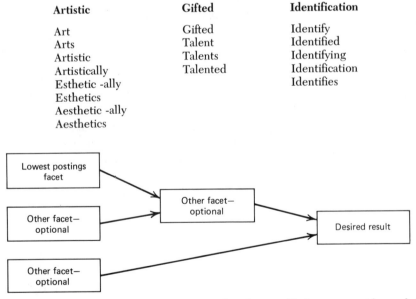

Figure 12.4.   Lowest postings facet first. Again, the other possible facets may not be needed.

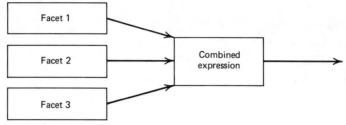

Figure 12.5. The building block approach. Several facets are used to build a logical structure.

In the DIALOG system, terms from each facet could then be assembled into search statements joined by *or* (Decision Point 3) and then combine the results of the subsearches for each concept by ***and*** (Step 10 in the following). The truncation symbol(?) indicates in what form the searcher decided to input the term in each concept group (Decision Point 2).

Formulation
1 *select art? ?*
2 *select artistic?*
3 *select esthetic?*
4 *select aesthetic?*
5 *combine 1-4/or*
6 *select gifted*
7 *select talent?*
8 *combine 6-7/or*
9 *select identif?*
10 *combine 5 **and** 8 **and** 9*

The building block approach has the advantage of providing a somewhat clearer history of the search logic, one that is easy to review and understand at a later time (or use, in part or as a whole, as a saved search). It tends to follow and read like the actual query formulation; however, two disadvantages of the approach are that more computer memory and online time are used in comparison to the other approaches, such as the single *facet* approach. The searcher establishes new sets with each command and introduces the main ***and*** conditions only at the final stage of formulation. This approach may use more online time than is necessary and is almost noninteractive, in the sense that the entire search formulation could be "batched" (using a semicolon between search statements entered all at once on DIALOG) since no intermediate results will affect the search strategy.

12.2.4   Citation Pearl Growing

The citation pearl growing strategy (Figure 12.6) starts with a very direct search on the *most specific term* for each of the concept groups in the search request in

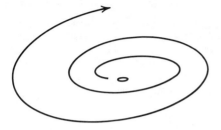

Figure 12.6. Citation pearl growing. From a beginning of a single facet, a larger structure is grown gradually, as need dictates.

order to find at least one citation. The searcher then calls up one or more of these citations for online review, noting index terms and free text found in some relevant citations. These new terms are incorporated into the revised search formulation to retrieve additional citations. (This could be a building block or specific facet first, etc.) After adding these terms to the formulation, one can again review more retrieved citations and continue this process in successive iterations until no additional terms that seem appropriate for inclusion are found.

This search strategy is the most interactive. Take the topic "Identification of the artistically gifted," again. If searched on DIALOG using this citation pearl growing strategy, it would look like this:

---

1 *s gifted(c)identification(c)artistic*

One citation is retrieved and printed in DIALOG's format 2 so that the descriptors can be reviewed for possible inclusion in a revised formulation.
ED104039 EC071443
THE IDENTIFICATION OF ACADEMIC, CREATIVE AND LEADERSHIP TALENT FROM BIOGRAPHICAL DATA. FINAL REPORT.
INSTITUTE FOR BEHAVIORAL RESEARCH IN CREATIVITY, SALT LAKE CITY, UTAH; NORTH CAROLINA STATE DEPT. OF PUBLIC INSTRUCTION, RALEIGH. DIV. FOR EXCEPTIONAL CHILDREN.
74   76P.
SPONSORING AGENCY: Z. SMITH REYNOLDS FOUNDATION, SAPELO ISLAND, GA.
EDRS PRICE MF-$0.76 HC-$4.43 PLUS POSTAGE
DESCRIPTORS: ACADEMIC ACHIEVEMENT/ ◆BEHAVIOR PATTERNS/ ◆CASE STUDIES (EDUCATION)/ CREATIVE ABILITY/ ◆CULTURAL FACTORS/ EXCEPTIONAL CHILD RESEARCH/◆GIFTED/ HIGH ACHIEVERS/ ◆IDENTIFICATION/ LEADERSHIP/RACIAL FACTORS

The three facets are represented by single terms. No retrieval features such as truncation are used to automatically combine variant forms of each term. The three terms are combined in DIALOG by using the operator (*c*) to indicate an *and* relationship in the citation or document. No requirement is made that the terms must appear in the same sentence or field of the record.

A quick glance at the descriptors in the retrieval record causes the searcher to think that the concept "artistic" might best be searched using the descriptor "creative ability." This results in a revision of the search. Substituting the descriptor phrase "creative ability", for the term "artistic," the search now reads as follows:

s creative **(w)** ability **(c)** identification **(c)** gifted
   Five citations are retrieved. Requesting the retrieved citations in DIALOG's format 6 allows the searcher
   to browse the titles of the set in order to find more words for searching if high recall is the search
   objective. Using format 8 would give descriptors as well.
1/6/1
ED104095
   THE GIFTED AND TALENTED: A HANDBOOK FOR PARENTS. WORKING DRAFT.
1/6/2
ED104094
   THE IDENTIFICATION OF THE GIFTED AND TALENTED.
1/6/3
ED104039
   THE IDENTIFICATION OF ACADEMIC, CREATIVE AND LEADERSHIP TALENT FROM BIOGRAPHICAL
DATA. FINAL REPORT.
1/6/4
ED102773
   SUGGESTIONS FOR IDENTIFICATION OF GIFTED AND TALENTED STUDENTS.
1/6/5
ED100102
   TEACHING GIFTED CHILDREN ART IN GRADES ONE THROUGH THREE.

Citation pearl growing is characterized by the development of the search formulation in a very dynamic, empirical manner. *Thinking* time associated with this approach may result in a longer online connect time, but online review of retrieved citations can be very helpful in the identification of search terms for addition or deletion, and the payoff from this approach can be incorporated into any of the other approaches.

12.2.5 Successive Fractions

The strategy of successive fractions (or divide and conquer, or file partitioning) implies that an initial bite of the file is made in order to assemble a set of documents that satisfies an essential condition of a multifaceted search, as illustrated in Figure 12.7. This may be the condition of year of publication, language of publication, document type, *major* descriptor to represent most specific concept group, and so on. Having built such a set online, when the chosen facet of the search query is represented, it is immediately combined as an *and* condition to the partitioned subfile. The result is the establishment of an even smaller set or subfile. The remaining search statements continue to be applied to the subfile resulting from the previous *and* conditions. This represents a built-in search revision strategy (see Decision Point 5, Figure 12.1).

DIALOG's *limitall* feature, when used at the beginning of a search, serves as an example of the successive fractions approach. In the following example, the *limitall* capability is employed to restrict searching to the partitioned subfile of only the *periodical* literature in the ERIC data base (called the CIJE (Combined Index of Journals in Education) portion which is represented by EJ accession numbers). We will use the same search topic, "Identification of the artistically gifted," to illustrate this approach.

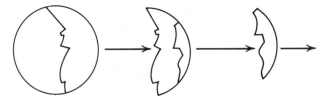

Figure 12.7. Successive fractions search. Typically, a fairly large initial set is created and this gradually is reduced until an acceptable set is reached.

Formulation	Comments
limitall/ej	
select identification (f) gifted/ti	The retrieved set will only contain the terms "Identification" and "Gifted" in the title of a *journal* article. These terms represent two of three concepts in the search.

In ORBIT, the stringsearch feature would be used for successive fractions. For example:

> *gifted*
> *strs (ti,ab) :identif: :artistic:*

12.3 SUMMARY

What terms will be searched, what forms these terms are given, and what features of the online system will be used are probably the most important decision points in search formulation. Different system features allow different term presentations (automatic linkage between controlled vocabulary terms, term truncation, or words in proximity, words within fields, etc.). This has been discussed in Chapters 7 and 8 and will not be repeated here. However, it must be emphasized that some search formulations will pose problems involving computer memory limitations, while others will reduce storage space. Search saves can reduce cost of searching. Searches done at off-peak times will give faster response time and result in a savings.

All these factors must be considered by the online searcher before going online; however, once the searcher is online, as indicated in Figure 12.1, all the plans decided on beforehand may go awry. At Decision Point 4, the online searcher must be prepared to handle unfavorable news about the terms selected and must always be on guard to check out mistakes made in input. If the step of compiling search terms is done carefully before going online, it will not be difficult to shift to other terms or to use the online thesaurus for term selection.

At Decision Point 5, if the step of conceptualizing the search as input to the retrieval system is planned beforehand in several different ways, then one strategy can be quickly replaced by another, always keeping search objectives in mind.

All this implies a quick evaluation of preliminary results and the recycling and use of different search terms. Revision of search logic can be done efficiently with practice if tools are used before going online as well as while online (see Figure 12.8). Before going online, the searcher must consult all the aids provided by the retrieval system and the data base supplier. These will have hints about how to prepare to make decisions at points 1–3 in Figure 12.1. Once online, however, the choices are the searcher's alone. As the clock ticks by, so do the computer charges, and it is an awesome responsibility to work online both efficiently and effectively.*

Before Online

Decision Points		Tools	
1	Concepts to be searched?	A	Information sheet from requester
		B	Presearch interview data
		C	Thesauri for relevant data bases
		D	Dictionaries and glossaries
2	Terms—in what form?	A	Inverted file word lists
		B	Thesauri
		C	Words in title and abstracts of some relevant items
		D	Classification schedules or category lists
		E	Data base user manuals
3	Features of retrieval system use?	A	Retrieval system user manual specific to data base to be searched
		B	Sample searches
		C	Sessions from update briefings

While Online

Decision Points		Tools	
4	Unfavorable results—how to react?	A	Information sheet from requester
		B	Online thesauri
		C	Data base dictionary online
		D	Brief search analysis
5	Revise search logic?	A	Presearch strategy notes
		B	System user manuals

Figure 12.8   Tools for critical decision points in search strategy.

---

*A more detailed discussion of search strategy appears in the second edition of F. W. Lancaster's *Information Retrieval Systems*, Wiley, 1979, pp. 156–177, and in the journal reports in such titles as *Online, Data Base, Online Review*.

A Summary of
Search Languages

INTRODUCTION

Each searching service maintains an encyclopedic user manual for its retrieval system. This documents and illustrates every feature of the system, the command language, the data base record structures, and other important topics. In many ways these manuals parallel the chapters in this book and give detailed information specific to that system, complete with examples of online experiences. Besides this and other training materials which they produce and make available at some cost, the services like ORBIT, DIALOG, and BRS, produce such things as a "Pocket Guide to Commands." We have reproduced the "Pocket Guide to DIALOG Commands" in this appendix (Part 1).

Many searchers, in search of as many data bases online as possible, are switching from one online service to another. Often they will search the same data base on all three systems because they know they will get different results and they want to make a comparison. For these reasons we are beginning to see *cross-system* searching aids. We reproduce in Part 2 of this appendix one such aid compiled by Karen L. Markey when she was a research assistant at the ERIC Clearinghouse for Information Resources at Syracuse University. These tables were done for a special ERIC workshop which explains why all the examples are searches in the ERIC data base. In each "box" of these tables is the prompt from the computer system and the user's response, a command, which when performed will result in the function listed in the first column of the table. The commands in each search language are arranged into groups by functional area: online assistance and procedures for operational control, search related tasks, and print related tasks. If a place in the table is blank, it means that the online service did not have a way of performing that function at the time this table was prepared. A quick reference to each system's user manual will determine if that is still the case as they are adding features very frequently. At press time we learned of another cross-system compilation of commands which includes the three in this appendix and four others. It is available from Online Command Chart Online, Inc., 11 Tannery Lane, Weston, CT 06883.

Contents of Appendix A
Part 1   Pocket Guide to DIALOG Commands
Part 2   A Summary of Online System Functions and Commands

LOCKHEED INFORMATION SYSTEMS

3251 Hanover Street (Code 5208)

Palo Alto, CA 94304

POCKET GUIDE TO

DIALOG®

COMMANDS

TELEPHONE:

(800) 227-1960 (toll free)

(800) 982-5838 (toll free in California)

(415) 493-4411, Ext. 45412

TELEX:

334499 (DIALOG)

145

A. COMMAND SUMMARY

A.1 BASIC COMMANDS

COMMAND	FUNCTION	EXAMPLE(s)
BEGINn Bn !n	To start a search in File n. Fastest way to start. Erases work done to that point; re-starts set numbers at 1.	BEGIN6 B10 !34
EXPAND E ''	To display a part of an index. May be used with words, prefix codes or online thesauri.	EXPAND ART E E7 ''AU=JONES
EXPAND (word)	To display subject related terms from a thesaurus. Applies only to databases with online thesaurus.	EXPAND(ENERGY)

SELECT
S
#
	To request postings to be retrieved from the Index. May be used with words, prefix codes or EXPAND numbers. (See Section B.1).	SELECT MIRAGE
		S DT=BIB
		#E6-E9, E3, R3
		SPY=1976:PY=1978

COMBINE C $	Used with Boolean operators AND, OR, NOT to relate sets. May only be used with set numbers. (See Section B.2).	COMBINE 1 AND 2 C 6-8/OR $ 4 AND (5 OR 6) C7NOT4
TYPE T	To type record(s) online on a print terminal. Used with either set numbers or DIALOG Accession numbers. Set/format/range. (See Section C.2).	TYPE 10 T 12/2/1-6 '899605/5
DISPLAY D %	To display a record online on a CRT terminal. Used with either set numbers or DIALOG Accession numbers. (See Section C.2).	DISPLAY 8 D780916 %9/6/2-9/CS
END =	Gives time elapsed and cost estimate since last BEGIN or END or file change. Does not interfere with search strategy. Starts new costing.	END =
PRINT PR &	To request offline prints. Used with either set numbers or DIALOG accession numbers. Format choice is required. (See Section C.2).	PRINT 7/5/1-49 PR 12/2/1-96/AU/TI &096389/2
PRINT- PR-	To cancel the previous print request. Must be used before LOGOFF, BEGIN, .FILEn, or END commands.	PRINT- PR-
LOGOFF	To signoff and disconnect from the system. Automatically gives cost estimate of connect time, offline print requests and tele-communication charges. (See Section F.2).	LOGOFF

1

A.2 SUPPLEMENTAL COMMANDS

COMMAND	FUNCTION	EXAMPLE(s)
•COST	Gives elapsed time and cost estimate since last BEGIN. Does not interfere with search strategy.	•COST
DISPLAY SETS DS	To display all sets made since previous BEGIN. Used for a recap of search strategy used.	DISPLAY SETS DS
DISPLAY SETSn DSn	Used with a set number (n) to start display from set n.	DISPLAY SETS 15 DS18
EXPLAIN ?	To request online explanations of command and file features. EXPLAIN EXPLAIN gives a list of all valid EXPLAIN commands.	EXPLAIN FILE 65 ?NEWS ?EXPLAIN
•FILEn	To change to another file without erasing previous results. Saves sets created to this point. Use not recommended for most searches.	•FILE7
KEEP K (	To request that certain records from online displays of citations be retained in set No. 99. Used to pre-edit output online before requesting offline prints. KEEP set or Accession no./record number or range of record numbers.	KEEP 5/3-6 K8/10 (AD510522) K9
LIMIT L)	To restrict SELECTed set to specified requirements. Capability varies per database.	LIMIT 5/MAJ L 8/ENG) 3/100009-999999
LIMITALL LALL)ALL	Used before SELECTing sets to limit all subsequent SELECTing to specified requirements. Capability varies per database.	LIMITALL/129665-200000 LALL/020089-999999
LIMITALL/ALL LALL/ALL)ALL/ALL	To cancel a LIMITALL command.	LIMITALL/ALL LALL/ALL)ALL/ALL
PAGE P	To request another screen (or page) of display after an EXPAND.	PAGE P -more-
•SORT	To sort online output according to specified parameters. Output may be SORTed offline using the PRINT command followed by specified parameters. Capability varies per database. (See Section C.2).	•SORT 8/1-48/AU TI •SORT 9/1-25/SD, D PRINT 10/5/1-36/AM, D

2

147

A.3 SEARCH·SAVE® COMMANDS

COMMAND	FUNCTION	EXAMPLE(s)
END/SAVE =/SAVE	To make a SEARCH·SAVE. Requests that all sets developed since the last BEGIN be saved for later use. User receives a serial #nnnn after entering the command. (See Section D.1).	END/SAVE =/SAVE
END/SAVETEMP =/SAVETEMP	To make a temporary SEARCH·SAVE. Saves a search formulation for use later in same search day. (See Section D.2).	END/SAVETEMP =/SAVETEMP
END/SDI =/SDI	SEARCH·SAVE for SDI (current awareness). Saves a search formulation to be automatically executed with each new update of database. Capability applies only to Files 1,4-6,8,10,11,13,16,50. (See Section D.2).	END/SDI =/SDI
●EXECUTEn	To recall and execute saved search with serial number n. Executes entire search strategy; gives final set number. (See Section D.3).	●EXECUTE1ST7 ●EXECUTE T010
●EXECUTE STEPSn	To recall and execute each line of saved search with serial number n. (See Section D.3).	●EXECUTE STEPS T008 ●EXECUTE STEPS 3A4Z
●RECALLnnnn	To recall a SEARCH·SAVE or SDI to review search strategy or to prepare to release it. (See Section D.4).	●RECALL1V83 ●RECALL A6YZ
●RELEASE	To release both permanent SEARCH·SAVEs and SDIs. (See Section D.4).	●RELEASE

B. SEARCH COMMANDS
B.1. SELECT

TRUNCATION
? (question mark)

There are four capabilities in truncation:
1) Unlimited number of characters after the stem.
      SELECT EMPLOY?
      SELECT AU=JONES, R?
      SELECT PY=197?

2) Specified maximum number of characters after the stem.
      SELECT HORSE? ?
      SELECT THEAT?? ?

3) Embedded variable character.
      SELECT WOM?N
      SELECT ADVERTI?E

4) Combinations of the above.
      SELECT WORKM?N?

B.1.2. BASIC INDEX FIELD INDICATORS

Suffix symbols; used to specify searching on field(s) which make up the Basic Index.
Number of fields in the Basic Index varies per database.

COMMON FIELD SYMBOLS	FIELD
. . . /AB	Abstract
. . . /DE, . . . /DE*	Descriptors
. . . /DF, . . . /DF*	Full Descriptors (single word)
. . . /ID, . . . /ID*	Identifiers
. . . /IF, . . . /IF*	Full Identifiers (single word)
. . . /TI	Title
. . . /NT	Note

*Indicates MAJOR in some databases

- SELECTing single terms:
      SELECT BUDGETS/TI
- Specifying more than one field:
      SELECT TENSION/TI, DE, ID
- With full-text operators:
      SELECT POP(W)TOP(F)CANS/TI, AB

B.1.3. ADDITIONAL INDEXES

Always used with two-letter prefix code. Additional Indexes may be composed of
individual words or full-character strings. Some Additional Indexes are numerical fields.
The number of Additional Indexes varies per database.

COMMON PREFIX CODES	FIELD
AU=	Author
CC=	Category Code or Classification Code
CS=	Corporate Source
DT=	Document Type
JN=	Journal Name
LA=	Language
PY=	Publication Year
UD=	Update

- SELECTing with a full character string:
      SELECT AU=JOHNSON, ROBERT R.
- With a single word:
      SELECT LA=GERMAN
- With truncation:
      SELECT PY=197?
- With full-text operators:
      SELECT CS=LOS(W)CS=ANGELES
- Combinations of Prefix Codes:
      SELECT CC=60050(C)LA=FRENCH

4

B.1.4. FULL-TEXT OPERATORS
Used only with the SELECT command.

SYMBOL	FUNCTION	EXAMPLE
(W)	To request Word A immediately adjacent to Word B, and in this sequence	S SOLAR(W)ENERGY
(nW)	To request Word A within n words of Word B, and in this sequence	S SOLAR(3W)ENERGY
(F)	To request Word A in the same field as Word B, in any order and in any field	S SOLAR(F)ENERGY
(C)	To request Word A in the same citation as Word B, in any order, and in any field. Equivalent to: S Word A; S Word B; C1AND2.	S SOLAR(C)ENERGY
(L)	To link parts of multilevel Descriptors. Capability varies per database.	S SOLAR(L)ENERGY
(S)	To link sub-field parts within the same field and in any order. Capability varies per database.	S SOLAR(S)ENERGY

- Used in the Basic Index, with or without suffix indicators:

    SELECT MANAGEMENT(1W)OBJECTIVES
    SELECT DATA(W)BASES/TI

- Used with Prefix Codes of Additional Indexes:

    SELECT CS=NEW(W)CS=ORLEANS
    SELECT CC=013892(C)BC=893415

- Used with both Basic Index and Additional Indexes:

    SELECT URANIUM(C)LA=GERMAN
    SELECT RN=50-81-7(C)ABSORPTION

- Used with more than one operator (most limiting operator precedes):

    SELECT FOOD(W)SCIENCE(F)MILK/DE
    SELECT CS=NEW(W)CS=YORK(C)BANKING

- Command allows up to 50 characters without spaces, i.e. bound multiword phrases may not be used.

B.1.5. RANGE SEARCHING
: (colon)

Use to SELECT a range from prefixed numerical fields. Causes logical ORed sum to be performed.

    SELECT PY=1976:PY=1978
    SELECT CC=64072:CC=64078

When used with E or R numbers from EXPAND displays, causes separate sets to be created for each E or R number.

    SELECT E6:E10

5

B.2. COMBINE

Boolean Operators are used only with the COMBINE command and set numbers.

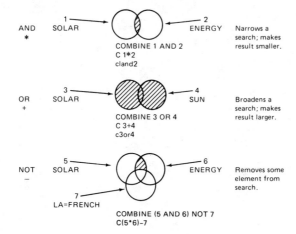

AND *	1 ──→ SOLAR ◯◯ 2 ──→ ENERGY COMBINE 1 AND 2 C 1*2 c1and2	Narrows a search; makes result smaller.

OR +	3 ──→ SOLAR ◯◯ 4 ──→ SUN COMBINE 3 OR 4 C 3+4 c3or4	Broadens a search; makes result larger.

NOT —	5 ──→ SOLAR ◯◯ 6 ──→ ENERGY 7 ──→ LA=FRENCH COMBINE (5 AND 6) NOT 7 C(5*6)–7	Removes some element from search.

PRIORITY OF EXECUTION:

    NOT
    AND
    OR

NESTING TO SPECIFY ORDER OF EXECUTION:

    COMBINE 1 AND (2 OR 3)
    COMBINE((4 OR 5 OR 6) AND (7 OR 8))NOT 9

SHORTCUTS:

    COMBINE 1-5/OR (Same as: COMBINE 1 OR 2 OR 3 OR 4 OR 5)
    COMBINE 6-8/AND (Same as: COMBINE 6 AND 7 AND 8)

A maximum of 29 sets may be COMBINEd in one statement.

6

C. COMMAND ENTRY AND OUTPUT FEATURES

C.1. ENTRY AND CONTROL

STACKING COMMANDS (semicolon)	Use to separate a series o commands to be executed with one carriage return: SELECT E6-E8; SELECT E12; SELECT LABOR; SELECT EMPLOY?; SELECT WORKM?N?; COMBINE 1-5/OR; TYPE 6
BREAK	To stop online output. Key is labeled BREAK or INTERRUPT on most terminals.
BACKSPACE and ERASE	Use CONTROL H . Hold down the CONTROL (CTRL) key and press the H key for each character to be backspaced. This process automatically erases internally in the computer. Then re-enter all desired characters from that point on.
ERASING A LINE	Use ESCAPE or ESC key followed by the RETURN or CR key. The system will ignore the line and give another prompt mark.
CARRIAGE RETURN	Use for two purposes: 1. To send a command for processing. 2. To interrupt a command execution already sent but not yet responded to by the system.

C.2. OUTPUT CONTROL

C.2.1. COMMON FORMAT OPTIONS

Format 1	DIALOG Accession Number	Used with TYPE, DISPLAY,
Format 2	Full Record Except Abstract	or PRINT commands.
Format 3	Bibliographic Citation	Number and type of format
Format 4	Abstract and Title	options varies per database.
Format 5	Full Record	
Format 6	Title and DIALOG Accession Number	
*Format 7	Bibliographic Citation and Abstract	
*Format 8	Title and Indexing	

*To be added to backfiles in 1979.

TYPE set =/format =/range	TYPE 11/2/1-6
If no range is given, defaults to first citation.	T16/3/1-10
DISPLAY set =/format =/range	DISPLAY 12/5
If no range is given, defaults to first citation.	D6/6/1-10
PRINT set =/format =/range	PRINT 21/5/1-56
If no range is given, defaults to first 50 citations.	PR 25/3/1-92

C.2.2. SPECIAL OUTPUT FEATURES

.SORT	To sort output online according to specified parameters. Capability varies per database. Set=/range/ field, sequence/field, sequence	.SORT 8/1-48/AU/TI .SORT 9/1-25/SD,D
PRINT (with SORT capability)	To sort output offline according to specified parameters. Capability varies per database. Set=/format=/ range/field sequence	PRINT 7/5/1-82/CS/AM,D PR 10/3/1-250/AU/TI PR 15/5/1-48/AU
VARIABLE LINE LENGTH	To vary online output line length. Use at LOGON. Enter Wnn after password and before carriage return to request output line length change between 40 and 79 characters. (Normal line length is 72 characters).	

ENTER YOUR DIALOG PASSWORD
XXXXXXXX W65

7

D. SEARCH·SAVE® FEATURE

D.1 TO PREPARE A SEARCH·SAVE

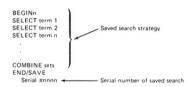

```
BEGINn
SELECT term 1
SELECT term 2          Saved search strategy
SELECT term n
    .
    .
COMBINE sets
END/SAVE
    Serial #nnnn          Serial number of saved search
```

D.2 TYPES OF SEARCH·SAVES

a) END/SAVE

Permanent (until released by user).

b) END/SAVETEMP

Temporary, automatically released
at end of search day (as defined
by Pacific Coast Time).

c) END/SDI

SDI, for automatic routine run of
saved search against updates of a file.
Available on DIALOG files 1, 4, 5,
6, 8, 10, 11, 13, 16, 50. (Permanent
until released by user.)

D.3 TO EXECUTE A SEARCH·SAVE

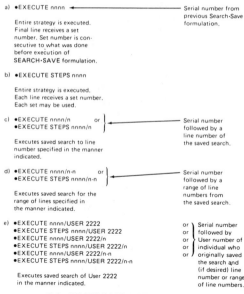

a) ●EXECUTE nnnn   Serial number from
                         previous Search·Save
                         formulation.

Entire strategy is executed.
Final line receives a set
number. Set number is con-
secutive to what was done
before execution of
SEARCH·SAVE formulation.

b) ●EXECUTE STEPS nnnn

Entire strategy is executed.
Each line receives a set number.
Each set may be used.

c) ●EXECUTE nnnn/n   or   Serial number
   ●EXECUTE STEPS nnnn/n   followed by a
                              line number of
                              the saved search.
Executes saved search to line
number specified in the manner
indicated.

d) ●EXECUTE nnnn/n-n   or   Serial number
   ●EXECUTE STEPS nnnn/n-n   followed by a
                               range of line
                               numbers from
Executes saved search for the   the saved search.
range of lines specified in
the manner indicated.

e) ●EXECUTE nnnn/USER 2222   or   Serial number
   ●EXECUTE STEPS nnnn/USER 2222   or   followed by
   ●EXECUTE nnnn/USER 2222/n   or   User number of
   ●EXECUTE STEPS nnnn/USER 2222/n or   individual who
   ●EXECUTE nnnn/USER 2222/n-n   or   originally saved
   ●EXECUTE STEPS nnnn/USER 2222/n-n   the search and
                                        (if desired) line
Executes saved search of User 2222   number or range
in the manner indicated.   of line numbers.

D.4 TO RELEASE A SEARCH·SAVE

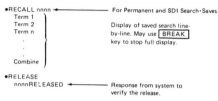

●RECALL nnnn   For Permanent and SDI Search·Saves.
    Term 1
    Term 2   Display of saved search line-
    Term n   by-line. May use BREAK
       .   key to stop full display.
       .
    Combine

●RELEASE
    nnnnRELEASED   Response from system to
                         verify the release.

●Temporary SEARCH·SAVE formulations are automatically
released at the end of the search day.

8

E. TROUBLE SHOOTING

E.1. SYSTEM MESSAGES

Error messages can originate either from the telecommunications network or the DIALOG system when typographical, procedural or format errors are detected. Some error messages related to online searching are shown below.

DIALOG Message	Probable Cause	User Action
BUSY PASSWORD	Password already in use or not proper LOGOFF from previous online session	Wait 10 minutes; if message repeats, call Customer Services
DISK STORAGE OVERFLOW	Search storage capacity exceeded (1,000,000 citations)	Use BEGINn command, re-enter search using E range numbers, or the C full-text operator and avoid higher posted nonspecific terms; if condition persists, call Customer Services
INPUT I/O ERROR	Momentary, hardware error	Re-try command immediately
INVALID . . .	User error	Correct and re-enter
NO CORE AVAILABLE	Momentary, system task switch	Re-try command immediately
OUTPUT I/O	Momentary, hardware error	Re-try command immediately
> 800 TERMS; RESPECIFY	Truncation or range search exceeded more than 800 terms	Make term more specific or decrease length of range or enter separate words
> 8000 TERM LOOKUP; RESPECIFY	Embedded truncation search exceeded 8000 terms	Enter separate words
(n sets to go)	Warning about approach to the 98 set limit	Complete search within number of sets left to go
(n items to go)	Warning about approaching the 1,000,000 item limitation	Complete search as soon as possible. To erase all results and start over, use BEGINn command

E.2. TELECOMMUNICATION DIFFICULTIES

PROBLEM	DIAGNOSIS
System doesn't respond to password	Check: 1. Shift lock on terminal (if locked, system is reading upper case of numbers instead of numbers). 2. "Online" key on terminal—is it 'on'? 3. Modem switch—is it on? 4. Telephone in acoustic coupler—is it placed with cord in correct direction? Is it coupled securely without obstruction? 5. "Baud" rate or "Characters-per-second" switch—is it set correctly for number dialed or terminal type used? 6. Entry of password—was an 0 (OH) used instead of a 0 (ZERO) or an I (ELL) instead of a 1 (ONE)?
System gives double letters when commands and entries are typed, e.g., SSEELLEECCTT CCAATT	Check duplex switch on terminal and/or modem—should be at HALF.
System responds but entry commands are not typed or displayed, e.g.,. ? (blank) 1 546 CAT	Check duplex switch on terminal and/or modem—should be at FULL.
Message appears: DROPPED BY HOST SYSTEM Please log in	TYMNET failure. Dial back immediately. Do not issue a BEGIN command; enter DS to show previous search strategy.
Message appears: 415 20 DISCONNECTED @	TELENET failure. Dial back immediately. Do not issue a BEGIN command; enter DS to show previous search strategy.
No reaction from terminal for longer than acceptable period of time.	Lockheed system failure. Dial back immediately; if phone continues ringing, dial back at 5-minute intervals. (Most failures are corrected within 10 minutes.) Do not issue a BEGIN command; enter DS to show previous search strategy.

9

F. LOGON AND LOGOFF

F.1. LOGON AND TELECOMMUNICATIONS

DIRECT DIAL: Set terminal: HALF DUPLEX

Telephone number: 415/493-7580 — 30 cps
                     415/493-1093 — 120 cps (Bell 202)
                     415/494-8672 — 120 cps (Bell 212A)
                     415/493-8805 — 120 cps (VADIC)

ENTER YOUR DIALOG PASSWORD
XXXXXXXX

Fast or slow carriage return control may be added to the login process for direct dialing
by specifying "F" (for fast) or "S" (for slow) immediately after entering the password,
e.g.,

ENTER YOUR DIALOG PASSWORD
XXXXXXXX F

TELENET: Set terminal: FULL DUPLEX

Telephone no.: _____
Terminal identifier: _____

(CR) (CR) two carriage returns after dial-up

TELENET

nnn lln

TERMINAL=
        (CR)—give carriage return for 30 cps
        (see TELENET brochure for other)

@C 415 20   Key in TELENET code for Lockheed
             Retrieval Service: C 415 20   (spacing is important)

415 20 CONNECTED

ENTER YOUR DIALOG PASSWORD
XXXXXXXX

TYMNET: Set terminal: FULL DUPLEX

Telephone no.: _____
Terminal identifier: _____

Please type your terminal identifier
-1010-02—   Key in E for 30 cps.
                                  (See TYMNET brochure
                                  for other)

Please log in: LRS ◄─────────── Key in code for Lockheed
                                  Retrieval Service

password: DIALOG ◄───────────── Key in word DIALOG (does
                                  not print)

HOST IS ONLINE

ENTER YOUR DIALOG PASSWORD
XXXXXXXX

F.2. LOGON AND LOGOFF FEATURES

LOGON   Use to LOGON again without re-dialing telephone. Type in LOGON
            instead of LOGOFF. Responds with normal LOGOFF information
            for previous terminal session and a new:

                   ENTER YOUR DIALOG PASSWORD
                   XXXXXXXX

LOGOFF   Use to complete search session. Gives elapsed time and cost estimate
            of connect time, telecommunication time, and offline print charges
            since last BEGIN. Disconnects user from the DIALOG system.

10

PART 2 A SUMMARY OF ONLINE SYSTEM FUNCTIONS AND COMMANDS

Online Assistance and Procedures	BRS Bibliographic Retrieval Services	DIALOG Lockheed Information Systems	ORBIT System Development Corporation
Change or choose data base	——: . . CHANGE/ERIC	? BEGIN 1 {or} ? B1	USER: FILE ERIC
Help!		? ?EXPLAIN	USER: HELP
Available data bases	——: . . CHANGE/NEWS	? ?FILES	USER: FILES?
Unit record description		? ?FIELDS1	USER: EXPLAIN ERIC
Data base description		? ?FILE1	USER: EXPLAIN ERIC
System news	——: . . CHANGE/NEWS	? ?NEWS	USER: NEWS
Obtain amount of connect time since sign-on to retrieval system	——: . . TIME	? END	USER: TIME I
Delete *all* search statements	——: . . PURGEALL	? BEGIN1	USER: ERASEALL

Search Related Tasks	BRS Bibliographic Retrieval Services	DIALOG Lockheed Information Systems	ORBIT System Development Corporation
Delete select number of search statements	___: . PURGE 1,9 ___: . PURGE 12, 24		USER: KEEP 10, 11, 25
Change length of system messages	___: . SET DETAIL=ON {or} ___: . SET DETAIL=OFF		USER: TERMINAL MESSAGE LENGTH TUTORIAL {or} TERM ML SHORT
Enter search mode	R0201 ENTER COMMAND: ___: . SEARCH BRS-SEARCH MODE- ENTER QUERY 1___: GIFTED	? SELECT GIFTED (or) ? S GIFTED	(Always in search mode; to enter search disguised as a command when ORBIT asks a question, use command FIND): FIND GIFTED (or) FD GIFTED
Select search term	1___: GIFTED	? S GIFTED	USER: GIFTED
Select multi-term descriptor or identifier	1___: TALENT-IDENTIFICATION	? S TALENT IDENTIFICATION/DF	USER: TALENT IDENTIFICATION
Select single-term descriptor or identifier	1___: IDENTIFICA-TION.MJ,MN.	? S IDENTIFICATION/DF	USER: IDENTIFICATION/IT

Search Related Tasks	BRS Bibliographic Retrieval Services	DIALOG Lockheed Information Systems	ORBIT System Development Corporation
Select adjacent free text terms	1___: GIFTED ADJ CHILD$	? S GIFTED(W)CHILDREN	USER: GIFTED AND ALL CHILD: PROG: SS 1 PSTG (98) USER: STRS 1 (TI, AB) :GIFTED#CHILD:
Select terms using word proximity		? S GIFTED(3W)CHILDREN	
Select terms in same sentence	1___: GIFTED WITH CHILD$3		
Select terms in same field	1___: GIFTED SAME CHILDREN	? S GIFTED(F)CHILDREN	USER: (TI)GIFTED AND CHILDREN
Author searching	1___: SMITH ADJ (R OR RICHARD)	? S AU=SMITH, R	/USER: SMITH, R:/AU
Select year of publication	2___: . LIMIT/1 YR GT 77	? S YR=77 ? C 1 AND 2	USER:
Unlimited character truncation	1___: IDENTIF$	? S IDENTIF?	USER: ALL IDENTIF:

Operation			
Embedded character truncation	1___: NAVA$0	? S NAVA?0	USER: ALL NAVA#0
Limited character truncation	1___: TALENT$2	? S TALENT?? ?	USER: ALL TALENT# #
View online alphabetic display	1___: ROOT IDENTIF	? E IDENTIF	USER: NBR IDENTIF
View online thesaurus		? E (IDENTIFICATION)	
Save search permanently	___: . SAVE PS (4-letter word of your choice) ___: . SAVE PS (IDEN)	? END/SAVE	
Save search for one day	___: . SAVE (4-letter word of your choice) ___: . SAVE IDEN	? END/SAVE (searcher must .RELEASE the Search Save)	USER: SAVE
Execute a saved search	___: . EXEC IDEN	? . EXECUTE (serial number) ? . EXECUTE 1KLM	USER: RECALL (saved search name) RECALL IDENTIFICATION
Release permanent/temporary saved search	___: . PURGE IDEN	? . RECALL 1KLM ? . RELEASE 1KLM	USER: PURGESEARCH IDEN TIFICATION
Review online interaction	___: . DISPLAY ALL (or) ___: . DISPLAY 15,25	? DISPLAY SETS (or) ? DS	USER: HISTORY (or) HISTORY 15—25

159

Search Related Tasks	BRS Bibliographic Retrieval Services	DIALOG Lockheed Information Systems	ORBIT System Development Corporation
Limit to CIJE or RIE subfile	___: . . LIMIT/1 AN EQ ED ___: . . LIMIT/1 AN EQ EJ	? LIMIT 1/ED (or)	USER: 1 AND RIE/FS (or)
Positional and logical operators	L___: LOCUS ADJ CONTROL AND WOMEN	? S LOCUS(W) CONTROL AND WOMEN	
Nesting with positional and logical operators	L___: LOCUS ADJ CONTROL AND DEPRESS$ AND (WOMEN GIRL$ FEMALE$)	? S LOCUS(W) CONTROL AND DEPRESS? AND (WOM?N OR GIRL? OR FEMALE?)	
Nested boolean and set numbers	L___: LOCUS ADJ CONTROL AND 1 AND (WOMAN GIRL$ FEMALE$)	? S LOCUS(W) CONTROL AND #1 AND (WOM?N OR GIRL OR FEMALE)	
Select terms with truncation using field delimiters	L___: GIFTED ADJ CHILD$/TI, ID		USER: GIFTED AND ALL CHILD:/TI, ID

Display and Print Related Tasks

	BRS Bibliographic Retrieval Services	DIALOG Lockheed Information Systems	ORBIT System Development Corporation
Online prints, full format, five prints	_:. PRINT 1 ALL/ DOC=1,5	? TYPE 1/5/1—5	PROG: SS 1 PSTG (1) USER: PRT SS 1
Online prints, bibliographic citation, two prints	_:. PRINT 1 BIBL/ DOC=1,2	? T 1/3/1—2	USER: PRT 5 SS 1 FULL
Online prints, specified fields, three prints	_:. PRINT 1 AU, TI, MJ, MN/DOC=1,3		USER: PRT 1 SS 1
			USER: PRT 3 SS 1 AU, TI, IT
Receive online explanations of print commands or formats		? ?TYPE	USER: EXPLAIN PRINT

Operational Control	BRS Bibliographic Retrieval Services	DIALOG Lockheed Information Systems	ORBIT System Development Corporation
Starting after login	In Search mode by default	BEGIN or B or !	FILE
Terminating and disconnecting	. . OFF	LOGOFF	STOP YES or Y
Determining elapsed connect time	. . TIME	END or = LOGOFF or .COST	TIME INTERVAL OR TIME I
Determining elapsed cost from beginning of login	. . COST	END or = LOGOFF or .COST	TIME INTERVAL or TIME I

Appendix B

Databases Available Online

CONTENTS OF APPENDIX B

Estimates of the online data bases now exceed 400. The number changes almost daily. It would be inappropriate to list the data bases available as we prepare this manuscript as it would be out of date before the copies of this book were bound. Instead, let us give you two very good ways of getting the most information about these data bases and their availability.

First, every online system has a means for informing you about the data bases available on their service. For BRS, you type the command: . . CHANGE/NEWS. For DIALOG, you type the command: ?FILES. For ORBIT, you type the command: FILES? In each case this command will give you the most up to date list of the files (data bases) available as of that very day. For additional information, you can enter another command and obtain a short note about the data base. On DIALOG, the command is: ?FILEn, where n is the number of the file on DIALOG. On ORBIT, the command is: EX-PLAINxxxx, where xxxx is the name of the file, for example, ERIC. Every service also maintains a printed list of their data bases, sometimes even producing a subject guide to these data bases. This material is available on request and there is a new feature appearing online that also serves this purpose. In this appendix we have included as a sample listing portions of the DIALOG list which was distributed in late 1980.

Second, there exist several directories of available online data bases, giving valuable descriptive information. These are kept up to date by supplements or revised editions. We cite two of the most comprehensive directories:

Ruth N. Landau, J. Wanger, and M.C. Berger (Compilers),
***Directory of Online Databases*. Santa Monica, Calif., Cuadra Associates.**
Martha E. Williams, (Ed.), *Computer-Readable Data Bases: A Directory and Data Source Book*.
White Plains, N. Y., Knowledge Industry Publications

162

The databases available on the DIALOG System are listed below. Each entry includes the file coverage dates, number of searchable records, producer name, cost, and DIALOG file number.

ABI/INFORM   August 1971—present, 107,000 records, monthly updates (Data Courier, Inc., Louisville, KY)
The *ABI/INFORM* database is designed to meet the information needs of executives and covers all phases of business management and administration.
$75 per online connect hour, 20¢ per full record printed offline   *File 15*

AGRICOLA   1979—present, 1,340,000 records, monthly updates (National Agricultural Library, Beltsville, MD)
AGRICOLA (former *CAIN*) is the cataloging and indexing database of the National Agricultural Library (NAL). This massive file provides comprehensive coverage of worldwide journal and monographic literature on agriculture and related subjects.
$25 per online connect hour, 5¢ per full record printed offline   *Files 10, 110*

AIM/ARM   September 1967—1976, 17,500 citations (The Center for Vocational Education, The Ohio State University, Columbus, OH)
AIM/ARM is a specialized index for locating materials on vocational and technical education as well as the related areas of manpower economics and development, employment, job training, and vocational guidance.
$25 per online connect hour, 10¢ per full record printed offline   *File 9*

AMERICA: HISTORY AND LIFE   1964—present, 91,400 records, quarterly updates (ABC—Clio Inc., Santa Barbara, CA)
AMERICA: HISTORY AND LIFE (AHL), covering the full range of U.S. and Canadian history, area studies, and current affairs, is a comprehensive and current aid to bibliographic research.
$65 per online connect hour, 15¢ full record printed offline   *File 38*

APTIC   1966—September, 1978, 89,000 records (Manpower and Technical Information Branch, U.S. Environmental Protection Agency, Research Triangle Park, NC)
APTIC comprehensively covers all aspects of air pollution, its effects, prevention, and control from 1966-1976.
$35 per online connect hour, 10¢ per full record printed offline   *File 45*

AQUACULTURE   1970—present, 4300 records, irregular updates (National Oceanic and Atmospheric Administration, Rockville, MD)
AQUACULTURE provides access to information on the growing of marine, brackish, and freshwater organisms.

$35 per online connect hour, 15¢ per full record printed offline, 10¢ per full record typed online   *File 112*

★**AQUALINE**   1974−present, 21,000 citations, monthly updates (Water Research Centre, Medmanham, Buckinghamshire, England)

AQUALINE provides access to information on every aspect of water, waste water, and the aquatic environment.

$35 per connect hour, 30¢ per full record printed offline, 25¢ per full record typed online   *File 116*

ART MODERN   1974−present, 28,000 records, quarterly updates (ABC−Clio, Inc., Santa Barbara, CA)

$60 per online connect hour, 15¢ per full record printed offline   *File 56*

ASFA   1978−present, 46,500 records (FAO, Rome and the Intergovernmental Oceanographic Commission of UNESCO)

AQUATIC SCIENCES AND FISHERIES ABSTRACTS (ASFA) is a comprehensive database on life sciences of the seas and inland waters as well as related legal, political, and social topics.

$35 per online connect hour, 15¢ per full record printed offline   *File 44*

★**ASI**   1973−present, 55,000 records, monthly updates (Congressional Information Service, Inc., Washington, D.C.)

$90 per online connect hour, 15¢ per full record printed offline   *File 102*

★**BHRA FLUID ENGINEERING**   1974−present 33,000 records, quarterly updates (British Hydromechanics Research Association, Cranfield, Bedford MK43 OAJ, England)

$65 per online connect hour, 15¢ per full record printed offline   *File 96*

BIOSIS PREVIEWS   1969−present, 2,600,000 records, monthly updates (Biosciences Information Service, Philadelphia, PA)

BIOSIS PREVIEWS contains citations from both *Biological Abstracts* and *Biological Abstracts/RRM (formerly entitled Bioresearch Index)*, the major publications of BioSciences Information Service of *Biological Abstracts*.

$45 per online connect hour, 10¢ per full record printed offline   *Files 5, 55*

CA SEARCH   1967−present, 4,362,000 records, biweekly updates (Chemical Abstracts Service, Columbus, OH)

CA SEARCH is an expanded database which was produced by the merge of two files: the *CA CONDENSATES* file, which contains the basic bibliographic information appearing in the printed *Chemical Abstracts*, and the *CASIA* file, which contains a CA General Subject Headings from a controlled vocabulary and the CAS Registry Numbers, a unique number assigned to each specific chemical compound.

$70 per online connect hour, 20¢ per full record printed offline   *Files 2, 3, 4*

CAB ABSTRACTS January 1973−present, 966,000 records, monthly up-dates (The Commonwealth Agricultural Bureaux, Farnham House, Farnham Royal, Slough, SL2 3BN, England)

CAB ABSTRACTS is a comprehensive file of agricultural and biological information containing all records in the 26 main journals published by Commonwealth Agricultural Bureaus.

$35 per online connect hour, 25¢ per full record printed offline or typed online

File 50

CAIN (See AGRICOLA)

CDA (See COMPREHENSIVE DISSERTATION ABSTRACTS)

CEC (See EXCEPTIONAL CHILD EDUCATION RESOURCES)

Chemical Abstracts (See CA SEARCH, CHEMNAME™, CHEMSEARCH™, CHEMSIS™)

CHEMICAL INDUSTRY NOTES (CIN) 1974−present, 294,000 records, biweekly updates (American Chemical Society, Columbus, OH)

CHEMICAL INDUSTRY NOTES (CIN) extracts articles from over 75 world-wide business-oriented periodicals which cover the chemical-processing indus-tries.

$60 per online connect hour, 20¢ per full record printed offline   *File 19*

CHEMNAME™ 37,000 chemical substances derived from *CAS* Registry Nomenclature File, quarterly updates (Lockheed DIALOG Retrieval Service, Palo Alto, CA and Chemical Abstracts Service, Columbus, OH)

CHEMNAME (CA Chemical Name Dictionary) contains a listing of chemical substances in a dictionary-type, nonbibliographic file.

$70 per online connect hour, 20¢ per full record printed offline   *File 31*

CHEMSEARCH™ 45,000 chemical substances, derived from CA SEARCH (File 4), biweekly updates, (DIALOG Information Retrieval Service, Palo Alto, CA and Chemical Abstracts Service, Columbus, OH)

CHEMSEARCH is a dictionary listing of the most recently cited substances in *CA SEARCH* (File 4) and is a companion file to *CHEMNAME™* (File 31).

$55 per online connect hour, 16¢ per full record printed offline   *File 30*

★**CHEMSIS™** 1972−1976, 1,500,000 records, closed file (DIALOG Infor-mation Retrieval Service, Palo Alto, CA and Chemical Abstracts Service, Columbus, OH)

CHEMSIS (CHEM Singly Indexed Substances) is a dictionary, non-bibliographic file containing those chemical substances cited once during a Collective Index Period of Chemical Abstracts.

$70 per online connect hour, 20¢ per full record printed offline   *File 131*

CHILD ABUSE AND NEGLECT 1965−present, 8,800 citations, semi-annual updates (National Center for Child Abuse and Neglect, Children's

Bureau, U. S. Department of Health, Education, and Welfare, Washington, DC)

CHILD ABUSE AND NEGLECT will initially contain about 4,500 records of three sorts: ongoing research project descriptions, bibliographic references, and service program listings.

$35 per online connect hour, 10¢ per full record printed offline   *File 64*

★**CIS/INDEX**   1970−present, 110,000 records, monthly updates (Congressional Information Service, Inc., Washington, DC)

The *CIS/INDEX* database is the machine-readable form of the Congressional Information Service's *Index to Publications of the United States Congress.*

$90 per online connect hour, 15¢ per full record printed offline   *File 101*

CLAIMS™/CHEM   1950−1970, 265,000 citations, (IFI/Plenum Data Company, Arlington, VA)

The *CLAIMS/CHEM* database contains over 265,000 U.S. chemical and chemically related patents issued from 1950−1970.

$95 per online connect hour, 15¢ per full record printed offline   *File 23*

CLAIMS™/CHEM/UNITERM   1950−present, 452,576 records, quarterly updates (IFI/Plenum Data Company, Arlington, VA)

CLAIMS/CHEM/UNITERM gives access to chemical and chemically related patents.

$300 per online connect hour, 15¢ per full record printed offline. *Files 223, 224, 225*

CLAIMS™/CLASS   15,000 records (IFI/Plenum Data Co., Arlington, VA)

CLAIMS/CLASS is a classification code and title dictionary for all classes and selected subclasses of the U.S. Patent Classification System.

$90 per online connect hour, 10¢ per full record printed offline   *File 124*

CLAIMS™/U.S. PATENTS   1971−1977, 485,000 records, quarterly updates (IFI/Plenum Data Company, Arlington, VA)

The *CLAIMS/U.S. PATENTS* database contains all patents listed in the general, chemical, electrical, and mechanical sections of the *Official Gazette* of the U.S. Patent Office.

$95 per online connect hour, 15¢ per full record printed offline   *File 24*

CLAIMS™/U.S. PATENT ABSTRACTS   1978−present, 116,000 records, monthly updates (IFI/Plenum Data Company, Arlington, VA)

CLAIMS/U.S. PATENT ABSTRACTS contains citations and abstracts for all patents classified by the U.S. Patent Office in the areas of aerospace and aeronautical engineering, agriculture engineering, chemical engineering, chemistry, civil engineering, electrical and electronics engineering, electromagnetic technology, mechanical engineering, nuclear science, and general science and technology.

$95 per online connect hour, 50¢ per full record printed offline, 25¢ per full record typed online   *File 25*

CLAIMS®/U.S. PATENT ABSTRACTS WEEKLY   Current month, 3,000 citations, weekly updates (IFI/Plenum Data Company, Arlington, VA)

CLAIMS/U.S. PATENT ABSTRACTS WEEKLY is a companion to File 25. It includes the most current weekly update and records from the current month.

$95 per online connect hour, 50¢ per full record printed offline, 25¢ per full record typed on line   *File 125*

Commonwealth Agricultural Bureaux Abstracts (See CAB Abstracts)

COMPENDEX   January 1970–present, 817,000 records, monthly updates (Engineering Index, Inc., New York, NY)

The *COMPENDEX* database is the machine-readable version of the *Engineering Index (Monthly/Annual)*, which provides the engineering and information communities with abstracted information from the world's significant engineering and technological literature.

$65 per online connect hour, 15¢ per full record printed offline, 10¢ per full record typed online   *File 8*

COMPREHENSIVE DISSERTATION ABSTRACTS   1861–present, 648,000 citations, monthly updates (Xerox University Microfilms, Ann Arbor, MI)

COMPREHENSIVE DISSERTATION ABSTRACTS is a definitive subject, title, and author guide to virtually every American dissertation accepted at an accredited institution since 1861, when academic doctoral degrees were first granted in the United States.

$55 per online connect hour, 12¢ per full record printed offline   *File 35*

Computer and Control Abstracts (See INSPEC)

CONFERENCE PAPERS INDEX   1973–present, 715,000 records, monthly updates (Data Courier, Inc., Louisville, KY)

CONFERENCE PAPERS INDEX provides access to records of more than 100,000 scientific and technical papers presented at over 1,000 major regional, national, and international meetings each year.

$75 per online connect hour, 15¢ per full record printed offline   *File 77*

Congressional Information Service (See CIS/INDEX)

CRIS   July 1974–present, 33,000 citations, quarterly updates (USDA Cooperative State Research Service, Washington, DC)

CRIS (Current Research Information System) is a valuable current–awareness database for agriculturally related research projects.

$40 per connect hour, 10¢ per full record printed offline.

Current Research Information System (See CRIS)

Defense Market Measures System (*See FROST & SULLIVAN DM²*)

DIALOG PUBLICATIONS   current information (DIALOG Information Retrieval Service, Palo Alto, CA)

DIALOG PUBLICATIONS is a special feature database which allows you to order DIALOG publications online.

$15 per onset connect hours   *File 200*

DISCLOSURE   1977–present, 18,000 records, weekly updates (Disclosure Incorporated, Washington, D.C.)

DISCLOSURE provides extracts of reports filed with the U.S. Securities and Exchange Commission (SEC) by publicly owned companies.

$90 per online connect hour, $3.00 per full reocrd printed offline, $1.50 per full record typed online   *File 100*

Dissertation Abstracts (See *COMPREHENSIVE DISSERTATION ABSTRACTS)*

ECER (See EXCEPTIONAL CHILD EDUCATION RESOURCES)

ECONOMICS ABSTRACTS INTERNATIONAL   1974–present, 89,000 citations monthly updates (Learned information, Ltd., London, England)

ECONOMICS ABSTRACTS INTERNATIONAL provides coverage of the world's literature on markets, industries, country-specific economic data, and research in the fields of economic science and management.

$65 per online connect hour, 20¢ per full record printed offline   *File 90*

EIS INDUSTRIAL PLANTS   current, 140,000 records, replaced three times per year (Economic Information Systems, Inc., New York, NY)

Access to the *EIS PLANTS* database offeres immediate answers to a broader range of questions concerning the U.S. industrial economy.

$90 per online connect hour, 50¢ per full record printed offline or typed online
                                                              File 22

EIS NONMANUFACTURING ESTABLISHMENTS   current, 247,000 records, replaced three times per year (Eonomic Information Systems, Inc., New York, NY)

EIS NONMANUFACTURING ESTABLISHMENTS provides such information as location, headquarters name, percenty of industry sales, industry classification, employment size class, etc. for nearly 200,000 nonmanufacturing establishments which employ 20 or more people.

$90 per online correct hour, 50¢ per full record printed offline or typed online
File 92

Electrical & Electronic Abstracts (See INSPEC)

ENCYCLOPEDIA OF ASSOCIATIONS   current year, 14,000 records, annual updates (Gale Research Company, Detroit, MI)

The *ENCYCLOPEDIA OF ASSOCIATIONS* database corresponds to the printed publication of the same name. The *ENCYCLOPEDIA OF ASSOCIATIONS* provides detailed information on several thousand trade associations, professional societies, labor unions, fraternal and patriotic organizations, and other types of groups consisting of voluntary members.

$55 per online connect hour, 15¢ per full record printed offline   *File 114*

ENERGYLINE™   1971–present, 29,000 citations, bimonthly updates (Environment Information Center, Inc., New York, NY)

ENERGYLINE is the machine-readable version of *Energy Information Abstracts* and also includes 8,000 energy/environment records dating back to 1971 from *The Energy Index*.

$90 per online connect hour, 20¢ per full record printed offline   *File 69*

Engineering Index (See COMPENDEX)

ENVIROBIB (See Environmental Bibliography)

ENVIROLINE®   1971–present, 79,000 citations, monthly updates (Environment Information Center, Inc., New York, NY)

ENVIROLINE, produced by the Environment Information Center, covers the world's environmental information.

$90 per online connect hour, 20¢ per full record printed offline   *File 40*

ENVIRONMENTAL BIBLIOGRAPHY   1973–present, 158,000 records, bimonthly updates. (Environmental Studies Institute, Santa Barbara, CA)

The ENVIRONMENTAL BIBLIOGRAPHY, covers the fields of general human ecology, atmospheric studies, energy, land resources, water resources, and nutrition and health.

$60 per connect hour, 15¢ per full record printed offline   *File 68*

EPB (See Environmental Bibliography)

ERIC   1966–present, 360,000 citations, mostly updates (National Institute of Education, Washington, D.C. and ERIC Processing and Reference Facility, Bethesda, MD)

ERIC is the complete database on educational materials from the Educational Resources Information Center.

$25 per online connect hour, 10¢ per full record printed offline   *File 1*

Exceptional Child Education Abstracts (See EXCEPTIONAL CHILD EDU-CATION RESOURCES)

EXCEPTIONAL CHILD EDUCATION RESOURCES   1966–present, 38,000 citations, bimonthly updates (The Council for Exceptional Children, Reston, VA)

EXCEPTIONAL CHILD EDUCATION RESOURCES (ECR) is a comprehensive database concerned with published and unpublished literature on the education of handicapped and gifted children.

$25 per online connect hour, 10¢ per full reocrd printed offline   *File 54*

EXCERPTA MEDICA   June 1974–present, 1,160,000 records, monthly updates (Excerpta Medica, Amsterdam, The Netherlands)

EXCERPTA MEDICA is one of the two principal sources for searching the biomedical literature. It consists of abstracts and citations of articles from over 3,500 biomedical journals published throughtout the world.

$55 per online connect hour, 15¢ per full record printed offline   *Files 72, 73*

Federal Index (See PTS FEDERAL INDEX)

Fludix (see BHRA FLUID ENGINEERING)

Food Science and Technology Abstracts (See FSTA)

FOODS ADLIBRA   1974–present, 39,000 citations, monthly updates (K&M Publications, Inc., Louisville, KY)

FOODS ADLIBRA contains up-to-date information on the lastest developments in food technology and packing.

$55 per online correct hour, 10¢ per full record printed offline   *File 79*

FOREIGN TRADERS INDEX   current five years, 155,000 records, quarterly updates (U.S. Department of Commerce, Washington, D.C.)

The *FOREIGN TRADERS INDEX* is a directory of manufacturers, service organizations, agent representatives, retailers, wholesalers, distributors, and cooperatives in 130 countries ouside the U.S.

$45 per online connect hour, 25¢ per full record printed offline or typed online
File 105

FOUNDATION DIRECTORY   current year's data, 3200 listings, semiannual updates (The Foundation Center, New York, NY)

FOUNDATION DIRECTORY provides descriptions of 3200 foundations which have assets of $1 million or more or which make grants of $100,000 or more annually.

$60 per online connect hour. 30¢ per full record printed offline   *File 26*

FOUNDATION GRANTS INDEX   January 1973–present, 68,000 records, bimonthly updates (The Foundation center, New York, NY)

FOUNDATION GRANTS INDEX contains information on grants awarded by more than 400 major American philanthropic foundations, representing all records from the *Foundation Grants Index* section of the bimonthly *Foundation News.*

$60 per online connect tour, 30¢ per full record printed offline   *File 27*

Foundations National (See NATIONAL FOUNDATIONS)

FROST & SULLIVAN DM² 1975–present, 271,000 records, quarterly updates (Frost & Sullivan, Inc., New York, NY)

The *DM²* database *(Defense Market Measures System)* provides access to announcements about U.S. Government contract awards, request-for-proposals, R&D sources sought, sole-source negotiations, long-range planning estimates, and advanced planning procurement information for the engineered systems and services market.

$90 per online connect hour, 25¢ per full record printed offline   *File 59*

FSTA 1969–present, 179,000 citations, monthly updates (International Food Information Service, Shinfield, Reading, Berkshire, England)

FSTA (FOOD SCIENCE AND TECHNOLOGY ABSTRACTS) provides access to research and new development literature in the areas related to food science and technology.

$65 per online connect hour, 15¢ per full record printed offline   *File 51*

Funk & Scott Indexes (See PTS F&S INDEXES and PTS PREDALERT)

GEOARCHIVE 1969–present, 290,000 citations, monthly updates (Geosystems, P.O. Box 1024 Westminster, London SW1, England)

GEOARCHIVE is the world's most comprehensive and best-indexed geoscience database, indexing more than 100,000 references each year.

$70 per online connect hour, 20¢ per full record printed offline   *File 58*

GPO MONTHLY CATALOG July, 1976–present, 75,000 records, monthly updates (U.S. Government Printing Office, Washington, D.C.)

The *GPO MONTHLY CATALOG* is the machine-readable equivalent of the printed *Monthly Catalog of United States Government Publications.*

$35 per online connect hour, 10¢ per full record printed offline   *File 66*

★GRANTS DATABASE 1977–present, 1,500 records, monthly updates (Oryx Press, Phoenix, Arizona)

GRANTS DATABASE is the source to more than 1500 grant programs available through government (federal, state, and local), commercial organizations, associations, and private foundations.

$60 per online connect hour, 30¢ per full record printed offline   *File 85*

HISTORICAL ABSTRACTS 1973–present, 54,000 citations, quarterly updates (ABC–Clio, Inc., Santa Barbara, CA)

HISTORICAL ABSTRACTS is a reference service that abstracts and indexes the world's periodical literature in history and the related social sciences and humanities.

$65 per online connect hour, 15¢ per full record printed offline   *File 39*

INFORM (See ABI/INFORM)

★**INPADOC**   most recent six weeks, 16,000 records, weekly updates (International Patent Documentation Center, Vienna, Austria)

INPADOC, corresponding to the COM (Computer Output Microfiche) publication, *INPADOC Patent Gazette*, provides references to approximately 16,000 patents per week from 45 countries.

$95 per connect hour, 20¢ per full record printed offline   *File 123*

INSPEC   1969–present, 1,404,000 citations, monthly updates (The Institution of Electrical Engineers, Savoy Place, London WS2R OBL, England)

The *Science Abstracts* family of abstract journals, indexes, and title bulletins commenced publication in 1898. Today it forms the largest English-language database in the fields of physics, electrotechnology, computers, and control.

$55 per online connect hour, 15¢ per full record printed offline   *Files 12,13*

International Patent Documentation Center (See INPADOC)

INTERNATIONAL PHARMACEUTICAL ABSTRACTS   1970–present, 56,000 citations, bimonthly updates (American Society of Hospital Pharmacists, Washington, DC)

INTERNATIONAL PHARMACEUTICAL ABSTRACTS (IPA) provides information on all phases of the development and use of drugs and on professional pharmaceutical practice.

$50 per online connect hour, 15¢ per offline record   *File 74*

IPA (See INTERNATIONAL PHARMACEUTICAL ABSTRACTS)

★**IRL LIFE SCIENCES COLLECTION**   1978–present, 250,000 records, monthly updates, (Information Retrieval Limited, London, England)

IRL LIFE SCIENCES COLLECTION contains abstracts of information in the fields of animal behavior, biochemistry, ecology, entomology, genetics, immunology, microbiology, toxicology, and virology among others, and corresponds to the series of 15 abstracting IRL journals.

$45 per online connect hour, 15¢ per full record printed offline   *File 76*

ISMEC   1973–present, 98,000 citations, monthly updates (Data Courier, Inc., Louisville, KY)

ISMEC (Information Service in Mechanical Engineering) indexes significant articles in all aspects of mechanical engineering, production engineering, and engineering management from approximately 250 journals published throughout the world.

$75 per online connect hour, 15¢ per full record printed offline   *File 14*

LANGUAGE AND LANGUAGE BEHAVIOR ABSTRACTS (LLBA)   band 1973−present, 33,000 records, quarterly updates, (Sociological Abstracts, Inc., San Diego, CA)

LANGUAGE AND LANGUAGE BEHAVIOR ABSTRACTS (LLBA) provides current selective access to the world's literature on language and language behavior as a service to all researchers and practitioners in disciplines concerned with the nature and use of language.

$55 per connect hour, 15¢ per full record printed offline   *File 36*

Library and Information Science Abstracts (See LISA)

LISA (LIBRARY AND INFORMATION SCIENCE ABSTRACTS)   BAND 1969−present, 22,000 records, bimonthly updates (Learned Information Ltd., Woodside House, Hinsky Hill, Oxford, OXI 5BP, England)

LISA is produced by the Library Association (London) and contains citations to the source material acquired by the British Library for library science and by the ASLIB Library (Association of Special Libraries and Information Bureaus) for information science materials.

$50 per online connect hour, 10¢ per full record printed offline   *File 61*

MAGAZINE INDEX   1977−present, 316,000 citations, monthly updates (Information Access Corporation, Los Altos, CA)

MAGAZINE INDEX is the first online database to offer truly broad coverage of general magazines. It is a new database created especially for general reference librarians who must handle a constant flow of diverse requests for information from the mundane to the scholarly to the light hearted.

$45 per online hour, 10¢ per full record printed offline   *File 47*

MANAGEMENT CONTENTS®   September, 1974−present, 63,000 citations, monthly updates (Management Contents, Inc., Skokie, IL)

The *MANAGEMENT CONTENTS* database provides current information on a variety of business and management related topics to aid individuals in business, consulting firms, educational institutions, government agencies or bureaus and libraries in decision making and forecasting.

$70 per online hour, 15¢ per full record printed offline   *File 75*

Maritime Research Information Service Abstracts (See TRIS)

Market Abstracts (See PTS PROMT)

METADEX (METALS ABSTRACTS/ALLOYS INDEX)   1966−present (Alloys Index, 1974−present) 374,000 records, monthly updates (American Society for Metals, Metals Park, OH)

The *METADEX* database, produced by the American Society for Metals (ASM) and the Metals Society (London), provides the most comprehensive coverage of international literature on the science and practice of metallurgy.

$80 per online connect hour, 12¢ per full record printed offline   *File 32*

MLA BIBLIOGRAPHY   1976–1978, 121,500 records, annual updates (Modern Language Association, New York, NY)

The *MLA BIBLIOGRAPHY* database provides the first online access to the distinguished and comprehensive bibliography of humanistic studies produced annually by the Modern Language Association. The *MLA BIBLIOGRAPHY* indexes books and journal articles published on the modern languages, literature, and on liguistics.

$55 per online connect hour, 15¢ per full record printed offline   *File 71*

Modern Language Association Bibliography (See MLA BIBLIOGRAPHY)

Monthly Catalog (See GPO MONTHLY CATALOG)

MRIS Abstracts (See TRIS)

National Criminal Justice Reference Service (See NCJRS)

NATIONAL FOUNDATIONS   current year's data, 21,800 records, annual updates (The Foundation Center, New York, NY)

NATIONAL FOUNDATIONS provides records of all 21,800 United States foundations which award grants, regardless of the assets of the foundation or of the total amount of grants it awards annually.

$60 per online connect hour, 30¢ per full record printed offline   *File 78*

National Institute of Mental Health (See NIMH)

NATIONAL NEWSPAPER INDEX   1979–present, 165,000 records, monthly updates (Information Access Corporation, Los Altos, CA)

The *NATIONAL NEWSPAPER INDEX* provides front page to back page indexing of *The Christian Science Monitor, The New York Times,* and *The Wall Street Journal.*

$75 per online connect hour, 10¢ per full record printed offline   *File 111*

NCCAN (See CHILD ABUSE AND NEGLECT)

★**NCJRS**   1972–present, 45,000 records, monthly updates (National Criminal Justice Reference Service, Rockville, MD).

The NCJRS (National Criminal Justice Reference Service) database covers all aspects of law enforcement and criminal justice from police; courts; corrections; juvenile justice; community crime prevention; criminal justice system; fraud, waste, and abuse in government programs.

$35 per online connect hour, 15¢ per full record printed offline, 10¢ per full record typed online   *File 21*

NEWSEARCH   current month only, daily updates (Information Access Corporation, Los Altos, CA)

NEWSEARCH is a daily index of more than 1,500 news stories, information articles and book reviews from nearly 400 of the most important newspapers, magazines, and periodicals.

$95 per online connect hour, 10¢ per full record printed offline   *File 211*

Subscription rates available on request   *File 911*

NICEM   1979 edition, 326,500 records, biennially replaced (National Information Center for Educational Media, U. Southern California, Los Angeles, CA)

The *NICEM* database offers comprehensive coverage of non-print educational material.

$70 per online connect hour, 20¢ per full record printed offline   *File 46*

NICSEM/NIMIS   1978 edition, 36,000 records (National Information Center for Special Educational Materials, Los Angeles, CA)

NICSEM/NIMIS (NATIONAL INSTRUCTIONAL MATERIALS INFORMATION SYSTEM) contains descriptions of media and devices for use with handicapped children. Audio visual materials and equipment, large print and braille books, and many types of equipment and adaptive devices for all handicap levels are included.

$35 per online connect hour, 10¢ per full record printed offline   *File 70*

★NIMH   1969—present, 375,000 records, monthly updates (National Clearinghouse for Mental Health Information (NCMHI), National Institute of Mental Health, Rockville, MD).

The *NIMH (National Institute of Mental Health)* database cites worldwide information relating to the general topic area of mental health.

$30 per online connect hour, 10¢ per full record printed offline   *File 86*

★NON-FERROUS METALS ABSTRACTS   1961—present, 60,000 records, monthly updates (British Non-Ferrous Metals Technology Centre, Wantage, Oxfordshire, England).

NON—FERROUS METALS ABSTRACTS covers all aspects of non—ferrous metallurgy and technology.

$45 per connect hour, 20¢ per full record printed offline, 10¢ per full record typed online   *File 118*

NTIS   1964—present, 765,000 citations, biweekly updates (National Technical Information Service, NTIS, U.S. Department of Commerce, Springfield, VA)

The *NTIS* database consists of government-sponsored research, development, and engineering plus analyses prepared by federal agencies, their contractors or grantees.

$35 per online connect hour, 10¢ per full record printed offline   *File 6*

OCEANIC ABSTRACTS   1964–present, 110,500 records, bimonthly updates (Data Courier, Inc., Louisville, KY)

OCEANIC ABSTRACTS organizes and indexes technical literature published worldwide on marine-related subjects.

$75 per online connect hour, 15¢ per full record printed offline   *File 28*

ONTAP CA SEARCH   special training and practice file

ONTAP CA SEARCH contains over 15,000 records from *CA SEARCH* (File 4). The purpose of *ONTAP CA SEARCH* is to provide a low cost database containing chemical information which may be used to demonstrate the DIALOG chemical information system to people unfamiliar with the DIALOG service, to train new searchers, and to practice and become more familiar with the type of information available in the *CA SEARCH* database. All of the DIALOG system's search capabilities are available in *ONTAP CA SEARCH* except offline printing and the Search+Save features.

$15 per online connect hour, records not available for printing offline   *File 204*

ONTAP CHEMNAME™   special training and practice file

ONTAP CHEMNAME contains the corresponding chemical substance information for the records in *ONTAP CA SEARCH*.

$15 per online connect hour, records not available for printing offline   *File 231*

ONTAP ERIC   special training and practice file

ONTAP (ONline Training And Practice) *ERIC* is a programmed instruction file, designed to provide an opportunity for low-cost training and practice in online searching.

$15 per online connect hour, records not available for printing offline   *File 201*

PAIS INTERNATIONAL   *Bulletin:* 1976–present, *Foreign Language Index:* 1972–present, 107,000 citations, quarterly updates (PAIS, Inc., New York, NY)

Band *PAIS (PUBLIC AFFAIRS INFORMATION SERVICE) INTERNATIONAL* contains references to information in all fields of social science including political science, banking, public administration, international relations, economics, law, public policy, social welfare, sociology, education and social anthropology.

$60 per online connect hour, 15¢ per full record printed offline   *File 49*

Patent Abstracts (See CLAIMS™**/U.S. PATENT ABSTRACTS)**

PHARMACEUTICAL NEWS INDEX   December, 1975–present, 43,000 citations, monthly updates (Data Courier, Inc., Louisville, KY)

PHARMACEUTICAL NEWS INDEX (PNI) is the online source of current news about pharmaceuticals, cosmetics, medical devices, and related health fields.

$90 per online connect hour, 20¢ per full record printed offline   *File 42*

PHILOSOPHER'S INDEX   1940–present, 81,300 citations, quarterly updates (Philosophy Documentation Center, Bowling Green, OH)

PHILOSOPHER'S INDEX provides indexing and abstracts from books and over 270 journals of philosophy and related interdisciplinary fields.

$55 per online connect hour, 15¢ per full record printed offline   *File 57*

Physics Abstracts (See INSPEC)

PIRA   1975–present, 48,000 citations, monthly updates (The Research Association for the Paper and Board, Printing and Packaging Industries, Randalls Road, Leatherhead, Surrey KT22 7RU England)

The *PIRA* database contains the records appearing in the four abstracting journals published by Pira. These are *Paper and Board Abstracts*, *Printing Abstracts*, *Packaging Abstracts*, and *Management and Marketing Abstracts*.

$55 per online connect hour, 15¢ per full record printed offline   *File 48*

Plants (See EIS INDUSTRIAL PLANTS)

PMLA (See MLA BIBLIOGRAPHY)

PNI (See PHARMACEUTICAL NEWS INDEX)

Political Science Documents (See USPSD)

POLLUTION ABSTRACTS   1970–present, 68,500 citations, bimonthly updates (Data Courier, Inc., Louisville, KY)

POLLUTION ABSTRACTS is a leading resource for references to environmentally related literature on pollution, its sources and its control.

$75 per online connect hour, 15¢ per full record printed offline   *File 41*

POPULATION BIBLIOGRAPHY   1966–present, 47,500 records, bimonthly updates (University of North Carolina, Carolina Population Center, Chapel Hill, NC)

POPULATION BIBLIOGRAPHY is the world's largest single database covering monographs, journals, technical reports, government documents, conference proceedings, dissertations, and many unpublished reports on population.

$55 per online connect hour, 10¢ per full record printed offline   *File 91*

PREDICASTS (See PTS)

PSYCHOLOGICAL ABSTRACTS   1967–present, 305,500 citations, monthly updates (American Psychological Association, Washington, DC)

PSYCHOLOGICAL ABSTRACTS covers the world's literature in psychology and related disciplines in the behavioral sciences.

$65 per online connect hour, 10¢ per full record printed offline   *File 11*

PTS CMA–EMA (See PTS PROMT)

PTS Domestic Statistics (See PTS U.S. TIME SERIES AND PTS U.S. FORECASTS)

PTS F&S INDEXES (FUNK & SCOTT)   1972–present, 1,470,000 citations, monthly updates (Predicasts, Inc., Cleveland, OH)

The *F&S Indexes* cover both domestic and international company, product, and industry information. It contains information on corporate acquisitions and mergers, new products, technological developments, and sociopolitical factors.

$90 per online connect hour, 20¢ per full record printed offline; 50¢ per full record printed offline or typed online for nonsubscribers after 3 months

Files 18, 98

PTS FEDERAL INDEX   October 1976–present, 130,000 citations, monthly updates (Predicasts, Inc., Cleveland, OH)

PTS FEDERAL INDEX provides coverage of such Federal actions as proposed rules, regulations, bill introductions, speeches, hearings, roll calls, reports, vetoes, court decisions, executive orders, and contract awards.

$90 per online connect hour, 20¢ per full record printed offline   *File 20*

PTS Federal Index Weekly (See PTS PREDALERT)

PTS INTERNATIONAL TIME SERIES   1972–present, 118,000 citations, replaced quarterly (Predicasts, Inc., Cleveland, OH)

PTS INTERNATIONAL TIME SERIES is composed of two subfiles:

Worldcasts Composites. Contains about 2,500 forecast time series consisting of about 50 key series for each of the 50 major countries of the world (excluding the U.S.). Time series include historical data (since 1957) and projected concensus of published forecasts through 1990. Coverage includes population, GNP, per capita income, employment, production or usage of major materials, products, energy and vehicles and other economic, demographic, industrial, and product data.

$90 per online connect hour, 20¢ per full record printed offline; 50¢ per full record typed online or printed offline for nonsubscribers after 3 months   *File 84*

PTS INTERNATIONAL FORECASTS   323,000 citations, monthly updates (Predicasts, Inc., Cleveland, OH)

PTS INTERNATIONAL FORECASTS contains abstracts of published forecasts with historical data for all countries of the world (excluding the United States).

$90 per online connect hour, 20¢ per full record printed offline; 50¢ per full record typed online or printed offline for nonsubscribers after 3 months   *File 83*

PTS International Statistics (See PTS INTERNATIONAL TIME SERIES and PTS INTERNATIONAL FORECASTS)

PTS PREDALERT   current month only, weekly updates (Predicasts, Inc., Cleveland, OH)

$90 per online connect hour, 20¢ per full record printed offline; 50¢ per full record typed offline or printed online for nonsubscribers after 3 months   *File 17*

PTS PROMT   1972–present, 305,000 citations, monthly updates (Predicasts, Inc., Cleveland, OH)

PROMT (Predicasts Overview of Markets and Technology) abstracts all significant information appearing in thousands of newspapers, business magazines, government reports, trade journals, bank letters, and special reports throughout the world. The *PROMT* database provides the following kind of information: Acquisitions, Capacities, End Uses, Environment, Foreign Trade, Market Data, New Products, Production, Regulations, and Technology.

$90 per online connect hour, 20¢ per full record printed offline; 50¢ per full record printed offline or typed online for nonsubscribers after 3 months   *File 16*

PTS U.S. TIME SERIES   July 1971–present, 35,000 citations, replaced monthly (Predicasts, Inc., Cleveland, OH)

PTS U.S. TIME SERIES is composed of two subfiles:

Predicasts Composites. Contains 500 time series on the U.S. giving historical data (since 1957) and projected consensus of published forecasts through 1990.

$90 per online connect hour, 20¢ per full record printed offline; 50¢ per full record printed offline or typed online for nonsubscribers after 3 months   *File 82*

PTS U.S. FORECASTS   July 1971–present, 196,000 citations, quarterly updates (Predicasts, Inc., Cleveland, OH)

PTS U.S. FORECASTS contains abstracts of published forecasts for the United States from trade journals, business and financial publications, key newspapers, government reports and special studies.

$90 per online connect hour, 20¢ per full record printed offline; 50¢ per full record printed offline or typed online for nonsubscribers after 3 months   *File 81*

PTS Weekly (See PTS PREDALERT)

Public Affairs Information Service (See PAIS)

RAPRA ABSTRACTS   1972–present, 110,000 records, monthly updates (Rubber and Plastics Research Association of Great Britain, Shawbury, Shrewsbury, Shropshire, England)

RAPRA (RUBBER AND PLASTICS RESEARCH ASSOCIATION) ABSTRACTS is a comprehensive database covering the commercial, technical, and research aspects of the rubber and plastics industries.

$65 per online connect hour, 15¢ per full record printed offline   *File 95*

Repertoire International de Litterature Musicale (See RILM)

RILM ABSTRACTS   1972–present, 20,000 records, irregular updates (City University of New York, International RILM Center, New York, NY)

RILM (REPERTOIR INTERNATIONAL DE LITTERATURE MUSICALE) ABSTRACTS is an international database containing abstracts of all significant literature on music.

$65 per online connect hour, 15¢ per full record printed offline   *File 97*

Rubber and Plastics Research Association (See RAPRA ABSTRACTS)

Science Abstracts (See INSPEC)

Science Citation Index (See SCISEARCH)

SCISEARCH®   January 1974–present, 2,970,000 citations, monthly updates (Institute for Scientific Information, Philadelphia, PA)

SCISEARCH is a multidisciplinary index to the literature of science and technology prepared by the Institute for Scientific Information (ISI). It contains all the records published in *Science Citation Index (SCI®)* and additional records from the *Current Contents* series of publications that are not included in the printed version of SCI.

Records from 1974–1977 are in File 94. File 34 contains records from 1978 through the present.

FILE 34: $120 per online connect hour, 20¢ per full record printed offline, nonsubscribers; $30 per online connect hour, 10¢ per full record printed offline, subscribers.

FILE 94: $130 per online connect hour, 20¢ per full record printed offline, nonsubscribers; $40 per online connect hour, 10¢ per full record printed offline, subscribers.   *Files, 34, 94*

Searchable Physics Information Notices (See SPIN)

Smithsonian Science Information Exchange (See SSIE CURRENT RE-SEARCH)

Social Science Citation Index (See SOCIAL SCISEARCH)

SOCIAL SCISEARCH®   1972–present, 765,000 records, monthly updates (The Institute for Scientific Information, Philadelphia, PA)

The *SSCI* is a multidisciplinary database indexing every significant item from the 1,000 most important social sciences journals throughout the world and social sciences articles selected from 2,200 additional journals in the natural, physical, and biomedical sciences.

$70 per online connect hour, 10¢ per full record printed offline   *File 7*

SOCIOLOGICAL ABSTRACTS   1963–present, 99,600 citations, quarterly updates (Sociological Abstracts, Inc., San Diego, CA)

SOCIOLOGICAL ABSTRACTS covers the world's literature in sociology and related disciplines in the social and behavioral sciences.

$55 per online connect hour, 15¢ per full record printed offline   *File 37*

SPIN   1975–present, 114,000 citations, monthly updates (American Institute of Physics, New York, NY)

SPIN (Searchable Physics Information Notices) is designed to provide the most current indexing and abstracting of a selected set of the world's most significant physics journals.

$35 per online connect hour, 10¢ per full record printed offline   *File 62*

SSIE CURRENT RESEARCH   last two years, e.g., 1978–present, 299,000 citations, monthly updates (Smithsonian Science Information Exchange, Washington, DC)

SSIE (SMITHSONIAN SCIENCE INFORMATION EXCHANGE) CURRENT RESEARCH is a database containing reports of both government and privately funded scientific research projects, either currently in progress or initiated and completed during the most recent two years.

$90 per online connect hour, 20¢ per full record printed offline   *File 65*

SURFACE COATINGS ABSTRACTS 1976−present, 25,000 citations, bimonthly updates (Paint Research Association of Great Britain, Middlesex, England)

SURFACE COATINGS ABSTRACTS (SCA) contains references to research literature on all aspects of paints and surface coatings including pigments, dyestuffs, resins, solvents, plasticisers, printing inks, insulations, fire retardants, occurrence and prevention of deterioration, testing, industrial hazards, pollution and marketing.

$65 per online connect hour, 15¢ per full record printed offline   *File 115*

Toxic Substances Control Act Initial Inventory (See TSCA INITIAL INVENTORY)

TRADE OPPORTUNITIES 1976−present, 57,700 records, quarterly updates, (U.S. Department of Commerce, Washington, D.C.)

TRADE OPPORTUNITIES provides leads to export opportunities for U.S. business; the information is supplied by Foreign Service officers directly to the U.S. Department of Commerce.

$45 per connect hour, 25¢ per full record printed offline   *File 106*

TRADE OPPORTUNITIES WEEKLY current three months, 7,800 records, weekly updates (U.S. Department of Commerce, Washington, D.C.)

TRADE OPPORTUNITIES WEEKLY, File 107, includes current records added on a weekly basis and transferred to *TRADE OPPORTUNITIES*, File 106, on a quarterly basis.

$45 per connect hour, 50¢ per full record printed offline   *File 107*

Transportation Research Information Service (See TRIS)

TRIS (Transportation Research Information Service) 1968−present, 145,000 records, monthly updates (U.S. Department of Transportation and Transportation Research Board, Washington, D.C.)

TRIS provides transportation research information in air, highway, rail, and maritime transport; mass transit; and other transportation modes.

$40 per online connect hour, 10¢ per full record printed offline   *File 63*

★TSCA INITIAL INVENTORY 1979, 43,300 records, irregular updates (DIALOG Information Retrieval Service, Palo Alto, CA and Environmental Protection Agency, Office of Toxic Substances, Washington, D.C.)

TSCA INITIAL INVENTORY (derived from the *Initial Inventory of the Toxic Substances Control Act Chemical Substance Inventory*) is a non-bibliographic dictionary listing chemical substances in commercial use in the U.S. as of June 1, 1979.

$45 per online connect hour, 15¢ per full record printed offline   *File 52*

*U.S. EXPORTS   100,000−200,000 records, annual updates (U.S. Department of Commerce, Washington, D.C.)

U.S. EXPORTS gives export statistics that reflect both government and non−government exports of domestic and foreign merchandise from the U.S. and Territories to foreign countries.

$45 per connect hour, 25¢ per full record printed offline, 25¢ per full record typed online   *File 126*

U.S. Patents (See CLAIMS™/U.S. PATENTS)

USPSD (UNITED STATES POLITICAL SCIENCE DOCUMENTS) 1975−1977, 12,500 records, irregular updates (University of Pittsburgh, University Center for International Studies, Pittsburgh, PA)

USPSD provides detailed abstracts and indexing from approximately 120 of the major American journals publishing scholarly articles in the broad area of political science.

$65 per online connect hour, 15¢ per full record printed offline   *File 93*

★**U.S. PUBLIC SCHOOL DIRECTORY** current year, 80,000 records, annual updates (National Center for Educational Statistics (NCES), Washington, D.C.)

U.S. PUBLIC SCHOOL DIRECTORY provides a variety of directory−type data on public schools throughout the U.S. and Territories. The data is applicable to monitoring trends in fields of public education and can be used to analyze public schools by type, location, and size; identify a specific school; or generate a list of schools.

$35 per connect hour, 10¢ per full record printed offline   *File 120*

WELDASEARCH 1967−present, 47,800 records, monthly updates (The Welding Institute, Abington, Cambridge CB1 6AL, England)

The *WELDASEARCH* database provides primary coverage of the international literature on all aspects of the joining of metals and plastics and related areas such as metals spraying and thermal cutting.

$65 per online connect hour, 15¢ per full record printed offline   *File 99*

WORLD ALUMINUM ABSTRACTS 1968−present, 70,600 citations, monthly updates, (American Society for Metals, Metals Park, OH)

WORLD ALUMINUM ABSTRACTS (WAA), provides coverage of the world's technical literature on aluminum, ranging from ore processing (exclusive of mining) through end uses.

$50 per connect hour, 10¢ per full record printed offline   *File 33*

WORLD TEXTILES   1970−present, 84,700 records, monthly updates (Shirley Institute, Didsbury, Manchester M20 8R4, England)

WORLD TEXTILES is the machine-readable version of *World Textile Abstracts* and indexes world literature on the science and technology of textile and related materials; on the technical economics, production, and management of the textile industry; and on the consumption of and international trade in textile materials and products.

$55 per online connect hour, 10¢ per full record printed offline   *File 67*

Worldcasts (See PTS INTERNATIONAL FORECASTS)

Appendix C

Examples of Data Base Descriptions and Search Aids

Both the data base suppliers and the searching services provide written documentation, searching aids, and user manuals for a particular data base. Occasionally a library or information specialist will gain substantial experience on the file and will provide yet another aid for other online searchers. These are now appearing in journal form or as separate pamphlets.

The information provided in these sources will cover the data base in terms of the following: major areas of coverage and time or language limits on the file, article selection policies, list of journals covered, indexing practices, a sample citation, a search guide for access to data elements in the citation, sample searches, related services such as document retrieval, a guide to online access via specified data base vendors, and other relevant aids.

We have included in this appendix examples of an online data base description produced by the data base supplier (ABI/Inform, a file of Data Courier, Inc.) and a description provided by each of the online services who allow you to search the file for a fee. A perusal of Parts 1–4 of this appendix will show what each has chosen to say about the data base. Often these descriptions can be quite lengthy. We have chosen the shortest versions available for reproduction. In one case (Part 1) we have shown only excerpts of the list of journals covered.

Because these data base search aids are now so numerous, there are directories to information about them. The directory we have included here (in Part 5 of this appendix) was produced by DIALOG Information Retrieval Service. The search aids referenced in this list are not necessarily specific to searching only on DIALOG.

As multiple data base searching becomes more prevalent, search aids *across* data bases are being developed. The *DIALOG Bibliographic Verification Aid* reproduced in Part 6 of this appendix is one such aid. It helps a DIALOG user remember what to enter if they are checking for authors in one, then another, data base. The other searching services provide other cross data base aids too.

Contents of Appendix C

ABOUT THE ABI/INFORM DATABASE

ABI/INFORM™ is known as **The Database for Decision Makers**. It was created in 1971 to fill a gap in the information available to executives and information managers in business, industry, government, universities, and other organizations.

ABI/INFORM is designed for use as a source of ideas, concepts, tested methods, tactics, and strategies of specific relevance to managers and administrators. It references information to be used in making the best possible decisions, recommendations, and judgments.

A search of the database provides both current and retrospective information on all phases of management and administration. ABI/INFORM is used, for example, to learn how to prevent a problem; who has tried a particular method of solving the problem and what the results have been; how to implement a new procedure; or how to predict the success or failure of a planned program.

A sweeping range of journal articles since 1971 is included in the database. Each was selected for its relevance to managers and administrators.

MAJOR AREAS OF COVERAGE:

> Accounting and Auditing
> Banking
> Economics
> EDP Systems and Information Science
> Finance and Financial Management
> General Management
> Insurance
> Law and Taxation
> Management Science
> Marketing, Advertising, and Sales Management
> Personnel, Employee Benefits, and Labor
>   Relations
> Public Administration and Government
> Real Estate
> Telecommunications

ABI/INFORM contains both full bibliographic information and a complete abstract for each article cited in the database. Articles are cited and abstracted from over 400 primary English-language management and administration journals. Although most of the journals selected for coverage in INFORM are published in the United States, there is increasing coverage of English-language journals published in other countries. The database currently contains over 88,000 abstracts and is growing at the rate of approximately 1900 abstracts per month.

ARTICLE SELECTION

Articles selected for inclusion in ABI/INFORM cover a variety of topics. They may contain highly technical discussions of econometric models or compare the planning process among companies within a specific industry. They may define the attitudes of successful decision-makers or describe case studies of establishing sales territories. They may discuss the impact of new technology, open office planning, participative budgeting, etc.

The same selection criteria have been used since the inception of the database in August 1971, although the specific journals and number of journals covered have varied. To be included in INFORM:

- An article must contain meaningful management ideas or concepts, usually defining or describing a method, technique, tactic, or strategy that would be of value to a manager or administrator.

- The article's content must be of lasting rather than passing value.

- Usually, the article must be at least a page in length; the average is over six pages.

- Personal interviews, feature interest stories, news items, and data-only articles are usually not included.

CORE JOURNALS

Beginning in January 1979, 135 journals will be abstracted in their entirety, omitting only news sections, letters to the editor, book reviews, and similar regular features or columns. Most of these Core Journals have been covered extensively in the ABI/INFORM database for several years. In the future, each issue will be abstracted on a cover-to-cover basis, excluding only those features and columns mentioned above. The list of Core Journals begins on page B-13.

JOURNAL SELECTION

Journal selection is an important ongoing responsibility of the ABI/INFORM editorial staff. The management literature is not static; new journals on existing topics are introduced every year, and such new areas as word processing and Eurodollar transactions, for example, become the subject of new management periodicals as they become of importance to

186

management decision-making. In addition, users of the ABI/INFORM database recommend new areas of coverage; in 1979, following recommendations of searchers of the database, several new journals covering telecommunications technology were added to the coverage list.

The editorial staff routinely acquires sample copies of new journals as well as journals recommended by online searchers. Each publication is reviewed thoroughly, and those journals having sound, long-term, meaningful management information are added to the acquisitions list.

In this user aid, in addition to the Core Journals list described above, are the following:

• Complete Journals List, alphabetical by journal title, including the two- or three-digit INFORM journal code, the date coverage began, and, when available, both CODEN and ISSN.

• Journals List by Subject Category to aid searchers who wish to limit to a specific set of topic area publications.

DATABASE UPDATES

The ABI/INFORM database invites use as a current awareness service, and every effort is made to ensure the currency of information entering the database. An article may, however, have been in print four to eight weeks before it is searchable online; the following description of the updating process indicates the ways in which this delay may occur.

Assuming the publication date on the cover of an incoming journal is correct (many organizations do not change the cover date when publication is delayed) and the Postal Service has not delayed delivery, each issue is scanned and articles are selected for abstracting in the first week after publication. Abstractors, chosen for their expertise in a particular subject area, receive material on a weekly basis; they read each article, assign appropriate controlled vocabulary terms, and write an abstract of 150 to 200 words.

When the abstracts are returned the following week, they are edited by a member of the editorial staff, who also monitors keyword assignment and checks all of the bibliographic information. Citations and abstracts are keyboarded each day. Proofreading and correcting add two more days to the process. At this point an article has been added to an update within two weeks of publication. Update tapes are run, however, on a monthly not daily basis. The tapes are forwarded to the vendors usually on the last Monday of a month. Cited articles being input just after an update has been run, therefore, will not be searchable for six or seven weeks after publication.

INDEXING: 1978 FORWARD

To increase the utility of the ABI/INFORM database, a controlled vocabulary was developed in late 1977. Beginning with the January 1978 update, each citation in the database includes an average of eight to twelve index terms assigned by the editorial staff. These terms, chosen from the Controlled Vocabulary included in the ABI/INFORM User Guide, represent the main points of the article.

The Controlled Vocabulary contains approximately 11,000 terms; it is not static but rather changes over time as management terminology changes and as management responsibilities broaden. When using the vocabulary, a searcher should note synonyms, broader terms, narrower terms, or acronyms for the search term.

A member of the editorial staff has indexed each abstract entering ABI/INFORM since January 1978. Abstracts in the database prior to 1978, however, were indexed by an automatic process; some false drops can be expected when searching citations added before 1978.

INDEXING: 1971-1977

When the Controlled Vocabulary was developed for ABI/INFORM, over 65,000 citations and abstracts were already in the database. It would have been impossible to manually index each citation; yet we wanted searchers to be able to limit to the index term field throughout the entire database. We decided, therefore, to index the 1971-1977 backfile through a computerized process: "auto-indexing."

In order for searchers to better understand the "false drops" that may result from a search including the 1971-1977 material, a brief description of the auto-indexing follows.

The basic operation of the auto-indexing process was to match terms in each article title and abstract with terms in a "bridge" vocabulary which included the following:

• Authorized index terms from the controlled vocabulary

• Synonyms

• Use/Related terms

• Normalized forms of terms

• Normalized names of companies, organizations, and countries

Each word in the title and abstract, except those on a short stop-word list, was examined for possible matching with the "bridge" vocabulary terms listed above. Whenever a match was made, the authorized term was posted to the index term field.

Despite recurrent checking of the bridge vocabulary, some terms that could generate false drops were overlooked. For example, a match of "Campbell" posted the authorized term for the Campbell Soup Company even though "Campbell" is a common surname. The imprecision of both the English language and management terminology led to other false drops, e.g., "diseases" has connotations other than physiological disorders; "go public" posted the authorized term "new SEC regulations" even when "go public" denoted disclosure of non-financial information.

The total bridge vocabulary was almost 19,000 terms; for each entry in the database, the number of words in the title plus abstract approximated 180-200 terms. In some abstracts, the number of matches exceeded 40 terms, although these are relatively few. The average number of index terms posted was approximately 16. Since 1977, the average number of terms assigned is approximately ten.

DATA ELEMENTS

Each citation in the ABI/INFORM database consists of three components:

- Bibliographic information, which provides all data necessary to locate the original article.

- An abstract, 150-200 words in length, which summarizes the content of the article.

- Index terms, chosen from the controlled vocabulary (in 1978 and thereafter, see above), which pinpoint the concepts discussed in the article.

In the sample citation below, each searchable data element is identified. Not all data elements, however, are searchable on all online systems.

SAMPLE CITATION

Accession number	78-03676
Title	**The upward mobility two incomes can buy**
Source publication	Business Week, n2522, pp. 80, 84-86, Feb. 20, 1978
CODEN, Journal code	BUWEA3, BWE, ISSN 0007-7135 _____ *ISSN*
Document type	J (Journal)
Language	English
Controlled terms	Dual career couples; Implications; Marketing; Inflation; Insurance; Social Change; Income; Social Issues; Standards of Living; Consumers
Abstract	In today's society, a new group of women is emerging. They are well-educated women, pursuing remunerative careers that have lifted their families into income brackets well above those they would have occupied if only their husbands worked. In light of the change in the overall status of families that this new group of women has occasioned, large numbers of businesses are struggling to re-identify their customers and their customers' wants. The marketers need new strategies because the affluent, dual-income family does not merely spend more money; it spends money differently. The dual-income situation also requires certain adjustments and realizations from the dual-income family itself. They must face the "marriage penalty" at tax time, and they must sacrifice certain family "togetherness" rewards. They have a need for more life insurance to protect the family's living standard against the effects of either spouse's demise. Graph.

A-3

CITATION NUMBER

A unique seven-digit citation number (accession number) is assigned to each entry in the database; the first two digits represent the year in which the article entered the database, and the following five digits indicate the sequence in which it was entered during that year. The sample citation, therefore, was the 3676th addition to ABI/INFORM in 1978. Currently around 1900 abstracts are added to the database each month. One can estimate, therefore, that the sample citation was in the March (7803) update.

In order to calculate roughly the update in which an abstract entered the database, one can use the following table.

Calendar year	Total items	Av. entries/month
1971	1,215	265
1972	4,285	360
1973	5,980	500
1974	10,390	865
1975	12,705	1,060
1976	13,550	1,130
1977	18,095	1,500
1978	19,445	1,620
Est. 1979	23,000	1,915

ARTICLE TITLE

Each article title is entered as it appears in the journal. Each meaningful word in the title is searchable; however, titles in the management literature are not necessarily indicative of article content, e.g., "Tender 'Bear Hugs' " and "Golden Apples of Antarctica." Although it is possible to limit a search term to this field, care should be exercised when using this limit capability as potentially good articles may be missed.

AUTHOR NAME

Author names are entered as they appear in the publication in the following format: last name, comma, space, first name, space, initial, period. To compensate for the possibility that an author's name has appeared in full, with nickname, or with initials only, it is helpful to use the appropriate online command to review the forms that have been used with a specific last name.

JOURNAL TITLE

Publication information includes the journal title (often abbreviated), volume and issue number, date of issue, and inclusive pagination of the cited article. Although the journal title may be searchable, we recommend limiting to a particular journal or journals by the codes discussed below rather than by the journal title.

JOURNAL CODES

A two- or three-character code has been assigned to each journal in the ABI/INFORM database. Care is taken to use the code consistently during the time period the journal is abstracted regardless of journal name changes, e.g., *Commerce Today* became *Commerce America* became *Business America,* but the journal code remained **CT**. We recommend limiting to a particular set of journals through use of this Journal Code.

Two additional codes—CODENs and ISSNs—are included for each journal to which either or both have been assigned. Although most scientific and technical journals have been assigned these codes, many business and management journals have not. The only code, therefore, that will appear for **all** journals cited in ABI/INFORM is the Journal Code.

ABSTRACT

Each abstract in the ABI/INFORM database since 1975 has been written under specific guidelines related to content, length, and style considerations. (These guidelines were more rigorously enforced after the database was acquired by Data Courier, Inc. in mid-1974.) The abstracts are informative rather than indicative, that is, they summarize the information in the article rather than describing the kind of information that is contained in the article.

Meaningful terms in the abstracts can be searched on a free-text basis; when conducting a free-text search, we recommend that a searcher:

- Input as many synonyms as possible for the concept.

- Use both acronyms and expanded forms of the terms.

- Use proximity or word adjacency capabilities when searching a multi-word term; "federal budget" will yield fewer hits but also fewer false drops than "federal" and "budget."

A-4

189

- Include British spellings, e.g., "labour" or "behaviour," where applicable or utilize a system truncation capability to include the alternate spellings.

INDEX TERMS

Since the January 1978 update, eight to twelve controlled index terms have been assigned to each article abstract in **ABI/INFORM**. It is possible to limit a search to only this field by entering a controlled vocabulary phrase or by adding the field limiter to a single term. Searches limited to the index term field will yield more accurate results for the 1978 and forward citations, less accurate results for the 1971-1977 citations.

OTHER SERVICES

● ARTICLE RETRIEVAL

An article retrieval service is provided for most articles abstracted in the **ABI/INFORM** database. Only those journals which have provided permission and only those articles which were published in 1975 or later are available under this program.

If an article which meets these criteria is not available in your library, you may obtain a copy by writing to:

ABI/INFORM Retrievals
Data Courier, Inc.
620 South Fifth Street
Louisville, KY 40202 U.S.A.

Customers with a deposit account (minimum deposit $100) will pay $5 per article; without a deposit account the fee is $6.50 per article. First class postage within the United States is included in the retrieval price. Orders outside the United States will require an additional $.50 per article for airmail postage. All orders are processed within 48 hours of receipt.

Some online vendors have an online ordering procedure through which searchers may order copies of articles when completing an online search. Please check with the representative of the system(s) you access.

● INDIVIDUAL INQUIRIES

Online searchers who have questions or suggestions are encouraged to write or call us. We promise fast, thorough, and courteous service. Please write:

ABI/INFORM
Data Courier, Inc.
620 South Fifth Street
Louisville, KY 40202 U.S.A.

Phone:

502/582-4111 -or-
800/626-2823
(Continental U.S. except Kentucky)

A-5

190

Search Guide

FIELD	BRS
ACCESSION NUMBER	Not searchable, displayed when document printed. Form: 78-0001
● **TITLE**	YES. Title words directly searchable. Hyphens & slashes removed for searching but appear when document printed. Qualifier: TI
● **AUTHOR**	YES. Allow for possible variations by inputting all likely forms. Must request that last name be adjacent to first name or initial, e.g., SMITH ADJ J. Qualifier: AU
● **SOURCE: TITLE**	NO.
● **CODE**	Not searchable, but limitable. Qualifier: JC
● **CODEN**	YES. Drop sixth character, e.g., BUNEA <u>not</u> BUNEA3 Qualifier: CD
● **ISSN NUMBER**	YES. Qualifier: IS
● **ABSTRACT**	YES. Directly searchable in free-text format. Hyphens & slashes removed for searching but appear when document printed. Qualifier: AB
● **CONTROLLED TERMS**	YES. 1971-1977 fields may be lengthy and contain excessive matches. Multiword terms must be hyphenated. Qualifier: DE
● **PUBLICATION YEAR**	Not directly searchable. Use Limit command with two-digit form of year. Qualifier: YR
● **DOCUMENT TYPE**	YES. Qualifier: 02 PT
● **UPDATES**	NO. Automatic SDI feature allows for automatic reprocessing of a search against each new update.

A-6

191

This chart is intended to be a helpful comparison of capabilities. It is **not** exhaustive. For details of capabilities and new
features, refer to each system's user manual and newsletters.

SDC/ORBIT	LOCKHEED/DIALOG
YES. Put a hyphen after the year. Only 5 digits follow the year. 78-00001/AN	YES. Number is eight digits: two denoting year; six following. Type 78000001
YES. Meaningful words part of the Basic Index. Qualifier—/TI	YES. Meaningful words part of the Basic Index. Qualifier—/TI
YES. Check for all variations using "NBR" command. Qualifier—/AU	YES. Check for all variations using "Expand" command. Qualifier—AU=
Not directly	YES. Check for variations in input form using "Expand" command. Qualifier—JN=
YES. Qualifier—/JC	YES. Qualifier—JC=
YES. Qualifier—/JC	YES. Qualifier—CO=
YES. Qualifier—/ISSN	YES. Qualifier—SN=
YES. All meaningful words are part of the Basic Index. Qualifier: cannot limit to this field.	YES. All meaningful words are part of the Basic Index. Qualifier—/AB
YES. 1971-1977 fields may be lengthy and contain excessive matches. Qualifier—/IT —/IW (index term words)	YES. 1971-1977 fields may be lengthy and contain excessive matches. Qualifier—/DF —/DE (index term words)
YES. Date Ranging	YES. Qualifier—PY=
YES. Qualifier—J/DT	YES. Qualifier—DT=Journal Paper
YES. File updated monthly. 1971-1977 were reloaded in 3 large updates. For current awareness, limit to recent update. Qualifier—7810/UP	YES. File updated monthly. 1971-1977 were reloaded in 1 large update. For current awareness, limit to recent update. Qualifier—UD=7810 or for always the most recent, UD=9999

A-7

192

SAMPLE SEARCHES

We asked our U.S. vendors to submit sample searches on specific topics utilizing the capabilities of their particular systems. Some of these are reprinted below for your examination.

None of these sample searches is intended as a definitive approach to the question, and alternate strategies will occur to many users. For illustration and clarity, we have converted the vendors' printouts to the formats shown below, and have added our comments.

●System: BRS

QUESTION:

What elements are involved in the controversy surrounding state taxation of software?

ENTER DATA BASE NAME	COMMENTS
__ : INFO	
1__ : SOFTWARE AND (STATE$1 OR SALES) ADJ TAX$5	Truncation of **STATE** limited to one additional character (plural). Truncation of **TAX** limited to five characters (ie., es, ing, ation).
RESULT 10	
2__ : ..PRINT 1 TI/DOC=1–5	Request that titles of first five documents be printed.

     1

TI ARE SOFTWARE TAXES INEVITABLE.

     2

TI "WE'LL PACK THE ROOM," SAYS STAG.

     3

TI N.Y. TAX LAW UNFAIR TO SERVICE INDUSTRY: LYNCH.

     4

TI CURRENT STATUS OF SOFTWARE TAX ISSUE.

     5

TI VERMONT EXCLUDES DP SERVICES FROM SALES TAX.

       END OF DOCUMENTS

..PRINT 2 ALL/DOC=1	Requesting all paragraphs of first document be printed.

     1

AN 77-08129

A-8

193

AU MYERS, EDITH D.

TI DATA PROCESSING AND TAXES.

SO PUB: DATAMATION. V23 N5. PAG: P155—160. MAY 1977.

PT 02.

CD DTMNA.

YR 77.

DE APPLICATIONS, COMPANIES, COURTS, DATA, DATA-PROCESSING,
   DRAFTING, HARDWARE, ISSUE, NEW, OPERATING-SYSTEMS-(DP),
   PERSONAL-PROPERTY, PROCESSING, PRODUCTS, PROPERTY,
   PROPERTY-TAXES, REGULATIONS, RETAIL, RULES, SALES, SALES-
   TAXES, SERVICES, SOFTWARE-(DP), STATES, STATUS, SUBJECTS,
   SYSTEMS, TAX-SALES, TAXATION, TAXES, USE-TAXES.

AB MANY STATES ARE DRAFTING REGULATIONS TO DEAL WITH TAXATION
   OF SOFTWARE, DATA PROCESSING SERVICES, AND RELATED SERVICES,
   WHILE OTHERS ARE ATTEMPTING TO RETROACTIVELY APPLY NEW
   INTERPRETATION OF OLD RULES. DATA PROCESSING PRODUCTS ARE
   BEING SUBJECTED TO PERSONAL PROPERTY TAX, SALES TAX, AND
   USE TAX. HARDWARE ALMOST ALWAYS IS CONSIDERED TANGIBLE
   AND SUBJECT TO PROPERTY TAX, BUT THE STATUS OF OPERATING
   SYSTEMS SOFTWARE IS NOT CLEAR. THE SALE, LEASE, OR RENTAL
   OF HARDWARE IS CONSIDERED A SALE, LEASE, OR RENTAL OF
   TANGIBLE PERSONAL PROPERTY IN ALL STATES HAVING A RETAIL
   SALES TAX. THE QUESTION IN MANY STATES IS WHETHER OR NOT
   APPLICATION SOFTWARE CONSTITUTES TANGIBLE PERSONAL PROPERTY
   FOR PURPOSES OF SALES TAXATION. AS MANY STATES HAVE CON-
   FLICTING OPINIONS, MANY COMPANIES HAVE FOUND DIFFERENT
   REACTIONS TO THESE TAXES. MANY HAVE DETERMINED TO FIGHT
   THEM THROUGH THE COURTS. THE SOFTWARE TAX ISSUE CAN BE
   WON — IT WAS WON IN FLORIDA. TABLE.

JC CD-DAT.

IS 0011-6963.

A-9

194

● QUESTION:

What articles are available on attitudes toward hiring the handicapped?

FILE INFORM	COMMENTS

SS 1: ALL HANDICAP:/IT (118)

SS 2: ALL HIR: OR ALL EMPLOY: OR ALL PLAC: (20704) .... Search statements may
be stacked.

SS 3: ALL ATTITUD: (3087)

SS 4: 1 AND 2 AND 3 (4)

SS 5/C?

USER:

PRT TI 4 .... Tailored print command
displays titles only.

PROG:

-1-

TI - EMPLOYEE SERVICES - A STUDENT PERSPECTIVE

-2-

TI - IBM CALLED EXCEPTION - DP INDUSTRY HIT FOR ATTITUDE
ON HANDICAPPED

-3-

TI - NOT ALL ILLNESSES ARE HANDICAPS

-4-

TI - TOTAL PERSON TRAINING

SS 6 /C?

USER:

PRT FULL 1 SKIP 1 .... Full information about
most likely title is requested.

PROG:

-2-

AN - 77-05588

TI - IBM CALLED EXCEPTION - DP INDUSTRY HIT FOR ATTITUDE
ON HANDICAPPED

AU - WISEMAN, TONI

SO - COMPUTERWORLD (CMPWAB, COW), V11 N14, P15, ISSN 0010-4841,
APR. 4, 1977

DT - J (JOURNAL)

LA - ENGLISH

IT - ADDITIONS; AREAS; CASES; COMPANIES; COMPUTER PROGRAM-
MING; COMPUTERS; COSTS; DEAFNESS; DISABILITIES; EMPLOYERS;
EXCEPTIONS; FIRMS; GOVERNMENT; HANDICAPPED; IBM-ARMONK
NY; INDUSTRIES; MANAGEMENT; MANUFACTURERS; NEGATIVE;
NOISE; PROGRAMMERS; SOLUTIONS; USERS

A-10

195

AB   WITH ONE EXCEPTION, THE DP INDUSTRY - BOTH USERS AND MANUFACTURERS - HAS DONE VERY LITTLE IN THE AREA OF EMPLOYING THE HANDICAPPED. IBM ALONE HAS BEEN 'IN THE FOREFRONT' ALMOST FROM ITS INCEPTION AS AN EMPLOYER OF THE HANDICAPPED. IN THE CASE OF SOME COMPUTER COMPANIES THERE HAS BEEN ALMOST A NEGATIVE REACTION, A FEELING OF 'I'M NOT GOING TO DO ANYTHING UNTIL THE GOVERNMENT FORCES ME TO.' IN MANY CASES, HOWEVER, IT IS THE DISABILITY WHICH MAKES THE HANDICAPPED PERSON SUITED TO A JOB. A DEAF PERSON, FOR INSTANCE, WAS THE IDEAL SOLUTION TO ONE COMPANY'S NOISE PROBLEM IN ITS BURSTING ROOM. THE OPERATOR WAS TRAINED TO DO THE JOB AND THE FIRM SAVED THE COST OF INSTALLING SOUNDPROOFING. DEAF PEOPLE ARE ALSO LESS DISTRACTED BY OTHER NOISES AND HAVE BEEN SHOWN TO HAVE A HIGHER PROGRAMMING OUTPUT THAN PROGRAMMERS WHOSE HEARING IS UNIMPAIRED. IN ADDITION, ACCORDING TO THE LAW, THE HANDICAPPED PERSON MUST ALSO BE HIRED IN THE MANAGEMENT AREA.

A-11

196

QUESTION:

Has worker productivity been affected by worker participation in the industrial workplace? Does worker participation significantly improve employee relations?

BEGIN 15   COMMENTS

? S PRODUCTIVITY; S PARTICIPATION
   1   2400 PRODUCTIVITY
   2   1663 PARTICIPATION
? C 1 AND 2
   3   82 1 AND 2
? T3/2
3/2/1
   78013175   ID NO: 78013175
   REBUILDING AN INCENTIVE PLAN
   BUSINESS WEEK N2549 40M—N AUG. 28, 1978 CODEN: BUWEA3
ISSN 0007-7135 JRNL CODE: BWE
   DOC TYPE: JOURNAL PAPER
   DESCRIPTORS: PRODUCTIVITY; SCANLON PLAN; GROWTH; PLANNING;
CASE STUDIES; EMPLOYEES; SUGGESTIONS; INCENTIVES; PROBLEMS

? S WORKER (W) PARTICIPATION; S SCANLON (W) PLAN; S WORKER (W)
CODETERMINATION ....   The descriptor "Scanlon Plan"
   4   86 WORKER (W) PARTICIPATION   is added to search statement.
   5   19 SCANLON (W) PLAN
   6   20 WORKER (W) CODETERMINATION
? S PARTICIPATORY (W) MANAGEMENT; S EMPLOYEE (W) INVOLVEMENT ..   The "w" operator requires
   7   47 PARTICIPATORY (W) MANAGEMENT   that terms be adjacent.
   8   21 EMPLOYEE (W) INVOLVEMENT
? C 1 AND (4 OR 5 OR 6 OR 7 OR 8)
   9   32 1 AND (4 OR 5 OR 6 OR 7 OR 8)
? T9/5/2 ....   Requesting a full record be
9/5/2   printed in order to scan
   78012123   ID NO: 78012123   abstract.
   HOW TO PROMOTE PRODUCTIVITY
   BUSINESS WEEK N2544 146, 151 JULY 24, 1978 CODEN: BUWEA 3
ISSN 0007-7135 JRNL CODE: BWE
   DOC TYPE: JOURNAL PAPER
   PRODUCTIVITY GROWTH IN THE U.S. MAY BE STAGNATING, BUT THE
NUMBER OF ORGANIZATIONS DEVOTED TO IMPROVING IT IS GROWING
SPECTACULARLY. SINCE 1973, MORE THAN A DOZEN GROUPS, SUP-
PORTED BY INDUSTRY, FOUNDATIONS, AND GOVERNMENT, HAVE BEEN
FORMED ALONG WITH OTHERS CONNECTED WITH UNIVERSITIES. IT IS
BECOMING A NATIONAL MOVEMENT. LAST YEAR, THE GROWTH WAS
ONLY 2.2%, 2/3 OF WHAT IT HAD BEEN IN THE 1960S AND LOWEST
AMONG MAJOR INDUSTRIAL COUNTRIES. AMERICA'S TECHNOLOGICAL
EDGE OVER OTHER NATIONS HAS ALL BUT DISAPPEARED. PRODUC-
TIVITY HAS BECOME URGENT, NOT JUST DESIRABLE; IT IS THE BEST
WAY TO CONTROL INFLATION. THE AMERICAN PRODUCTIVITY CENTER
LAUNCHED ITS FIRST "PRODUCT," A SERIES OF SEMINARS ON STARTING
PRODUCTIVITY-IMPROVEMENT PROGRAMS JUST LAST MONTH. UP
TO NOW, THERE HAS ONLY BEEN THE BASIC STUDY OF PRODUC-
TIVITY MEASUREMENT. THERE IS A VAGUENESS IN WHAT CON-

A-12

197

STITUTES A PRODUCTIVITY PROGRAM; WORKERS RESPOND BEST
TO PROGRAMS THEY HELP CREATE AND THAT BENEFIT THEM.
INDUSTRY IS A LONG WAY FROM AN ALL-ENCOMPASSING METHOD
TO IMPROVE PRODUCTIVITY.
    DESCRIPTORS: PROGRAMS; PRODUCTIVITY; IMPROVEMENTS;
PLANNING; MEASUREMENT; MANYCOMPANIES; WORKERS; PAR-
TICIPATORY MANAGEMENT ....

The controlled term "many-companies" is applied when an article discusses several companies, often applied to survey type articles.

? S EMPLOYEE (W) RELATIONS; S LABOR (W) MANAGEMENT (W)
RELATIONS ....

Additional search statements are added.

```
  10    134  EMPLOYEE (W) RELATIONS
  11     94  LABOR (W) MANAGEMENT (W) RELATIONS
? C (4 OR 5 OR 6 OR 7 OR 8) AND (1 OR 11)
? T 12/6/1-5
12/6/1
    78015417     ID NO: 78015417
    PERSONNEL'S ROLE IN PARTICIPATION

12/6/2
    78014819     ID NO: 78014819
    THE MITBESTIMMUNG MESS-UP

12/6/3
    78014702     ID NO: 78014702
    EMPLOYEE PARTICIPATION IN THE U.S. ENTERPRISE

12/6/4
    78010361     ID NO. 78010361
    WORKER PARTICIPATION IN WEST GERMAN INDUSTRY

12/6/5
    78009500     ID NO: 78009500
    HUMANIZATION OF WORK: A EUROPEAN PERSPECTIVE
```

A-13

198

Below are listed the approximately 400 journals which are searched by the ABI/INFORM editorial staff for articles worthy of abstracting in the data base. These journals have been searched continuously since the "start date" for articles which contain meaningful management ideas or concepts.

If you desire to limit a search to a single journal, please use the journal code rather than the journal title for searching. You may also use the CODEN or ISSN number, but these lists are less complete than the journal code list.

Journal entries preceded by an asterisk (*) are participating in the ABI/INFORM retrievals program.

	Journal Code	Journal Title	Start Date	CODEN	ISSN
		A			
*	AEE	AACE Transactions	1/78		
*	ABA	Abacus (Australia)	6/76	ABACAF	0001-3072
*	ABC	ABCA Bulletin	12/74	ABCACL	0001-0383
	AMA	Academy of Mgmt Jrnl	9/71	AMJOD6	0001-4273
*	AMR	Academy of Mgmt Review	1/76		
*	ACE	Accountancy (UK)	11/72	ACTYAD	0001-4664
	ACR	Accounting Review	10/71	ACRVAS	0001-4826
	CBR	Across the Board (formerly Conference Board Record)	9/71	ACBODW	0010-5546
*	ADH	Adherent	8/75		0360-9588
*	ADM	Administrative Mgmt	10/71	ADMAAF	0001-8376
	ASQ	Administrative Science Qtrly	9/71	ASCQAG	0001-8392
	AMJ	Advanced Mgmt Jrnl	Sum/75	ADVMAS	0036-0805
*	ADQ	Advertising (UK) (formerly Advertising Qtrly)	Fall/74	ADQUAR	0001-8961
*	ADA	Advertising Age	10/71	ADVAAQ	0001-8899
	AGE	Agency Sales Magazine	3/75		
*	AIR	Air Force Comptroller	1/76	AFCTB3	0002-2365
*	ABE	Akron Business & Economic Review	Fall/75	ABERDF	0044-7048
*	ABL	American Business Law Jrnl	Fall/71	ABLJAN	0002-7766
	AER	American Economic Review	9/71	AENRAA	0002-8282
*	AES	American Jrnl of Economics & Sociology	1/75	AJESA3	0002-9246
*	AMS	American Salesman	2/75	AMSLB6	0003-0902
	ANB	Antitrust Bulletin	Wint/74		0003-603X
	ALE	Antitrust Law & Economics Review	Spr/71		0003-6048
*	APJ	Appraisal Jrnl	10/71	APPJA5	0003-7087
*	ARB	Arbitration Jrnl	12/74		0003-7893
	REU	AREUEA Jrnl (Amer Real Estate & Urban Economics Assn)	Spr/75		0092-914X
*	ABB	Arizona Business	8-9/71	ABBUA6	0093-0717
*	ARK	Arkansas Business & Economic Review	Wint/74	ABRVBM	0004-1742
	AAC	Arthur Andersen Chronicle	1/74	ARACAP	
	AYJ	Arthur Young Jrnl	Spr/72	ARYJAU	0004-3613
*	AMG	Association Mgmt	1/75		0004-5578
*	AEC	Atlanta Economic Review	3/75	ATERA2	0004-671X
		B			
*	BKR	Banker (UK)	8/71	BNKRB2	0005-5395
*	BZE	Bankers Magazine	Fall/71	BNMGBD	0005-5441

B-1

199

ACCOUNTING & AUDITING

Abacus
Accountancy
Accounting Review
Air Force Comptroller
Arthur Young Jrnl
Canadian Chartered Accountant
CPA Jrnl
* Government Accountants Jrnl
Internal Auditor
* International Jrnl of Government Auditing
Jrnl of Accountancy
* Jrnl of Accounting, Auditing & Finance
Jrnl of Accounting Research
Management Accounting
Management Accounting
National Public Accountant
Ohio CPA
Practical Accountant
Price Waterhouse Review
RIA Cost & Mgmt
* Taxation for Accountants
Woman CPA

MARKETING, ADVERTISING & SALES MANAGEMENT

Advertising Age
Advertising
Agency Sales Magazine
American Salesman
Chain Store Age Executive
Direct Marketing
Discount Merchandiser
Distribution Worldwide
European Jrnl of Marketing
Industrial Marketing
Industrial Marketing Mgmt
Jrnl of Advertising
Jrnl of Advertising Research
Jrnl of Consumer Affairs
Jrnl of Consumer Research
Jrnl of Marketing
Jrnl of Marketing Research
Jrnl of the Market Research Society
Jrnl of Retailing
Mark II
Marketing
Marketing News
Marketing Times

Media Decisions
Product Marketing
Public Relations Jrnl
Public Relations Qtrly
Qtrly Review of Marketing
Sales & Marketing Mgmt
Southern Advertising/Markets

BANKING

Bankers Monthly
Banking
Bank Systems & Equipment
Canadian Banker & ICB Review
Eurofile (The Banker Supplement)
Federal Reserve Bank of New York - Monthly Review
* Issues in Bank Regulation
Jrnl of Bank Research
Jrnl of Commercial Bank Lending
Jrnl of Money, Credit & Banking
Lloyds Bank Review
Mortgage Banker
Savings Bank Jrnl
Savings & Loan News
The Banker
The Bankers Magazine
The Magazine of Bank Administration
United States Banker

ECONOMICS

Akron Business & Economic Review
American Economic Review
American Jrnl of Economics & Sociology
Antitrust Bulleting
* Antitrust Law & Economics Review
Arkansas Business & Economics Review
Atlanta Economic Review
Bell Jrnl of Economics
Business Economics
Carnegie-Rochester Conference Series on Public Policy
Challenge
Commerce America
Economic Development & Cultural Change
Economic Jrnl
Engineering Economist
Engineering & Process Economics
Futures
Growth & Change
Indiana Business Review
International Economic Review

* Referenced two or more categories

B-9

200

ABI/INFORM on BRS (April 1980)

BRS LABEL:	INFO
SCOPE:	Management and administration. Specific coverage of banking, insurance, real estate, accounting, finance, marketing, data processing, and telecommunications.
TIME SPAN:	1971-
TYPE OF MATERIAL:	Primarily English language journals; but books, chapters, conference papers and proceedings, patents, dissertations, and reports will also be included.
TOTAL SIZE:	122,600 (Apr. 1980)
UPDATES:	Monthly, approximately 1900 records per date.
BIBL PARAGRAPHS:	AN,AU,TI,SO
ROYALTIES:	$35/hour; $.10/citation offline
PRODUCER:	Data Courier, Inc. 620 South Fifth Street Louisville, KY 40202 800/626-2823 Contact: Dena Gordon or Sue Kennedy
PRINT COUNTERPART:	None
DOCUMENT DELIVERY:	Journals List for Article Retrieval is a brochure which contains order and account information for those journals for which document delivery is available.
SEARCH AIDS:	ABI/INFORM USER BUIDE, 2d. ed. 1979. $27.50. Available from producer.

KEY TO THE BRS/INFO CITATION ELEMENTS

Paragraph Label	Content of Paragraph	User Function
AN	Accession Number	search and limit
AU	Author/s	search
TI	Title	search
SO	Source	search
PT	Publication Type	search
CD	Coden	search
YR	Publication Year	search and limit
DE	Descriptors	search
JC	Journal Code	search
IS	ISSN	search
AV	Availability	search
AB	Abstract	search

-1-

AN   80-05123.
AU   PAVIT-KEITH.
TI   TECHNICAL INNOVATION AND INDUSTRIAL DEVELOPMENT-THE DANGERS OF
      DIVERGENCE.
SO   FUTURES. VOL: V12N1. PAG: 35-44. FEB 1980.
PT   02.
CD   FUTUB.
YR   80.
DE   INDUSTRIAL-DEVELOPMENT. TECHNOLOGICAL. INNOVATIONS. OECD.
      MANYCOUNTRIES. R&D. PRODUCTIVITY. COMPARATIVE-ANALYSIS.
      REGRESSION-ANALYSIS. CORPORATE. STRATEGY. PERFORMANCE.
JC   CD-FUR.
IS   0016-3287.
AB   GIVEN THE FACT THAT INNOVATION IS PLAYING AN INCREASINGLY IMPORTANT
      ROLE IN INDUSTRIAL GROWTH, AN ATTEMPT CAN REASONABLY BE MADE TO
      IDENTIFY THE COUNTRIES LIKELY TO SUCCEED AND THOSE LIKELY TO FAIL IN
      THIS AREA. AN ASSESSMENT IS PRESENTED OF QUESTIONS CONCERNING: 1. TO
      WHAT DEGREE EACH OF THE ORGANIZATION FOR ECONOMIC COOPERATION &
      DEVELOPMENT (OECD) COUNTRIES HAVE IN THE WAY OF CAPACITY FOR
      INDUSTRIAL INNOVATION, AND 2. WHAT THE IMPLICATIONS ARE OF ANY
      DIFFERENCES IN THIS CAPACITY. IT BECOMES EVIDENT THAT COUNTRIES CAN BE
      CLASSIFIED INTO 3 GROUPS, AND SOME COUNTRIES SUCH AS JAPAN MAY BE
      ABLE TO MAKE THE TRANSITION INTO HIGHER DIVISIONS. MOST COUNTRIES
      WILL REMAIN OUTSIDE THE FIRST DIVISION, WITH THE RESULT THAT NATIONAL
      ECONOMIES WILL TEND TO DIVERGE RATHER THAN CONVERGE. AT THE
      MICRO-LEVEL, COMPANIES WILL HAVE TO MAKE THE CHOICE BETWEEN
      DEVELOPING A CAPACITY FOR INNOVATION OR SELECTING A LESS COSTLY, BUT
      ALSO LESS EFFECTIVE, STRATEGY SUCH AS LOCATING OPERATIONS OFFSHORE.
      FIRST DIVISION COUNTRIES ARE WEST GERMANY, SWEDEN, AND SWITZERLAND,
      ALL WITH HIGH LEVELS OF INNOVATIVE ACTIVITIES, WITH THE US POSSIBLY
      ALSO A MEMBER. TABLES. REFERENCES.

AN   80-04789
AU   GODDEN-PAUL.
TI   WARC ENDS ON UPBEAT-BUT SOME DECISIONS ARE POSTPONED.
SO   TELEPHONY. VOL: V198N3. PAG: 70,72. JAN 21, 1980.
PT   02.
CD   TLPNA.
YR   80.
DE   TELECOMMUNICATIONS. CONFERENCES. ITU-TC. PROBLEMS.
      DECISION-MAKING. PROPOSALS. INTERNATIONAL. BROADCASTING.
      SATELLITE-COMMUNICATIONS. SERVICE.
JC   CD-TPH.
IS   0040-2656.
AB   THE INTERNATIONAL TELECOMMUNICATIONS UNION'S WORLD ADMINISTRATIVE
      RADIO CONFERENCE (WARC) 1979 HELD IN GENEVA, SWITZERLAND, SEEMED TO
      EMBODY THE SPIRIT OF COMPROMISE. THE MAIN BATTLEFRONTS OF THE
      CONFERENCE WERE LINED UP ALONG HIGH FREQUENCY (HF) BROADCASTING AND
      THE SPACE SERVICES ISSUES. THE CONFERENCE ALLOCATED SOME 60% MORE
      SPECTRUM IN THE 9, 11, 15, 17, AND 21, MHZ BANDS WHICH WILL BE
      AUCTIONED AT A HF BROADCASTING WARC TO BE HELD IN THE MID-1980S. THE
      SPACE SERVICES BATTLE MAINLY CONCERNED GEOSTATIONARY ORBIT AND
      PLANNING. EIGHTEEN AREAS COVERED BY THE CONFERENCE WERE: 1. FFS
      GENERAL, 2. FFS FEEDER LINKS, 3. FFS AND BSS, 4. MOBILE SATELLITE
      SERVICE (MSS) AT 7 TO 8 GHZ, 5. MSS (UHF), 6. MSS 1533 TO 1600 MHZ,
      7. SOLAR POWERED SATELLITE, 8. RADIO LOCATION, 9. MULTIFREQUENCY.

-2-

203

The content of each of the BRS/INFO citation elements is described below. Examples are used freely and the BRS SYSTEM REFERENCE MANUAL is referenced where applicable.

ACCESSION NUMBER (AN)

Each document in INFORM has a two part unique accession number (AN):

    AN 80-03696

The first part of the AN indicates the two digit year in which the document was entered in the database; the second part indicates the order in which the document was entered during that year.

The AN is searchable with the embedded hyphen:

    1_: 80-03684
    RESULT   1

The first part of the AN is also limitable for update purposes. To limit a search to documents which were put into the database after 1979, enter:

    1_: gold with price$1
    RESULT 117

    2_: ..limit/1 an gt 79
    RESULT   20

AUTHOR (AU)

Author names (AU) are entered into the database exactly as they appear on the original document, with last names first followed by first name and/or middle initial. Author names are bound with hyphens for prompt retrieval when searching or ROOTing:

    1_: root jenkins

        JENKINS$
    R1 JENKINS-GLENN-P   1 DOCUMENT
    R2 JENKINS-JAMES-W   1 DOCUMENT

    2_: rodriguez-carlos-alfredo
    RESULT   1

TITLE (TI)

The title (TI) will display exactly as it appears on the original document--with symbols, punctuation, etc. BRS has text-edited (i.e. removed punctuation and special characters) titles for ease in searching. The following examples illustrate how to retrieve some problematic titles:

-3-

204

Title: CREDIT SNAGS SEND BATH CLOTHIER ON-LINE.

    1_: clothier adj online.ti.   IN ON-LINE HYPHEN IS RE-
    RESULT   1   MOVED AND WORD CLOSED UP.
                                      ONLINE SEARCHERS N.B.

Title: SAMPLE SURVEYS: HELP FOR THE OUT-OF-HOUSE EVALUATOR.

    2_: out adj house adj evaluator.ti.   SEARCH WITH A STOPWORD
    RESULT   1   'OF' HYPHENS ARE REMOVED
                                      AND 'OF' IS AN INSIGNIFICANT
                                      WORD SO ADJ IS USED.

Title: THE CRAY-1 GOES COMMERCIAL.

    3_: cray adj '1'.ti.   USE LITERALS WHEN SEARCHING
    RESULT   1   NUMBERS. DROP HYPHEN.

Title: THE CANADIAN DOLLAR ON THE THRESHOLD OF THE '80s.

    4_: canadian adj dollar with 80s.ti.   DROP APOSTROPHE
    RESULT   1

SOURCE (SO)

The Source (SO) paragraph is directly searchable, which is an excellent feature for verification, or to determine if a journal is indexed in INFORM.

The SO paragraph is very clear. It contains the name of the publication, volume, pagination, and issue date. The volume and pagination are prefaced by the three character designations VOL and PAG:

    SO TRAINING & DEVELOPMENT JRNL. VOL: V34N2 PAG: 70-74.
       FEB 1980.

Sometimes abbreviations are used in journal titles as in the example above. Either use the most unique words in the journal title, or consult the "Journals List" in the ABI/INFORM USER GUIDE. Variations have also been used in the SO paragraph since 1971. For example, the journal title above also occurs as:

    SO TRAINING AND DEVEL JOUR. VOL: VOL28 NO 10. PAG:
       P 44-47. OCT 72.
                                                      AND

    SO TRAINING AND DE. VOL: V.25N. PAG: P2. DEC 71.

Use caution when searching SOURCE and consider supplementing searching journal titles with CODEN, ABI Journal Code, or ISSN searching as described below.

Not all journals in INFORM were included for the duration of the database. Consult the ABI/INFORM USER GUIDE for dates of coverage.

Non-U.S. journals are followed by their country of origin in parenthesis:

    SO LABOUR GAZETTE (CANADA)...

These designations are directly searchable:

    1_: labour adj gazette adj canada
    RESULT   63

They are also a convenient way of eliminating or limiting to non-U.S. journals:

    2_: telecommunications.so.
    RESULT   40

    3_: 2 not (uk canada)   ELIMINATES JOURNALS FROM
    RESULT   30   THE UNITED KINGDOM AND
                                         CANADA.

All of the elements of the SO paragraph are directly searchable. For example, to verify a citation on corporate development which a patron claims appeared in Long Range Planning in December 1979:

    1_: corporate adj development
    RESULT   27

    2_: 1 and (long adj range adj planning.so. and dec adj 1979
    RESULT   1

PUBLICATION TYPE (PT)

    Each type of document in INFORM is assigned a publication type (PT) by Data Courier. The PT is directly searchable. The majority of publications in INFO are journals, but the coding scheme allows for other publications types to be added:

01	N/A	07	N/A
02	Journal Paper	08	Patent
03	Book	09	N/A
04	Book Chapter	10	Dissertation
05	Conference Proceedings	11	Report
06	Conference Paper	12	Report Section

Publication types should be searched in literals (') and paragraph qualified to distinguish them from statement numbers and other searchable fields:

    1_: '02'.pt.
    RESULT 18795

When other publication types are added by Data Courier, this will be an additional method of refining a search as on databases such as ERIC and Psychological Abstracts which also have this feature.

206

CODEN (CD)

A CODEN (CD) is a standard five character alphabetic code for a journal title which is directly searchable. The CODENS for INFORM journals are listed in the ABI/INFORM USER GUIDE "Journals List" section.

To search for CODENS, enter the first five characters listed in the USER GUIDE. It is usually not necessary to paragraph qualify CODENs because they do not form meaningful words. The CODEN for <u>Training and Development Journal</u> is:

```
1_:  tdeja
RESULT  190
```

YEAR OF PUBLICATION (YR)

The year in which a document was published is standardized to two digits in the YR paragraph. This field is both searchable for quick response time and limitable for refining a search to ranges of years.

To restrict a search to articles published in 1980 only, enter in a single statement:

```
1_:  (silver gold) with price$1 and 80.yr.
RESULT    8
```

The limit function requires two steps. In a search about the use of computers in banking after 1973, enter:

```
1_:  (computer$ online database$1) with bank$3
RESULT   81

2_:  ..limit/1 yr gt 73
RESULT   21
```

Always use the YR paragraph to limit a search by publication date because the year listed in the AN paragraph is the year in which the document was entered into the database, and not necessarily the year in which it was published.

DESCRIPTORS (DE)

The descriptors used to index INFORM documents are listed in the ABI/INFORM USER GUIDE and occur in the DE paragraph. There are three separate sections of descriptors in the USER GUIDE--subject, geographic, and company/corporate names. The average number of descriptors assigned to pre-1978 citations is 16.

Multiword descriptors have been <u>double posted</u> so that free text searching will automatically retrieve <u>both</u> controlled vocabulary and free text terms.

```
1_:  employee adj stock adj options      RETRIEVES THESAURUS TERM
                                          EMPLOYEE-STOCK-OPTIONS PLUS
                                          ANY OCCURRENCES OF THE PHRASE
                                          'EMPLOYEE STOCK OPTIONS' IN
                                          OTHER SEARCHABLE PARAGRAPHS.
```

-6-

If only controlled vocabulary is required, searchers may enter multiword descriptors hyphenated under standard BRS practice:

2_:	employee-stock-options	RETRIEVES CITATIONS WITH THESAURUS TERM EMPLOYEE-STOCK-OPTIONS.
3_:	employee.de.	RETRIEVES SINGLE WORD DESCRIPTOR BY ITSELF AND AS PART OF A MULTI-WORD DESCRIPTOR (EMPLOYEE-STOCK-OPTIONS).
4_:	employee	RETRIEVES A SINGLE WORD DESCRIPTOR BY ITSELF, AS PART OF A MULTIWORD DESCRIPTOR OR AS IT OCCURS IN FREE TEXT PARAGRAPHS.

However, all multiword descriptors will be displayed with hyphens.

INFORM thesaurus terms are frequently assigned three character field codes such as (LBR) for 'Labor' to distinguish them. Entry of these terms follows standard BRS practice, i.e. parentheses are removed and the term closed up with hyphens. 'Back to work movement (LBR)' as it appears in the ABI/INFORM USER GUIDE would be entered and displayed online as:

```
1_: back-to-work-movement-lbr
RESULT    10
```

To free text search the topic as well, ignore the stopword, and supplement the strategy with related terms:

```
2_: back adj work or full adj employment
RESULT    278
```

JOURNAL CODE (JC)

Data Courier created original three-character journal codes (JC) for each journal. These are directly searchable and are prefaced by CD- to bypass paragraph qualification and so that the ROOT feature may be easily used. DO NOT CONFUSE THESE JOURNAL CODES WITH THE CODENS DESCRIBED ABOVE.

To restrict a search to several journals, use the following procedure:

```
1_: management-by-objectives
RESULT    76
```

2_: 1 and (cd-hbr cd-mbr cd-pej) RESULT 12	RESTRICTS SEARCH TO JOURNAL CODES FOR HARVARD BUSINESS REVIEW, MICHIGAN BUSINESS REVIEW, AND PERSONNEL JOURNAL.

These journal codes are also listed in the ABI/INFORM USER GUIDE. Data Courier recommends using the JC field to limit a search to particular journals.

INTERNATIONAL STANDARD SERIAL NUMBER-ISSN (IS)

The ISSN is a universal system of assigning a unique 8 digit number
with an embedded hyphen to each journal published. This number occurs
in the IS paragraph and is searchable exactly as it appears in the ABI/
INFORM USER GUIDE:

    1_: 0001-0782   ISSN FOR <u>COMMUNICATIONS</u>
    RESULT   26   <u>OF THE ACM</u>.

AVAILABILITY (AV)

With the June, 1980 update, Data Courier will add an availability
field (AV). For documents which are available through ABI/INFORM's
document delivery program, the field will simply list:

    AV ABI/INFORM

For other documents, full availability information will be listed.

ABSTRACT (AB)

INFORM abstracts (AB) are informative and contain 150-200 words. Like
the title (TI), they have been text-edited for easy searching.

Notice that the second sample citation on page 3 is full of abbreviations,
dates, and statistics. All of this information is directly searchable,
following BRS conventions as outlined in the BRS SYSTEM REFERENCE MANUAL,
Section 6.

A search for 'high frequency broadcasting' should include both the
term and the abbreviation:

    1_: high adj frequency or hf adj broadcasting
    RESULT   38

Question: The growth of the plastics industry.

      1_: plastic$1..so.   PLASTICS ELIMINATED FROM
      RESULT   102   SOURCE PARAGRAPH.

      2_: 1 and (new growth boom$3).ti,de.
      RESULT   50

      3_: ..print 2 ti/doc=4-6

      4
TI   MANY NEW PLASTICS SET FOR BIG GROWTH.

      5
TI   POLYACETAL BUCKS SHORTAGE AND PRICE TRENDS.

      6
TI   HOW TO BE BIG THOUGH SMALL.

Question: An article was published in the Harvard Business Review in the
              past five years on the right vs. the left brain in managers.
              Can you find it?

      1_: brain and management
      RESULT   29

      2_: 1 and cd-hbr   COMBINE TOPIC WITH JOURNAL
      RESULT   1   CODE FOR HARVARD BUSINESS
                                     REVIEW.

      3_: ..p 2 ti,so/doc=1

      1
TI   PLANNING ON THE LEFT SIDE AND MANAGING ON THE RIGHT.
SO   PUB: HARVARD BUSINESS REVIEW VOL: V34N4. PAG: P49-58. JUL-AUG 1976.

Question: I need articles comparing the Insurance Exchange with Lloyd's
              of London.

      1_: insurance adj exchange   FREE TEXT BECAUSE THERE IS
      RESULT   39   NO TERM FOR 'INSURANCE EX-
                                     CHANGE'.

      2_: lloyds-syndicate-ins   LLOYD'S IS A THESAURUS TERM
      RESULT   14   WITH AN 'INS' (INSURANCE)
                                     QUALIFIER. ENTER HYPHENATED.

      3_: lloyds adj (london syndicate)   SUPPLEMENT #2 WITH FREE TEXT
      RESULT   57   TERMS. DROP THE APOSTROPHE.

      4_: 1 and (2 3)
      RESULT   13

-9-

210

```
5_:   ..p 4 ti/doc=1-3

      1
TI    THE SCRAMBLE TO BEAT LLOYD'S OF LONDON.

      2
TI    BAD LUCK FORCES UPDATING AT LLOYD'S OF LONDON.

      3
TI    N.Y. EXCHANGE SHOULD GROW BUT WITH CAUTION.
```

Question: What are the economic effects of arson since 1974?

```
      1_:   arson
      RESULT    47

      2_:   (economy economic$1) with effect$1
      RESULT   681

      3_:   trend$1
      RESULT  6589

      4_:   insurance-industry fire-insurance
      RESULT  1000

      5_:   1 and (2 3 4)
      RESULT    23

      6_:   ..limit/5 yr gt 74            ALL CITATIONS WERE PUBLISHED
      RESULT    23                        AFTER 1974.
```

FILE 15

DIALOG* INFORMATION RETRIEVAL SERVICE
ABI/INFORM

FILE DESCRIPTION

The ABI/INFORM database was created in 1971 to meet the information needs of executives. All phases of management and administration are covered by the database. Since ABI/INFORM stresses functional information, it is highly transferable from one industry to another. Specific product and industry information is included but does not receive primary emphasis. There is no print counterpart to the ABI/INFORM database.

SUBJECT COVERAGE

The ABI/INFORM database covers the primary functions of management and administration including all aspects of the following major areas:

- Accounting
- Data Processing
- Finance
- Management
- Marketing
- Production

SOURCES

Approximately 400 primary publications in business and related fields are currently scanned for articles to be abstracted and included in ABI/INFORM. Some representative publications are: *Harvard Business Review, Sloan Management Review, Fortune, Journal of Marketing Research, Journal of Accountancy, IEEE Transactions on Software Engineering, American Economic Review, ABA Banking Journal,* and *Governmental Finance.*

DIALOG FILE DATA

Inclusive Dates: August 1971 to the present
Update Frequency: Monthly (approximately 1,900 records per update)
File Size: 92,900 records as of April 1979

DOCUMENT RETRIEVAL

Copies of articles from selected journals may be acquired in full from DCI. For pricing and ordering information call 800/626-2823, or 502/582-4111 (in Kentucky).

ORIGIN

ABI/INFORM is produced by DCI and questions concerning file content should be directed to:

Data Courier, Inc. (DCI)   Telephone: 502/582-4111 (in Kentucky)
620 South Fifth Street   800/626-2823
Louisville, KY 40202

No special terms or conditions.

---

*Trademark Reg. U.S. Pat. & Trademark Office.

(Revised September 1979)   15-1

FILE 15

ABI/INFORM
DIALOG FILE 15

SAMPLE RECORD

DIALOG Accession Number

```
       72000080    ID No: 72000080
       WHAT TO DO ABOUT BANK PROPERTY TAXES - AND WHY ◄──────────── /TI
PY=    SCHAFF, ROBERT J.
AU=    BANKING  VOL 6J  NO 6   P 30   DEC 71  Coden: BNKGA2  ISSN 0005-5492
JN=    Jrnl Code: BNK
CO=    Doc Type: JOURNAL PAPER
JC=    PROPERTY-TAXES ARE ONE OF THE FASTER GROWING ITEMS OF CORPORATE
SN=    EXPENSE, DUE TO THE MULTIPLIER EFFECT OF RISING TAX RATES COMBINED
DT=    WITH INCREASING ASSESSED VALUATIONS. YET PROPERTY TAXES ARE ONE OF THE
       MOST UNDERRATED OF EXPENSES. BANKS HAVE P.T. PROBLEMS FOR AT LEAST
       FOUR REASONS, 1- BANKS ARE HIGHLY VISIBLE AND ALWAYS GET FULL
       ATTENTION, 2- BANKS DONT VOTE - HOMEOWNERS DO, 3- BANKS ARE THE OBJECT
       OF ASSESSMENT DISCRIMINATION, EITHER CONSCIOUSLY OR UNCONSCIOUSLY, AND   /AB
       4- BANKS HAVE TAX PROBLEM WHICH ARE THEIR OWN FAULT. ARTICLE SAYS
       BANKS SHOULD MEET THE PROBLEM BY, 1- CENTRALIZING THE RESPONSIBILITY
       IN THE BANK, 2- ANALYZING ASSESSED VALUATIONS CAREFULLY, 3-
       QUESTIONING ASSESSED VALUATIONS, 4- COMMINICATING WITH THE ASSESSOR,
       AND BY DOCUMENTING EVERY OPINION SYSTEMATICALLY.
         Descriptors: ARTICLES; ASSESSED VALUATION; ATTENTION; BANKS;
       CORPORATIONS; COSTS; DISCRIMINATION; EXPENSES; FULL; HOME OWNERSHIP;   /DE
       HOMEOWNERS; OPINIONS; PROBLEMS; PROPERTY; PROPERTY TAXES; RATES;
       RESPONSIBILITIES; TAX RATES; TAXES; VALUATION
```

SEARCH OPTIONS

BASIC INDEX

PAGE	SUFFIX	FIELD NAME	EXAMPLES	
15-3	None	Basic Index (Includes Abstract, Descriptor, and Title)	E BANKS	S TAX
			S HOME(W)OWNERSHIP	
15-3	/AB	Abstract	S RISING(F)TAXES/AB	
15-3	/DE	Descriptor[1]	S ASSESSED VALUATION/DE	
15-4	/TI	Title	S BANK(W)PROPERTY/TI	

[1]Also /DF

ADDITIONAL INDEXES

PAGE	PREFIX	FIELD NAME	EXAMPLES	
15-5	AU=	Author	E AU=SAXE, EMANUEL	S AU=SCHAFF, ROBERT J.
15-5	CO=	CODEN	E CO=ASLOAL	S CO=BNKGA2
15-5	DT=	Document Type	E DT=JOURNAL	S DT=JOURNAL?
15-5	JC=	Journal Code	E JC=BIP	S JC=BNK
15-6	JN=	Journal Name	E JN=BANKER	S JN=BANKING
15-6	PY=	Publication Year	E PY=1972	S PY=1971
15-6	SN=	ISSN Number	E SN=0005-7087	S SN=0005-5492
15-6	UD=	Update	E UD=9999	S UD=7904

LIMITING

PAGE	SUFFIX	FIELD NAME	EXAMPLES
15-7	None	DIALOG Accession Number	LIMIT 12/77000001-79999999

FORMAT OPTIONS

PAGE	NUMBER	RECORD CONTENT	NUMBER	RECORD CONTENT
15-12	Format 1	DIALOG Accession Number	Format 5	Full Record
	Format 2	Full Record except Abstract	Format 6	Title and DIALOG Accession Number
	Format 3	Bibliographic Citation	Format 7	Bibliographic Citation and Abstract
	Format 4	Abstract and Title	Format 8	Title and Indexing

DIRECT RECORD ACCESS

PAGE	PREFIX	FIELD NAME	EXAMPLES	
15-14	None	DIALOG Accession Number	TYPE 77000053/2	PRINT 78006916/5

NB: Page numbers refer to detailed discussion in *Guide to DIALOG - Databases.*

INFORM
on ORBIT

General Description

SUPPLIER	ABI/INFORM, a division of Data Courier, Inc. 620 South Fifth Street Louisville, Kentucky 40202 (502) 582-4111
CONTENT COVERAGE	Covers nearly 300 periodicals in the areas of business management and administration, accounting, advertising, area development, banking, data processing, economics, employee benefits, finance, general management, insurance, international trade, labor relations, marketing, market research, operations research, pensions, personnel, physical distribution, planning, production, real estate, sales management, social conditions, stocks and bonds, taxes and taxation, training and education.
PERIOD OF COVERAGE	1971 to date
UNIT RECORD	Bibliographic citation and abstract
SIZE OF FILE	Approximately 14,400 records per year of coverage
UPDATING FREQUENCY	Monthly

Sample Record

AN	78-07686
TI	Britain and Economic Miracles
AU	Pratten, Cliff
SO	Management Today (UK) (MANTAI, MTO), PP. 7–8, ISSN 0025-1925, March 1978
DT	J (Journal)
LA	English
IT	UK: Germany; SWEDEN: Wages & salaries; PRICES: PRODUCTION: Exports; Balance of payments; R&D: Economic analysis; UNEMPLOYMENT
AB	During the 1950s and 1960s, Britain had a comparatively slow growth rate while Germany and Sweden experienced rapid growth of output led by exports. Differences in growth rates narrowed during 1970–75, but inflation became the major problem. Since 1975, there have been changes in performance of all three countries. Now unemployment is the center of concern with Britain having the highest level. In Germany, wages and prices have risen more slowly because of adherence to pay norms. Sweden's wage-price record has deteriorated due in part to world economic recession, rapid wage increases, recession of export industries, and changes in control of the country. Without the North Sea, Britain would have a strong deficit. The nation is finding its alternatives include increasing the competitiveness of its industries faster than those overseas and using the North Sea project as a means to increase the use of capacity and employment. Tables.

Inform (5/79)

Inform Record Description

Search Qualifier	Element Name	Print/STRS Qualifier	Standard Print Commands		
			Print	Trial	Full
—	Basic Index (*single words from Titles, Abstracts, and Index Terms*)	—	—	—	—
/IT	Index Terms	IT	—	X	X
/IW	Index Term Words	—	—	—	—
/TI	Titles	TI	X	X	X
(IN BI)	Abstract	AB	—	—	X
/AN	Accession Number	AN	X	X	X
/AU	Authors	AU	X	—	X
/JC	Journal Code/Coden	—	—	—	—
/ISSN	Intl. Std. Ser. No.	—	—	—	—
Ranging	Publication Year (PY)	—	—	—	—
/DT	Document Type	DT	X	—	X
/LA	Language	LA	X	—	X
—	Source (*includes JC, ISSN, PY*)	SO	X	—	X

Searching Tips

Element Name	Notes	User:
Basic Index	Single words from Titles, Abstracts, and Index Terms. No qualifier required.	*HEALTH AND INSUR-ANCE AND ALL PLAN:*
Index Terms	Single words and multi-word controlled vocabulary in *Thesaurus* format. /IT qualifier optional for multi-words.	*FOREIGN INVESTMENTS* *FORGERY/IT*
Index Term Words	Use /IW for single-word terms derived from assigned Index Terms.	*NATIONAL/1W AND HEALTH/1W AND INSURANCE/1W*
Authors	Variable format; use truncated entry.	*PRATTEN, C: /AU*
Journal Code/Coden	Use ABI-assigned code of 3 letters up through 1977 and standard 6-character journal coden beginning in 1978. (See user manual for list.)	*FBR/JC* retrieves *FORBA5/JC* Forbes
International Standard Serial Number	Search journals using /ISSN qualifier. (See user manual for list. Alternative method to search journal code/coden.)	*0015-6914/ISSN* retrieves Forbes
Document Type	Search with /DT qualifier.[1]	*J/DT*
Language	Search with /LA qualifier.[2]	*ENGLISH/LA*

Notes:

1 Document type field is limited to journals only at present.

2 Language field is limited to English-language documents at present. ENGLISH/LA retrieves the entire file.

DIALOG® Information Retrieval Service

SEARCH AIDS FOR USE WITH DIALOG DATABASES

ABI/INFORM (File 15)

ABI/INFORM User Aid. Data Courier, Inc., 620 South Fifth Street, Louisville, KY 40202. Telephone: 800/626-2823. Free. Includes database description; discussion of the citations, field by field; list of journals giving codes, CODEN, ISSN, and start date; list of core journals; list of journals by subject area; search guide chart; sample searches.

ABI/INFORM User Guide. Data Courier, Inc., 620 South Fifth Street, Louisville, KY 40202. Telephone: 800/626-2823. 108p. $27.50. Includes step-by-step instructions on how to use ABI/INFORM and search strategy suggestions, plus the controlled vocabulary, journals lists, selection criteria, database fields, and additional services. Inclusion of the controlled vocabulary now offers the user the option of searching by controlled terms or by the free text of article titles and abstracts.

AGRICOLA (File 10)

AGRICOLA Online Users Guide. 1979 edition. U.S.D.A. Science and Education Administration, Technical Information Systems, Rm. 300, NAL Bldg., Beltsville, MD 20705. Telephone: 301/344-3704. Free.

Agricultural/Biological Vocabulary. Volumes 1 and 2 and supplements. (1967 & 1968; reprinted 1976). Limited copies available from: U.S.D.A. Science and Education Administration, Technical Information Systems, Rm. 300, NAL Bldg., Beltsville, MD 20705. Telephone: 301/344-3704. Free.

Bibliography of Agriculture. 2 volume annual cumulation including subject index. Oryx Press, 3930 East Camelback Road, Phoenix, AZ 85018. Telephone: 602/956-6233. $195.00.

FNIC Controlled Vocabulary. U.S.D.A. Science and Education Administration, Technical Information Systems, Rm. 300, NAL Bldg., Beltsville, MD 20705. Telephone 301/344-3704. Free. Vocabulary for the Food and Nutrition Information Center part of AGRICOLA.

List of Journals Indexed. U.S.D.A. Science and Education Administration, Technical Information Systems, Rm. 300, NAL Bldg., Beltsville, MD 20705. Telephone: 301/344-3704. Free.

(June 1979)   1

Thesaurus of Agricultural Terms. Second edition. Oryx Press, 3930 East
Camelback Road, Phoenix, AZ 85108. Telephone: 602/956-6233. $13.95.

AIM/ARM (File 9)

See ERIC

AMERICA: HISTORY AND LIFE (File 38)

America: History and Life, Online Vocabulary Aid. ABC-Clio Inc., P.O. Box 4397,
Santa Barbara, CA 93103. Telephone: 805/963-4221. $35.00. Includes index of
terms, search hints, list of periodicals.

List of Periodicals. Revised 1978. ABC-Clio, Inc., P.O. Box 4397, Santa Barbara,
CA 93103. Telephone: 805/963-4221. Free.

APTIC (File 45)

Microthesaurus of Air Pollution Terms. September 1976. Science and Services
Dept., The Franklin Institute of Research Laboratories, 20th and Race Streets,
Philadelphia, PA 19103.

Standard Air Pollution Classification Network: A Thesaurus of Terms (as used in
the APTIC Database), Second Edition by Peter Halpin. EPA 450/1-78-002
USEPA, Research Triangle Park, NC 27711. March 1978. Order from: National
Technical Information Service, 5285 Port Royal Road, Springfield, VA 22161.
(Document No. PB-292 038) Price code A09, currently (May 1979) $9.00.

AQUATIC SCIENCES AND FISHERIES ABSTRACTS (File 44)

ASFA (Aquatic Sciences and Fisheries Abstracts) Data Base Users Guide.
Environmental Science Information Center, D8, 11400 Rockville Pike, Rockville,
MD 20852. Will be available early in 1980. Price to be determined. May
also be available from: Research Information Unit, Fishery Information, Data
and Statistics Service, FAO, Via delle Term di Caracalla, Rome 00100, Italy.

Geographic Authority List for the Aquatic Sciences and Fisheries Information
System and Draft Geographic Indexing Guidelines. 1976. Research Information
Unit, Fishery Information, Data and Statistics Service, FAO, Via delle Term di
Caracalla, Rome 00100, Italy. Out-of-Print. (Future uncertain).

List of Periodicals Monitored for ASFA. 1978. Research Information Unit, Fishery
Information, Data and Statistics Service, FAO, Via delle Term di Caracalla,
Rome 00100, Italy. Free.

Thesaurus of Terms for Aquatic Sciences and Fisheries. 1976. Research
Information Unit, Fishery Information, Data and Statistics Service, FAO, Via
delle Term di Caracalla, Rome 00100, Italy. Out-of-Print. To be revised and
reissued in 1980. Price to be determined.

World List of Aquatic Sciences and Fisheries Serial Titles. 1975. Research

Information Unit, Fishery Information, Data and Statistics Service, FAO, Via delle Term di Caracalla, Rome 00100, Italy. Free.

ARTBIBLIOGRAPHIES MODERN (File 56)

ARTbibliographies Modern. (brochure) ABC-Clio, Inc., P.O. Box 4397, Santa Barbara, CA 93103. Telephone: 805/963-4221. Includes list of periodicals. Free.

BIOSIS (Files 5 and 55)

BIOSIS Guide to the Indexes. BioSciences Information Service of Biological Abstracts, 2100 Arch Street, Philadelphia, PA 19103. Telephone: 800/523-4806, 215/568-4016. Free.

BIOSIS Previews Memo. BioSciences Information Service of Biological Abstracts, 2100 Arch Street, Philadelphia, PA 19103. Telephone: 800/523-4806, 215/568-4016. Free. Provides news and updates for searchers of BIOSIS PREVIEWS. Topics covered include: changes in Previews, tips for searching, user information exchanges and training schedules.

BIOSIS Search Guide/BIOSIS Previews Edition. 1979 edition. BioSciences Information Service of Biological Abstracts, 2100 Arch Street, Philadelphia, PA 19103. Telephone: 800/523-4806, 215/568-4016. $70.00 or $50.00 to holders of 1977 ed. This 500 page, color-coded, looseleaf manual is the reference tool which unifies the multiple-index approach of the database.

BIOSIS Training Course/BIOSIS Previews Edition. BioSciences Information Service of Biological Abstracts, 2100 Arch Street, Philadelphia, PA 19103. Telephone: 800/523-4806, 215/568-4016. $25.00. This user aid helps teach the use of the BIOSIS database to yourself and others. It includes an instruction book and 35mm slides.

A Guide to the Vocabulary of the Biological Literature. BioSciences Information Service, 2100 Arch Street, Philadelphia, PA 19103. Telephone: 800/523-4806, 215/568-4016. $25.00.

1978 Serial Sources for the BIOSIS Database. BioSciences Information Service, 2100 Arch Street, Philadelphia, PA 19103. Telephone: 800/523-4806, 215/568-4016. $30.00. This new listing of serials gives information about over 10,000 serials including publisher's addresses, journal frequency and CODENs. Updated annually.

CA PATENT CONCORDANCE (File 43)

No special search aids are available for this database.

CA SEARCH (Files 2, 3, and 4)

Chemical Abstracts Index Guide 1967-1971 (Vol. 66-75 Cumulative). Chemical Abstracts Service, P.O. Box 3012, Columbus, OH 43210. Telephone: 614/421-6940. $50.00.

(June 1979) 3

Chemical Abstracts Index Guide 1972-1976 (Vol. 76-85 Cumulative). Chemical Abstracts Service, P.O. Box 3012, Columbus, OH 43210. Telephone: 614/421-6940. $50.00.

Chemical Abstracts Index Guide 1977 (plus supplements). A guide to the 10th Collective Period. Chemical Abstracts Service, P.O. Box 3012, Columbus, OH 43210. Telephone: 614/421-6940. $50.00.

Chemical Abstracts Service Information Tools--1979 Catalog. Chemical Abstracts Service, P.O. Box 3012, Columbus, OH 43210. Telephone: 614/421-6940. Free. An 89 page catalog to the full range of Chemical Abstracts information products and services.

Chemical Abstracts Service Source Index--Cumulative 1907-1974, plus Quarterly Supplements. Chemical Abstracts Service, P.O. Box 3012, Columbus, OH 43210. Telephone: 614/421-6940. $200.00 plus $100.00 per year for supplements plus postage.

Headings List. Chemical Abstracts Service, P.O. Box 3012, Columbus, OH 43210. Telephone: 614/421-6940. $50.00 (microfiche form). Includes the list of controlled vocabulary headings for: 1) General subject index headings of the 9th and 10th Collective Index periods and 2) Plant and Animal headings for the 9th and 10th Collective Index periods.

Merck Index. Publications Department, Merck & Co., Inc., P.O. Box 2000, Rahway, NJ 07065. $15.00.

Naming and Indexing of Chemical Substances for Chemical Abstracts; reprint of Appendix 4 of the 1977 Index Guide (for the 10th Collective Period). Chemical Abstracts Service, P.O. Box 3012, Columbus, OH 43210. $5.00.

A Natural Language Term List. Chemical Abstracts Service, P.O. Box 3012, Columbus, OH 43210. Telephone: 614/421-6940. $50.00 (microform format—either film or fiche). Words which occur five or more times within eight volumes. Includes word frequencies and key letter in context (KLIC) format.

1000 Most Frequently Cited Journals. Chemical Abstracts Service, P.O. Box 3012, Columbus, OH 43210. Telephone: 614/421-6940. Free.

A Rotated Title Phrase List. Chemical Abstracts Service, P.O. Box 3012, Columbus, OH 43210. Telephone: 614/421-6940. $50.00 (microform format--either film or fiche). Multiword phrases from titles and alphabetical access to each word and phrase. Gives frequency of occurrence on basis of four volumes.

Subject Coverage and Arrangement of Abstracts by Sections in Chemical Abstracts (Subject Coverage Manual). Chemical Abstracts Service, P.O. Box 3012, Columbus, OH 43210. Telephone: 614/421-6940. $5.00.

CAB ABSTRACTS (File 50)

Ainsworth and Bixby's Dictionary of Fungi, by G. C. Ainsworth. The Commonwealth Agricultural Bureaux, Farnham House, Farnham Royal, Slough, SL2 3BN, United Kingdom. £8.45 UK; £10.15 overseas.

4 (June 1979)

Anthelmintic Index, by J. H. Bard. 1972. The Commonwealth Agricultural Bureaux, Farnham House, Farnham Royal, Slough, SL2 3BN, United Kingdom. £3.80 UK; £4.55 overseas.

CAB Abstracts Online Manual. August 1979. Commonwealth Agricultural Bureaux, Farnham House, Farnham Royal, Slough, SL2 3BN, United Kingdom. (Price to be determined)

CAB Abstracts Word List. Commonwealth Agricultural Bureaux, Farnham House, Farnham Royal, Slough, SL2 3BN, United Kingdom. £5.50 UK; £6.60 overseas.

A Dictionary of Livestock Breeds, by I. R. Mason. The Commonwealth Agricultural Bureaux, Farnham House, Farnham Royal, Slough, SL2 3BN, United Kingdom. £7.60 UK; £9.10 overseas.

Nematicide Index, by J. H. Bard. The Commonwealth Agricultural Bureaux, Farnham House, Farnham Royal, Slough, SL2 3BN, United Kingdom. £5.00 UK; £6.00 overseas.

The Nematode Parasites of Plants Cataloged under Their Hosts, by J. B. Goodex, M. T. Franklin and D. J. Hooper. Third revised edition. The Commonwealth Agricultural Bureaux, Farnham House, Farnham Royal, Slough, SL2 3BN, United Kingdom. £5.00 UK; £6.00 overseas.

Veterinary Subject Headings, by R. Mack. 1972. The Commonwealth Agricultural Bureaux, Farnham House, Farnham Royal, Slough, SL2 3BN, United Kingdom. £4.40 UK; £5.25 overseas.

Weed Abstracts List. The Commonwealth Agricultural Bureaux, Farnham House, Farnham Royal, Slough, SL2 3BN, United Kingdom. A list of common names and abbreviations used for herbicides and plant growth regulators. Printed in every issue of Weed Abstracts.

CHEMICAL INDUSTRY NOTES (File 19)

No special search aids are available for this database.

CHEMNAME™ (File 31)

Naming and Indexing of Chemical Substances for Chemical Abstracts; reprint of Appendix 4 of the 1977 Index Guide (for the 10th Collective Period). Chemical Abstracts Service, P.O. Box 3012, Columbus, OH 43210. Telephone: 614/421-6940. $5.00.

Naming Organic Compounds: A Programmed Introduction to Organic Chemistry, by James E. Banks. Second edition, 1976. W.B. Saunders, West Washington Square, Philadelphia, PA 19105. $5.95 (paperback).

"Substructure Searching of Computer-Readable Chemical Abstracts Service Ninth Collective Index Chemical Nomenclature Files", by W. Fisanick, L.D. Mitchell, J.A. Scott and G.G. Vander Stouw. In Journal of Chemical Information and Computer Science, 15(2) (1975) 73-84.

Substructure Searching Via Nomenclature Manuals and Search Aids (9CI). Chemical Abstracts Service, P.O. Box 3012, Columbus, OH 43210. Telephone: 614/421-6940. $50.00 (microform format—either film or fiche). Materials to help users develop search profiles for accessing CA SEARCH and CHEMNAME.

CHILD ABUSE AND NEGLECT (File 64)

Child Abuse and Neglect Thesaurus of Subject Descriptors. 1978. National Center on Child Abuse and Neglect, P.O. Box 1182, Washington, DC 20013. Free.

CLAIMS™ (Files 23, 24, 25, 124, and 125)

Assignee Name/Number Lists for the IFI Chemical Patent Data Bases 1950-1976. IFI/Plenum Data Company, 2001 Jefferson Davis Highway, Arlington, VA 22202. $25.00. For an additional $25.00 IFI will send 2 years of quarterly cumulative updates.

International Classification of Patents. IFI/Plenum Data Company, 2001 Jefferson Davis Highway, Arlington, VA 22202. $145.00.

Manual of Classification of Patents. IFI/Plenum Data Company, 2001 Jefferson Davis Highway, Arlington, VA 22202. $60.00 (U.S.), $75.00 (elsewhere).

Thesaurus of General Terms. 1950-1976. Descriptors for chemical patents. IFI/Plenum Data Company, 2001 Jefferson Davis Highway, Arlington, VA 22202. $75.00.

COMPENDEX (File 8)

CAL Classification Brochure. 1977. Engineering Index, Inc., 345 East 47th Street, New York, NY 10017. Telephone: 212/644-7600. Free. This brochure was originally produced to describe the CARD-A-LERT service from Engineering Index, Inc. The service has been discontinued, but the brochure remains as a useful guide which describes the scope of Engineering Index/COMPENDEX. In addition, the CAL classification codes are identified and the scope of each code is described; the codes can still be used in computer searching.

The Engineering Index COMPENDEX: Online User's Manual for the Lockheed DIALOG Information Retrieval Service. Engineering Index, Inc., 345 East 47th Street, New York, NY 10017. Telephone: 212/644-7600. $10.00. This manual gives specific details on the form of COMPENDEX as the tapes are processed by the Lockheed Information Retrieval Service. Specific techniques for searching COMPENDEX with DIALOG are detailed. A CAL Classification Brochure and a sample issue of Engineering Index Monthly are also included.

PIE: Publications Indexed for Engineering. Annual. Engineering Index, Inc., 345 East 47th Street, New York, NY 10017. Telephone: 212/644-7600. $10.00 (1979), paperback. Published as part of the Engineering Index Annual; reflects only those publications actually abstracted and indexed by Engineering Index, Inc., for that year. It is also available as a separate. The list is arranged in two parts: CODEN-designated publications (listing the abbreviated title, full

6 (June 1979)

publication or key title and the CODEN) and non-CODEN-designated publications (listing the abbreviated title, bibliographic information, and the published title).

SHE: Subject Headings for Engineering. 1972. Engineering Index, Inc., 345 East 47th Street, New York, NY 10017. Telephone: 212/644-7600. $15.00, supplement $5.00. The alphabetical list of terms currently in use as a controlled vocabulary for indexing the transdisciplinary literature of engineering and related sciences. Includes cross-references, scope notes and category codes. The introduction on the structure and format of SHE gives several examples which illustrate its use. Supplement, 1977, includes over 400 entries updating the 1972 edition of SHE. Included are lists of those terms added, changed and/or deleted from 1973 through January 1977, and remarks, scope notes, and subheadings are also included.

Subheading Index. Engineering Index, Inc., 345 East 47th Street, New York, NY 10017. Telephone: 212/644-7600. $15.00. A compilation of terms used by technical editorial specialists to 1) divide broad terms (Main headings) listed in SHE and its Supplement, 2) permit a Main heading listed in SHE to be used also as a subheading, and 3) express concepts not otherwise expressed in SHE. Use of subheadings enables more specific search statements and additional access points to the accumulated information in COMPENDEX.

Subject Heading Guide to Engineering Categories. Second edition, 1977. Engineering Index, Inc., 345 East 47th Street, New York, NY 10017. Telephone: 212/644-7600. $10.00. Clusters related terms from SHE and its Supplement. Although not a thesaurus, the numerical CAL classification codes found in SHE and the CAL Brochure provide subject entry to the indexing vocabulary.

COMPREHENSIVE DISSERTATION INDEX (File 35)

Comprehensive Dissertation Index (printed form). University Microfilms International, 300 North Zeeb Road, Ann Arbor, MI 48106. Telephone: 800/521-0600, x367. The printed form of the Comprehensive Dissertation Index contains information that may be helpful to DIALOG users. Each volume has a list of sources consulted when compiling CDI, a subject cross-reference list, specific information on abbreviations, special characters, scientific nomenclature, and information on ordering dissertation copies from University Microfilms International.

Dissertation Data Base Service Brochure. University Microfilms International, 300 North Zeeb Road, Ann Arbor, MI 48106. Telephone: 800/521-0600, x367. Includes school and subject lists as well as overview of database.

CONFERENCE PAPERS INDEX (File 77)

Conference Papers Index User Aid. Data Courier, Inc., 620 South Fifth Street, Louisville, KY 40202. Telephone: 800/626-2823. Free. Includes database description; discussion of the citations, field by field; search guide chart; sample searches; partial list of the the conferences cited in 1978.

(June 1979) 7

CRIS (File 60)

See USDA/CRIS

DISCLOSURE (File 100)

Disclosure OnLine User's Manual. Disclosure, Inc., 4827 Rugby Avenue, Washington, DC 20014. Telephone: 301/951-0100. $25.00. Includes sections on database content, database fields, usage on DIALOG, conventions and abbreviations, and document fulfillment. Many sample searches also included.

ECER/EXCEPTIONAL CHILD EDUCATION RESOURCES (File 54)

Thesaurus of ERIC Descriptors. Macmillan Information, 866 Third Avenue, New York, NY 10022. $9.95.

ECONOMICS ABSTRACTS INTERNATIONAL (File 90)

User Manual. Learned Information (Europe) Ltd., 37-39 Oxford Street, London W1R 2LL, United Kingdom. Telephone: (01) 434 1788, Telex: 837704 (INFORM G). U.S. $30.00 (includes subscription to automatic updating). Looseleaf. Includes lists of publications abstracted, an English language thesaurus with cross references and UDC numbers, and UDC numbers cross-indexed to related terms.

EIS NONMANUFACTURING ESTABLISHMENTS (File 92)

EIS Information Retrieval Users Manual. Economic Information Systems, Inc., 9 East 41st Street, New York, NY 10017. Telephone: 212/697-6080. $15.00. The examples included in this manual illustrate how sales, marketing, and financial analysts can use EIS PLANTS data. Similar search techniques can be applied to data on EIS NONMANUFACTURING ESTABLISHMENTS.

Input/Output Databases: Uses in Business and Government, by Jay M. Gould, with Foreword by Wassily Leontief. Economic Information Systems, Inc., 9 East 41st Street, New York, NY 10017. Telephone: 212/697-6080. $19.95.

PTS Users Manual. Predicasts, Inc., 200 University Circle Research Center, 11001 Cedar Ave., Cleveland, OH 44106. Telephone: 216/795-3000. Includes code thesauri used to index the firm records included in the EIS NONMANUFACTURING ESTABLISHMENTS. There is also an alphabetical listing of proper and alternative terms with code references.

EIS PLANTS (File 22)

EIS Information Retrieval User's Manual. Economic Information Systems, Inc., 9 East 41st Street, New York, NY 10017. Telephone: 212/697-6080. $15.00. This manual Includes numerous examples illustrating how the EIS PLANTS database is used to obtain information needed by sales managers, sales representatives, marketing managers and analysts, product managers, and financial analysts.

8 (June 1979)

Input/Output Databases: Uses in Business and Government, by Jay M. Gould, with Foreword by Wassily Leontief. Economic Information Systems, Inc., 9 East 41st Street, New York, NY 10017. Telephone: 212/697-6080. $19.95.

PTS Users Manual. Predicasts, Inc., 200 University Circle Research Center, 11001 Cedar Ave., Cleveland, OH 44106. Telephone: 216/795-3000. Included are code thesauri used to index the firm records in the EIS NONMANUFACTURING ESTABLISHMENTS. There is also an alphabetical listing of proper and alternative terms with code references.

ENERGYLINE (File 69)

Connectimes. EIC-Environment Information Center, Inc., 292 Madison Avenue, 3rd floor, New York, NY 10017. Telephone: 212/949-9471. A newsletter focussing on energy and environmental information in general and online searching in particular. Free.

ENERGYLINE User's Manual. EIC-Environment Information Center, Inc., 292 Madison Avenue, 3rd floor, New York, NY 10017. Telephone: 212/949-9471. $25.00 prepaid, $30.00 billed.

ENVIROLINE (File 40)

Connectimes. EIC-Environment Information Center, Inc., 292 Madison Avenue, 3rd floor, New York, NY 10017. Telephone: 212/949-9471. A newsletter focussing on energy and environmental information in general and online searching in particular. Free.

ENVIROLINE User's Manual. EIC-Environment Information Center, Inc., 292 Madison Avenue, New York, NY 10017. Telephone: 212/949-9471. $25.00 prepaid, $30.00 billed.

ENVIRONMENTAL PERIODICALS BIBLIOGRAPHY (File 68)

EPB Online Vocabulary Aid. Environmental Studies Institute, International Academy at Santa Barbara, 2074 Alameda Padre Serra, Santa Barbara, CA 93103. Telephone: 805/965-5010. $45.00.

ERIC (File 1)

A Bibliography of Publications about the Educational Resources Information Center. 1978. ERIC Processing and Reference Facility, 4833 Rugby Avenue, Suite 303, Bethesda, MD 20014. Telephone: 301/656-9723. Free.

Directory of ERIC Microfiche Collections. Biannual. ERIC Processing and Reference Facility, 4833 Rugby Ave., Suite 303, Bethesda, MD 20014. Telephone: 301/656-9723. Free. A listing of the libraries and information centers that have a standing order to the ERIC microfiche collection. The directory gives collection scope/size, equipment and services and accessibility data, as well as the name and phone number of a contact person at each collection. Many of these facilities are open to the general public, and will duplicate microfiche and/or hardcopy.

(June 1979) 9

224

Directory of ERIC Search Services. Biannual. ERIC Processing and Reference Facility, 4833 Rugby Avenue, Suite 303, Bethesda, MD 20014. Telephone: 301/656-9723. Free. A listing of the sites which provide search services on a regular basis—irrespective of whether the service is available only to a circumscribed community or to all users without restrictions.

ERIC Contract/Grant Number Index. Annual. ORI, Inc., 4833 Rugby Avenue, Suite 303, Bethesda, MD 20014. Telephone: 301/656-9723. $10.00 (domestic) and $12.00 (foreign).

ERIC Descriptor and Identifier Usage Report. 1966-1977. ERIC Clearinghouse on Science, Mathematics and Environmental Education, Ohio State University, 1200 Chambers Road, 3rd Floor, Columbus, OH 43212. Telephone: 614/422-6717. $3.50. Lists each ERIC descriptor and identifier, the number of times it has been used to date, and the accession numbers where used.

ERIC Processing Manual. 1974. ERIC Processing and Reference Facility, 4833 Rugby Ave., Suite 303, Bethesda, MD 20014. Telephone: 301/656-9723. $33.32 (hardcopy) and $1.00 (microfiche). (ED 092164).

ERIC Report/Project Number Index, Cumulative. ORI, Inc., 4833 Rugby Avenue, Suite 303, Bethesda, MD 20014. Telephone: 301/656-9723. $30.00 (domestic) and $36.00 (foreign). Annual subscription price: $50.00 (domestic) and $57.00 (foreign).

ERIC Title Index, 1966-1976. Annual cumulations with quarterly supplements, 1977- . ERIC Processing and Reference Facility, 4833 Rugby Avenue, Suite 303, Bethesda, MD 20014. Telephone: 301/656-9723. $50.00 (domestic) and $60.00 (foreign). Annual subscription price for the cumulations: $45.00 (domestic) and $60.00 (foreign).

ERIC: What It Can Do for You/How to Use It, by James Brown and others. 1975. ERIC Clearinghouse on Information Resources, Stanford University, Stanford, CA 94305. Available from: Box E, School of Education, Stanford University, Stanford, CA 94305. $3.75; make checks payable to "Box E". Also available from ERIC Document Reproduction Service: $3.32 (hardcopy) and $.83 (michrofiche). (ED 110095)

How to Prepare for a Computer Search of ERIC; a Nontechnical Approach, by Judith Yarborough. 1975. ERIC Clearinghouse on Information Resources, Stanford University, Stanford, CA 94305. Available from: Box E, School of Education, Stanford University, Stanford, CA 94305. $1.00; make checks payable to "Box E". Also available from ERIC Document Reproduction Service: $3.32 (hardcopy) and $.83 (michrofiche). (ED 110096)

How to Use ERIC. Educational Resources Information Center, National Institute of Education, Washington, DC 20208. Free.

Institutional Source Directory. Annual. ERIC Processing and Reference Facility, 4833 Rugby Ave., Suite 303, Bethesda, MD 20014. Telephone: 301/656-9723. Published semiannually, $15.00 domestic, $18.00 foreign. Annual subscription: $25.00 domestic, $30.00 foreign. An alphabetical listing of the names of all institutions by which documents in the ERIC system have been indexed in the Institutional Name and Sponsoring Agency Name fields of the citation, together with the corresponding alphanumeric code which appears in either the Institution or Sponsoring Agency Code field of each record.

Interchange [Newsletter]. ERIC Processing and Reference Facility, 4833 Rugby Ave., Suite 303, Bethesda, MD 20014. Telephone: 301/656-9723. Free. The newsletter used by the ERIC Processing and Reference Facility to communicate with ERIC users. Published 4-6 times a year.

Thesaurus of ERIC Descriptors. Seventh edition, 1977. Macmillan Information, 866 Third Ave., New York, NY 10022. $9.95 (Paperback)

EXCERPTA MEDICA (Files 72 and 73)

The Excerpta Medica Mark II Biomedical Information System. Second edition. Excerpta Medica, P.O. Box 3085, Princeton, NJ 08540, or Excerpta Medica, P.O. Box 1126, 1000-BC Amsterdam, The Netherlands. Telephone: Amsterdam 26 44 38. Free. A brochure providing an overview of the MARK II system and covering the total procedure from the arrival of the primary journals to the production of the publications and computer tapes from the database.

Guide to Excerpta Medica Classification and Indexing System. Excerpta Medica, P.O. Box 3085, Princeton, NJ 08540, or Excerpta Medica, P.O. Box 1126, 1000-BC Amsterdam, The Netherlands. Telephone: Amsterdam 26 44 38. Dfl. 25.00, U.S. $10.00 (paperback).

List of Journals Abstracted. 1979 edition. Excerpta Medica, P.O. Box 3085, Princeton, NJ 08540, or Excerpta Medica, P.O. Box 1126, 1000-BC Amsterdam, The Netherlands. Telephone: Amsterdam 26 44 38. Orders must be prepaid. Hardcopy: Dfl 10.00, U.S. $5.00; microfiche: Dfl 8.00, U.S. $4.00. The 1979 edition contains about 15% more entries than the 1978 edition and provides information on those journals that have been dropped from the previous collection.

MALIMET, EMCLAS and EMTAGS on Microfiche. Excerpta Medica, P.O. Box 3085, Princeton, NJ 08540, or Excerpta Medica, P.O. Box 1126, 1000-BC Amsterdam, The Netherlands. Telephone: Amsterdam 26 44 38. Dfl 400.00, $160.00, or $80.00 to subscribers of printed EM (approximately 360 fiche).

User Manual. Excerpta Medica, P.O. Box 3085, Princeton, NJ 08540, or Excerpta Medica, P.O. Box 1126, 1000-BC Amsterdam, The Netherlands. Telephone: Amsterdam 26 44 38. Dfl 20.00, U.S. $10.00. An 80-page booklet which shows the most cost-effective methods of searching journals and computer files. Sample searches are included and the different types of records used by Excerpta Medica are described in detail.

FOOD SCIENCE & TECHNOLOGY ABSTRACTS (File 51)

Food Science and Technology Abstracts. International Food Information Service, Shinfield, Reading, Berkshire, United Kingdom, and International Food Information Service, Arabella Center, Lyoner Strasse 44-48, Frankfurt/Main, Federal Republic of Germany. Telephone: Frankfurt 6687/338 or 6687/339, Telex: 41 43 51. Each issue of the printed form includes a list of standard abbreviations, language abbreviations, and an introduction to the subject index which may be helpful to searchers.

IFIS Magnetic Tape Manual (Version 2, Revised edition). International Food

Information Service, Arabella Center, Lyoner Strasse 44-48, Frankfurt/Main, Federal Republic of Germany. Telephone: Frankfurt 6687/338 or 6687/339, Telex: 41 43 51. Free.

IFIS List of Headings. International Food Information Service, Arabella Center, Lyoner Strasse 44-48, Frankfurt/Main, Federal Republic of Germany. Telephone: Frankfurt 6687/338 or 6687/339, Telex: 41 43 51. Includes approximately 1,000 terms. U.S. $3.00.

FSTA Thesaurus. International Food Information Service, Shinfield, Reading, Berkshire, United Kingdom. £18.00. Includes approximately 10,000 terms.

FOODS ADLIBRA (File 79)

No special search aids are available for this database.

FOREIGN TRADERS INDEX (File 105)

Numerical List of Manufactured Products, New (1972) SIC Basis, 1972 Census of Manufactures. May 1973. (Series MC 7212) Superintendent of Documents, U.S. Government Printing Office, Washington, DC 20402. $3.45 (paperback), C56.244/2:P94/2/972, Item 135.

Schedule C-E: Classification of County and Territory Designations for U.S. Export Statistics. Superintendent of Documents, U.S. Government Printing Office, Washington, DC 20402. Prepared by the U.S. Department of Commerce, Bureau of the Census, Foreign Trade Division. C3.150:C-E/976. Supersedes Schedule C: Classification of Country Designations.

Standard Industrial Classification Manual 1972. Superintendent of Documents, U.S. Government Printing Office, Washington, DC 20402. Prepared by the Statistical Policy Division. (S/N4104-0066) $6.75. PrEx 2.6/2:/N27/972.

FOUNDATION DIRECTORY (File 26)

About Foundations. Second edition. The Foundation Center Library, 888 Seventh Ave., New York, NY 10019. Telephone: 212/975-1120. $5.00.

FOUNDATION GRANTS INDEX (File 27)

About Foundations. Second edition. The Foundation Center Library, 888 Seventh Ave., New York, NY 10019. Telephone: 212/975-1120. $5.00.

FROST & SULLIVAN DM^2 (File 59)

List of Codes. Frost and Sullivan, Inc., 106 Fulton Street, New York, NY 10038. Telephone: 212/233-1080. Free.

Master Code Book of Companies. Frost and Sullivan, Inc., 106 Fulton Street, New York, NY 10038. Telephone: 212/233-1080. Free.

GEOARCHIVE (File 58)

Geoarchive User's Guide, by Graham Lea and others. Second edition, 1979. Geosystems, P.O. Box 1024 Westminster, London SW1, United Kingdom. Telephone: 01-222-7305. $20.00.

Geosaurus: Geosystems Thesaurus of Geoscience, by Rosalind Charles and others. Third edition, 1979. Geosystems, P.O. Box 1024, Westminster, London SW1, United Kingdom. Telephone: 01-222-7305. $50.00.

Geosources: Geoserials and Geopublishers, by James Shearer and others. Third edition, 1979. Geosystems, P.O. Box 1024, Westminster, London SW1, United Kingdom. Telephone: 01-222-7305. $50.00.

All three of these user aids for $100 if purchased as a package.

GPO MONTHLY CATALOG (File 66)

Anglo-American Cataloging Rules: North American Text. American Library Association, Chicago, IL 60611. ISBN 0-8389-3119-7.

Anglo-American Cataloging Rules: North American Text, Chapter 6, Separately Published Monographs. American Library Association, Chicago, IL 60611. ISBN 0-8389-3156-1.

Composite MARC Format: A Tabular Listing of Content Designators Used in the MARC Formats. MARC Development Office, Library of Congress, Washington, DC 20540. For sale by the Superintendent of Documents, U.S. Government Printing Office, Washington, DC 20402. $2.50. S/N 030-000-00089-7.

Geographic Area Code. MARC Development Office, Library of Congress, Washington, DC 20540.

Library of Congress Subject Headings. Eighth edition. Cataloging Distribution, Service Division, Library of Congress, Bldg. 159, Navy Yard Annex, Washington, DC 20541. $35.00 (two volumes).

List of Classes of United States Government Publications Available for Selection by Depository Libraries. Superintendent of Documents, Government Printing Office, Washington, DC 20402. Free. Gives the "stem class" of Superintendent of Document numbers.

HISTORICAL ABSTRACTS (File 39)

List of Periodicals. Revised 1978. ABC-Clio, Inc., P.O. Box 4397, Santa Barbara, CA 93103. Telephone: 805/963-4221. Free.

INSPEC (Files 12 and 13)

Concordance to the INSPEC Classification, 1969-1977. Revised edition, 1978. IEEE, 445 Hoes Lane, Piscataway, NJ, 08854. Telephone: 201/981-0060, or INSPEC: IEE, Station House, Nightingale Road, Hitchin Herts SG5 1RJ, England. Telephone: 0462 53331. $12.00.

Guide to INSPEC Classification Codes with Changed Meanings, 1969-1977. IEEE, 445 Hoes Lane, Piscataway, NJ 08854. Telephone: 201/981-0600, or INSPEC: IEE, Station House, Nightingale Road, Hitchin Herts SG5 IRJ, England. Telephone: 0462 53331. $4.00.

INSPEC Classification, 1978. IEEE, 445 Hoes Lane, Piscataway, NJ 08854. Telephone: 201/981-0060, or INSPEC: IEE, Station House, Nightingale Road, Hitchin Herts SG5 IRJ, England. Telephone: 0462 53331. $20.00 or £12.00.

INSPEC Database User's Guide. Third edition. IEEE, 445 Hoes Lane, Piscataway, NJ 08854. Telephone: 201/981-0060, or INSPEC: IEE, Station House, Nightingale Road, Hitchin Herts SG5 IRJ, England. Telephone: 0462 53331. $15.00.

INSPEC List of Journals, 1978. IEEE, 445 Hoes Lane, Piscataway, NJ 08854. Telephone: 201/981-0060, or INSPEC: IEE, Station House, Nightingale Road, Hitchin Herts SG5 IRJ, England. Telephone: 0462 53331. $5.00.

INSPEC Thesaurus, 1979. IEEE, 445 Hoes Lane, Piscataway, NJ 08854. Telephone: 201/981-0060, or INSPEC: IEE, Station House, Nightingale Road, Hitchin Herts SG 5 IRJ, England. Telephone: 0462 53331. $70.00.

INTERNATIONAL PHARMACEUTICAL ABSTRACTS (File 74)

Index Nominum. Drug Intelligence Publications, Hamilton Press, Inc., Dept. Y-26, Hamilton, IL 62341. $65.75.

International Pharmaceutical Abstracts. International Pharmaceutical Abstracts, 4630 Montgomery Ave., Washington, DC 20014. Telephone: 301/657-3000. A current semi-annual cumulative index. Use as a guide to the controlled vocabulary descriptors.

USAN and the USP Dictionary of Drug Names. 1980 edition. United States Pharmacopei Convention, Inc., 12601 Twinbrook Parkway, Rockville, MD 20852. $19.50.

ISMEC (File 14)

ISMEC User Aid. Data Courier, Inc., 620 South Fifth Street, Louisville, KY 40202. Telephone: 800/626-2823. Free. Includes subject category listing and codes, database description; discussion of the citations, field by field; search guide chart; sample searches; journals list; the controlled vocabulary listed both alphabetically and by subject category.

LANGUAGE AND LANGUAGE BEHAVIOR ABSTRACTS (File 36)

LLBA User's Manual. Sociological Abstracts, Inc., P.O. Box 22206, San Diego, CA 92122. Telephone: 714/565-6603. $17.50. This manual discusses LLBA editorial, indexing and classification practices. It also includes listings of the controlled vocabulary terms, abbreviations used in abstracts, serial publications covered, editorial practices, and retrieval methods.

14   (June 1979)

LISA/LIBRARY AND INFORMATION SCIENCE ABSTRACTS (File 61)

No special search aids are available for this database.

MAGAZINE INDEX (File 47)

Access Information: An Online User's Guide to IAC Databases. Information Access Corporation, 885 N. San Antonio Road, Los Altos, CA 94022. Telephone: 800/227-8431 (in California: 415/941-1100). $20.00. This guide includes a list of titles indexed. Available Fall 1979.

List of Magazines Covered by MAGAZINE INDEX. Information Access Corporation, 885 N. San Antonio Road, Los Altos, CA 94022. Telephone: 800/227-8431 (in California: 415/941-1100).

MANAGEMENT CONTENTS (File 75)

MANAGEMENT CONTENTS Database Thesaurus. Revised edition, 1979. Management Contents, Inc., Box 1054, Skokie, IL 60077. Telephone: 312/967-1122. $40.00. Updated at no extra charge. Includes controlled vocabulary, related terms, general subject divisions, journal listings plus description code. Also included is a detailed explanation of record structure, article and journal selection policy, indexing and abstracting procedures, database coverage and vendor manuals.

METADEX (File 32)

Alloys Index. American Society for Metals, Metals Park, OH 44073. Telephone: 216/338-5151. Guidelines for optimum use and listings such as subject sections, journals indexes and translation sources, in addition to the actual indexes.

Metals Abstracts and Metals Abstracts Index. American Society for Metals, Metals Park, OH 44073. Telephone: 216/338-5151. These publications include guidelines for optimum use and listings such as subject sections, journals indexed, and translation sources, in addition to the actual indexes.

Thesaurus of Metallurgical Terms. American Society of Metals, Metals Park, OH 44073. Telephone: 216/338-5151. $30.00.

METEOROLOGICAL AND GEOASTROPHYSICAL ABSTRACTS (File 29)

Cumulative Index for Volumes 21-26 (1970-75). American Meteorological Society, 45 Beacon Street, Boston, MA 02108. Two volumes: 1) Author, 2) Subject; $200 each (as separates) or both for $300. The cumulative index is the only vocabulary tool available for 1972-75.

MGA Annual Indexes. American Meteorological Society, 45 Beacon Street, Boston, MA 02108. Vol. 27 (1976) and Vol. 28 (1977) available for $150 each or $200 for both. The annual index is useful for determining subject terminology to be used in searching the database.

(June 1979) 15

MLA BIBLIOGRAPHY (File 71)

No special search aids are available for this database.

MRIS (File 63)

MRIS Cumulative Index: 1970-1976. Maritime Research Information Service, Transportation Research Board, National Research Council, 2101 Constitution Ave., N.W., Washington, DC 20418. Telephone: 202/389-6687 or 202/389-6452. $15.00.

MRIS Subject Term (Key Word) Index: Feb. 1979. National Academy of Sciences, 2101 Constitution Ave., Washington, DC 20418. $21.00. Contains 5700 maritime terms, including a frequency count for each term.

NATIONAL FOUNDATIONS (File 78)

About Foundations. Second edition. The Foundation Center Library, 888 Seventh Ave., New York, NY 10019. Telephone: 212/975-1120. $5.00.

NATIONAL NEWSPAPER INDEX (File 111)

Access Information: An Online User's Guide to IAC Databases. Information Access Corporation, 885 N. San Antonio Road, Los Altos, CA 94022. Telephone: 800/227-8431 (in California 415/941-1100). $20.00. This guide includes a list of titles indexed. Available Fall 1979.

NICEM (File 46)

No special search aids are available for this database.

NICSEM/NIMIS (File 70)

Instructional Materials Thesaurus for Special Education. 1976. Publications Sales Division, Ohio State University Press, Columbus, OH 43210. $2.00.

NTIS (File 6)

COSATI Subject Category List. National Technical Information Service, 5285 Port Royal Road, Springfield, VA 22161. Telephone: 703/557-4650. (NTIS order #: AD-612200). $5.25 paper, $3.00 microfiche. Gives subject matter scope notes for all COSATI fields.

DDC Retrieval and Indexing Terminology. May 1979. National Technical Information Service, 5285 Port Royal Road, Springfield, VA 22161. Telephone: 703/557-4650. (NTIS order #: AD-A068500) $6.50 paper, $3.00 microfiche.

Energy Information Data Base: Corporate Author Entries. National Technical Information Service, 5285 Port Royal Road, Springfield, VA 22161. Telephone: 703/557-4650. (NTIS order #: TID-4585). $16.50 paper, $3.00 microfiche.

16   (June 1979)

Energy Information Data Base: Subject Categories. National Technical Information Service, 5285 Port Royal Road, Springfield, VA 22161. Telephone: 703/557-4650. (NTIS order #: TID-4584-R3). $6.00 paper, $3.00 microfiche. Lists subject categories which appear in the Identifier field of DOE reports.

Energy Information Data Base: Subject Thesaurus. June 1978. Used from June 1975 to the present. National Technical Information Services, 5285 Port Royal Road, Springfield, VA 22161. Telephone: 707/5557-4650. (NTIS order #: TID-7000-R3). $21.50 paper, $3.00 microfiche.

Energy Microthesaurus-A Hierarchical Listing of Energy Index Terms Used in the NTIS Database. July 1976. National Technical Information Service, 5285 Port Royal Road, Springfield, VA 22161. Telephone: 703/557-4650. (NTIS order #: PB-254-800). $10.50 paper or microfiche.

Environmental Microthesaurus-A Hierarchical List of Indexing Terms Used by NTIS. May 1977. National Technical Information Service, 5285 Port Royal Road, Springfield, VA 22161. Telephone: 703/557-4650. (NTIS order #: PB-265261). $10.50 paper or microfiche. Lists keywords from the "Major Thesauri" as well as free-language keywords for air pollution, noise pollution, water pollution, and solid waste disposal.

Health Care Microthesaurus-A Hierarchical List of Indexing Terms Used by NTIS. April 1979. National Technical Information Service, 5285 Port Royal Road, Springfield, VA 22161. Telephone: 703/557-4650. (NTIS order #: PB-290776). $10.50 paper or microfiche.

Medical Subject Headings Annotated. Alphabetical List. 1979. National Technical Information Service, 5285 Port Royal Road, Springfield, VA 22161. Telephone: 703/557-4650. (NTIS order #: PB-285-356) $15.00 paper, $3.00 microfiche. Used from 1974 to the present and is updated.

Microthesaurus of Soil Mechanics Terms. National Technical Information Service, 5285 Port Royal Road, Springfield, VA 22161. Telephone: 703/557-4650. (NTIS order #: AD-A003812). $12.50 paper, $3.00 microfiche. Used from 1974 to the present.

Microthesaurus of Vehicle Mobility, Environment and Pavement Terms. National Technical Information Service, 5285 Port Royal Road, Springfield, VA 22161. Telephone: 703/557-4650. (NTIS order #: AD-A011269). $7.25 paper, $3.00 microfiche. Used from 1975 to the present.

NASA Thesaurus. National Technical Information Service, 5285 Port Royal Road, Springfield, VA 22161. Telephone: 703/557-4650. Volume 1: Alphabetical listing. $24.00 paper, $3.00 microfiche (NTIS order #: N76-17992). Volume 2: Access vocabulary. $14.00 paper, $3.00 microfiche (NTIS order #: N76-17993). Used from 1964 to the present and is updated.

NHTSA/SASI Cooperative Thesaurus of Highway and Motor Vehicle Safety Literature Terms. 1973. National Technical Information Service, 5285 Port Royal Road, Springfield, VA 22161. Telephone: 703/557-4650. (NTIS order #: PB-226870/4). $31.00 paper or microfiche.

NTIS Price Code Lists. National Technical Information Service, 5285 Port Royal Road, Springfield, VA 22161. Telephone: 703/557-4650. (NTIS order PR-360-3 for price code tables for addresses within the North American Continent or NTIS PR-360-4 for price code tables for all other addresses.) Free.

NTIS Subject Classification (Past and Present). National Technical Information Service, 5285 Port Royal Road, Springfield, VA 22161. Telephone: 703/557-4650. (NTIS PB- 270 575). $6.00 paper, $3.00 microfiche. Includes subject matter scope notes and historical scope notes for all NTIS subject categories.

Reference Guide to the NTIS Bibliographic Data File. National Technical Information Service, 5285 Port Royal Road, Springfield, VA 22161. Telephone: 703/557-4650. (NTIS order PR-253). Free. Provides background material on the database and its bibliographic content.

Source Header List. National Technical Information Service, 5285 Port Royal Road, Springfield, VA 22161. Telephone: 703/557-4650. (NTIS order #: AD-A041700). $21.50 paper, $3.00 microfiche. DDC corporate authors with codes.

Subject Headings Used by the USAEC Division of Technical Information. Tenth revised edition. National Technical Information Service, 5285 Port Royal Road, Springfield, VA 22161. Telephone: 703/557-4650. (NTIS order #: TID-5001-REV 10). $10.75 paper, $3.00 microfiche.

TEST: Thesaurus of Engineering and Scientific Terms. Engineers Joint Council, 345 East 47th Street, New York, NY 10017. $25.00 paper.

Thesaurus of ERIC Descriptors. Seventh edition, 1977. CCM Information Corp., 866 Third Avenue, New York, NY 10022. $9.95.

Water Resources Thesaurus. National Technical Information Service, 5285 Port Royal Road, Springfield, VA 22161. Telephone: 703/557-4650. (NTIS order #: PB-245-673). $13.00 paper or $3.00 microfiche. Used from 1974 to the present.

OCEANIC ABSTRACTS (File 28)

OCEANIC ABSTRACTS User Aid. Data Courier, Inc., 620 South Fifth Street, Louisville, KY 40202. Telephone: 800/626-2823. Free. Includes database description; discussion of the citations, field by field; search guide chart; sample searches; list of source materials regularly cited with CODENs when available; controlled vocabulary; lists of the acronyms, abbreviations, prefixes, symbols used in the citations.

ONTAP CA SEARCH (File 204)

No special search aids are available for this database.

ONTAP CHEMNAME™ (File 231)

No special search aids are available for this database.

18 (June 1979)

ONTAP ERIC (File 201)

ONTAP: Online Training and Practice Manual for ERIC Data Base Searching, by Karen Markey and Pauline Atherton. Syracuse University Printing Services, 115 College Place, Syracuse, NY 13210. Order #IR-24. $6.60.

PAIS INTERNATIONAL (File 49)

PAIS Bulletin. Public Affairs Information Service, Inc., 11 West 40th Street, New York, NY 10018. Telephone: 212/736-6629. Includes listing of abbreviations used for English language documents.

PAIS Foreign Language Index. Public Affairs Information Service, Inc., 11 West 40th Street, New York, NY 10018. Telephone: 212/736-6629. Includes list of abbreviations used in indexing non-English language documents. Abbreviations used for non-English language documents correspond as closely as possible with equivalent English abbreviations.

PAIS Selection Policy and Periodicals List. Public Affairs Information Service, Inc., 11 West 40th Street, New York, NY 10018. Telephone: 212/736-6629.

PHARMACEUTICAL NEWS INDEX (File 42)

PHARMACEUTICAL NEWS INDEX User Aid. Data Courier, Inc., 620 South Fifth Street, Louisville, KY 40202. Telephone: 800/626-2823. Includes database description; discussion of the citations, field by field; search guide chart; sample searches; listings of the acronyms regularly used in PNI, alphabetical by both the acronym and the phrase.

PHILOSOPHER'S INDEX (File 57)

The PHILOSOPHER'S INDEX Thesaurus. June 1979. Philosophy Documentation Center, Bowling Green State University, Bowling Green, Ohio 43403. Telephone: 419/372-2419. $10.00.

PIRA (File 48)

PIRA Online User Manual. Pira, the research association for the paper and board, printing and packaging industries, Randalls Road, Leatherhead, Surrey KKT22 7RU, United Kingdom. £15.00 (Pira members), £20.00 (Pira non-members). Add £5.00 airmail outside U.K. Includes database subject coverage, database journal coverage, and guidance on database structure.

POLLUTION ABSTRACTS (File 41)

POLLUTION ABSTRACTS User Aid. Data Courier, Inc., 620 South Fifth Street, Louisville, KY 40202. Telephone: 800/626-2823. Free. Includes database description; discussion of the citations, field by field; search guide chart; sample searches; list of source materials regularly cited with CODENs when available; controlled vocabulary; list of acronyms, abbreviations, prefixes, symbols used in the citations.

(June 1979) 19

PREDICASTS (Files 16-22, 81-82, 86-87)

PTS User's Manual. Predicasts, Inc., 200 University Circle Research Center, 11001 Cedar Avenue, Cleveland, OH 44106. Telephone: 216/795-3000. Free to DIALOG users.

Who Makes What, When and How Much. Economic Information Systems, Inc., 9 East 41st Street, New York, NY 10017. Telephone: 212/697-6080. $10.00.

PSYCHOLOGICAL ABSTRACTS (File 11)

PSYCHOLOGICAL ABSTRACTS Information Services Users Reference Manual. American Psychological Association, 1200 Seventeenth Street, N.W. Washington, DC 20036. Telephone: 800/336-4980. $25.00. Updating service provided. Includes selection and coverage, bibliographic recording practices, indexing practices, and appendices which list source publications, subject codes, and the number of times descriptors have been used to date. Sections are included on retrieval methods and DIALOG searching.

Thesaurus of Psychological Index Terms. Second edition. American Psychological Association, 1200 Seventeenth Street, N.W. Washington, DC 20036. Telephone: 800/336-4980. $10.00. Includes a relationship section, rotated alphabetical terms section, and a postable terms & term codes section.

RAPRA ABSTRACTS (File 95)

Controlled Descriptors Including Chemicals, Polymers, Applications and Properties. Rubber and Plastics Research Association of Great Britain, Shawbury, Shrewsbury, Salop SY4 4NR, England. Telephone: Shawbury (0939) 250383. Telex: 35134. £45.00. Computer printout format.

Journals List. Rubber and Plastics Research Association of Great Britain, Shawbury, Shrewsbury, Salop SY4 4NR, England. Telephone: Shawbury (0930) 250383. Telex: 35134. Free.

RAPRA Classification Code. Rubber and Plastics Research Association of Great Britain, Shawbury, Shrewsbury, Salop SY4 4NR, England. Telephone: Shawbury (0939) 250383. Telex: 35134. £10.00.

Trade Names and Company Names. Rubber and Plastics Research Association of Great Britain, Shawbury, Shrewsbury, Salop SY4 4NR, England. Telephone: Shawbury (0930) 250383. Telex: 35134. £80.00. Computer printout format.

SCISEARCH (Files 34 and 94)

User's Guide to Online Searching of SCISEARCH and SOCIAL SCISEARCH. Revised edition, 1978. Database Marketing, Institute for Scientific Information, 325 Chestnut Street, Philadelphia, PA 19106. Telephone: 800/523-1850 toll free in Pennsylvania, or 215/923-3300, x357, collect. Free. Included are current source publication listings for the two databases.

20 (June 1979)

SOCIAL SCISEARCH (File 7)

User's Guide to Online Searching of SCISEARCH and SOCIAL SCISEARCH. Revised edition, 1978. Database Marketing, Institute for Scientific Information, 325 Chestnut Street, Philadelphia, PA 19106. Telephone: 800/523-1850 toll free in Pennsylvania, or 215/923-3300, x357, collect. Free. Included are current source publication listings for the two databases.

SOCIOLOGICAL ABSTRACTS (File 37)

SOCIOLOGICAL ABSTRACTS User's Manual. Sociological Abstracts, Inc., P.O. Box 22206, San Diego, CA 92122. Telephone: 714/565-6603. $25.00. This manual discusses SA editorial, indexing and classification practices. It also includes a listing of the controlled vocabulary terms, a journal coverage list, and a section on retrieval methods.

SPIN (File 62)

AIP Style Manual. American Institute of Physics, 335 East 45th Street, New York, NY 10017. Telephone: 212/661-9404. $7.50. This manual discusses AIP editorial practices.

List of Titles and Codens. American Institute of Physics, 335 East 45th Street, New York, NY 10017. Telephone: 212/661-9404. Free.

Physics and Astronomy Classification Scheme. American Institute of Physics, 335 E. 45th Street, New York, NY 10017. Telephone: 212/661-9404. $15.00. Covers from 1975 to the present.

SSIE CURRENT RESEARCH (File 65)

SSIE Subject Indexes. Smithsonian Science Information Exchange, 1730 M Street N.W., Room 300, Washington, DC 20036. Telephone: 202/381-4211. $25.00. A "top down" listing of all five levels of SSIE subject indexes, about 40,000 terms in all.

SSIE Subject Terms and Synonyms. Smithsonian Science Information Exchange, 1730 M Street N.W., Room 300, Washington, DC 20036. Telephone: 202/381-4211. $50.00. A single alphabetical listing of all 40,000 SSIE subject index terms, plus 50,000 synonyms cross referenced to SSIE index terms, in a three-volume computer printout.

U.S. POLITICAL SCIENCE DOCUMENTS (File 93)

Political Science Thesaurus: Revised and Expanded. 1979. University Center for International Studies, 4G30 Forbes Quad, University of Pittsburgh, Pittsburgh, PA 15260. Telephone: 412/624-3341. Casebound: $65.00.

(June 1979)   21

236

USDA/CRIS (File 60)

Agricultural/Biological Vocabulary. 1967. Vol. I, II and Supplement. Reprinted 1976. National Agricultural Library, U.S. Dept. of Agriculture, Beltsville, MD 20705. Telephone: 301/344-3704.

Keyword Bank in CRIS. Current Research Information System, U.S. Dept. of Agriculture, National Agricultural Library Bldg., Beltsville, MD 20705. Telephone: 301/344-3850. Cumulative updates prepared annually. To be made available through NTIS.

Manual of Classification of Agricultural and Forestry Research. Revision III. 1978. Current Research Information System, U.S. Dept. of Agriculture, National Agricultural Library Bldg., Beltsville, MD 20705. Telephone: 301/344-3850. Available from National Technical Information Service (NTIS), 5285 Port Royal Road, Springfield, VA 22161. Telephone: 703/557-4650. (NTIS order #: PB 286099/AS). $8.00 paper, $3.00 microfiche.

WELDASEARCH (File 99)

International Welding Thesaurus. First edition, 1974, plus 2 Addenda. Published for the International Institute of Welding. Order from: The Welding Institute, Abington Hall, Abington, Cambridge CB1 6AL, United Kingdom. Price: £27.00 in the U.K. and £32.40 outside the U.K. £24.00 for members of the Welding Institute. (Price includes the 2 Addenda.) A second edition of the Thesaurus will be available early in 1980.

WORLD ALUMINUM ABSTRACTS (File 33)

Alloy Tables. 1978. The Aluminum Association, 818 Connecticut Avenue, N.W., Washington, DC 20006. Chemical compositions of commercial alloys.

Frequency Counts for WAA. The Aluminum Association, 818 Connecticut Avenue, N.W., Washington, DC 20006. $5.00. A cumulative frequency listing of terms in the WAA database. Republished at 6 month intervals.

List of Journals Abstracted. The Aluminum Association, 818 Connecticut Avenue, N.W., Washington, DC 20006. Available in WAA Annual Index and bound volumes.

Thesaurus of Aluminum Technology. Second edition. The Aluminum Association, 818 Connecticut Avenue, N.W., Washington, DC 20006. $25.00 (or $30.00 outside North America). Terms selected for inclusion in the Thesaurus cover aluminum technology from ore processing through end uses. The Thesaurus is compatable with the ASM Thesaurus of Metallurgical Terms and with the Thesaurus of Engineering and Scientific Terms.

World Aluminum Abstracts. The Aluminum Association, 818 Connecticut Avenue, N.W., Washington, DC 20006. This publication includes an introduction, guidelines for optimum use, and detailed information on subject sections, in addition to the actual indexes.

WORLD TEXTILES (File 67)

On Line to Textile Literature. Library and Information Department, Shirley
Institute, Manchester M20 8RX, England. Telephone: 061-445-8141. Telex:
668417 SHIRLY G. Free. Provides an introduction to the use of the WORLD
TEXTILES database within the DIALOG system and encloses, as a separate
document, a description of the facilities in this database and their use in the
conduct of online searches.

Register of Keyterms. Annual. Vol. 1: Keyterm List; Vol. 2: Advisory Lists.
Library and Information Department, Shirley Institute, Manchester M20 8RX,
England. Telephone: 061-445-8141. Telex: 668417 SHIRLY G. $30.00. Volume
1 provides a complete list of all the keyterms that can be assigned in indexing
and of the preferred keyterms (and additional keyterms) that are recorded in
the database on input of assigned indexing terms. Volume 2 provides lists of
keyterms, for advisory purposes only, that have subject-oriented relationships
with each other. Both volumes contain introductions with explanatory notes.

World Textile Abstracts. Library and Information Department, Shirley Institute,
Manchester M20 8RX, England. Telephone: 061-445-8141. Telex: 668417
SHIRLY G. $152.00 payable in advance. This is a twice-monthly review of
world literature, presented in classified order, of relevance to the textile and
related industries. Detailed indexes are presented at the end of each annual
volume. The abstracts in the periodical are cross referenced to records in the
database by abstract number.

DIALOG® BIBLIOGRAPHIC VERIFICATION AID*

FILE NO.	DATABASE+	YEAR†	AUTHOR**	JOURNAL	CORPORATE SOURCE	TITLE
1	ERIC	YR=66	AU=NAME, I?	JO=	/CS	/TI
2	CA SEARCH (1967-1971)	PY=70	AU=NAME, I?	JN=	/CS	/TI
3	CA SEARCH (1972-1976)	PY=72	AU=NAME, I?	JN=	/CS	/TI
4	CA SEARCH (1977+)	PY=77	AU=NAME, I?	JN=	/CS	/TI
5	BIOSIS PREVIEWS (1974+)	-	AU=NAME I?	JN=	CS=	/TI
6	NTIS	-	AU=NAME, I?	-	/CS	/TI
7	SOCIAL SCISEARCH®	-	AU=NAME I?	JO=	/CS	/TI
8	COMPENDEX	-	AU=NAME, I?	CO=	/CS	/TI
9	AIM/ARM	-	AU=NAME, I?	JO=	-	/TI
10	AGRICOLA	SY=1970	AU=NAME, I?	JN=	/CS	/TI
11	PSYCHOLOGICAL ABS	YR=67	AU=NAME, I?	JN=	/CS	/TI
12	INSPEC (1969-1977)	-	AU=NAME, I?	JN=	/CS	-
13	INSPEC (1978+)	PY=1978	AU=NAME, I?	JN=	CS=	/TI
14	ISMEC	-	AU=NAME, I?	JN=	/CS	-
15	ABI/INFORM	PY=1971	AU=NAME, I?	JN=	-	/TI
16	PTS PROMT	DT=72/01	-	JO=	-	-
17	PTS PREDALERT	DT=79/05	AU=NAME	JO=	-	-
18	PTS F&S INDEXES (1976+)	DT=76/01	-	JO=	-	/TI
19	CHEM INDUSTRY NOTES	DT=74/01/01	-	JO=	-	-
20	PTS FEDERAL INDEX	DT=76/01	AU=NAME	JO=	/CS	-
22	EIS INDUSTRIAL PLANTS	-	-	-	-	-
23	CLAIMS™/CHEM (1950-1970)	-	-	-	AN=	/TI
24	CLAIMS™/US PAT (1971-1977)	PY=1971	AU=NAME I?	-	AN=	/TI
25	CLAIMS™/US PAT ABS (1978+)	PY=1978	AU=NAME I?	-	AN=	/TI
26	FOUNDATION DIRECTORY	-	-	-	-	-
27	FOUNDATION GRANTS INDEX	-	-	-	-	-
28	OCEANIC ABS	PY=64	AU=NAME, I?	JN=	-	/TI
29	MET/GEOASTRO ABS	-	AU=NAME, I?	-	/CS	/TI
31	CHEMNAME™	-	-	-	-	-
32	METADEX	PD=1966	AU=NAME, I?	JO=	-	/TI
33	WORLD ALUMINUM ABS	PY=1968	AU=NAME, I?	JN=	CS=	/TI
34	SCISEARCH® (1978+)	-	AU=NAME I?	JN=	CS=	/TI
35	COMP DISSERTATION ABS	YR=1861	AU=NAME, I?	-	/CS	/TI
36	LLBA	PD=1973	AU=NAME, I?	JO=	/CS	/TI
37	SOCIOLOGICAL ABS	PD=1963	AU=NAME, I?	JO=	/CS	/TI
38	AMERICA: HISTORY & LIFE	YR=1963	AU=NAME, I?	PB=	-	/TI
39	HISTORICAL ABS	YR=1973	AU=NAME, I?	JO=	-	/TI
40	ENVIROLINE®	-	AU=NAME I? or AU=NAME, I?	-	/CS	/TI
41	POLLUTION ABS	PY=1970	AU=NAME, I?	JN=	CS=	/TI
42	PHARM NEWS INDEX	PY=1977	-	JN=	-	/TI
43	CA PATENT CONCORDANCE	-	-	-	-	-
44	ASFA	PY=1965	AU=NAME, I?	-	CS=	/TI
45	APTIC	PD=1966	AU=NAME I? or AU=NAME, I?	JO=	/CS	/TI

IOD Provides photocopies of published material in any form from any country. No special order forms or verification required. Telephone orders are accepted.¹ IOD staff daily accesses UC Berkeley, UCLA, UC Davis, LC, NLM, Linda Hall, John Crerar, Countway, NAL, & Cornell. $4.50 plus .15 a page from IOD sources, $7.50 plus costs from other sources.*

*Plus royalty payments to the CCC where appropriate.   ¹ On line ordering available through DIALOG®.

INFORMATION on DEMAND, P.O. BOX 4536, BERKELEY, CA 94704   (415) 841-1145   CABLE: INFODEMAND

FILE NO.	DATABASE +	YEAR†	AUTHOR**	JOURNAL	CORPORATE SOURCE	TITLE
46	NICEM	PD=64	-	-	-	/TI
47	MAGAZINE INDEX	PY=1978	AU=NAME, I?	JN=	-	/TI
48	PIRA	PY=1975	AU=NAME, I?	JN=	-	/TI
49	PAIS INTERNATIONAL	YR=72	AU-NAME, I?	JN=	CS=	/TI
50	CAB ABS	PD=1972	AU=NAME, I?	JO=	/CS	/TI
51	FSTA	PD=1969	AU=NAME, I?	JO=	CS=	/TI
54	ECER/EXCEP CHILD	PD=65	AU=NAME, I?	JO=	-	/TI
55	BIOSIS PREVIEWS (1969-1973)	-	AU=NAME I?	JN=	-	/TI
56	ART MODERN	-	AU=NAME, I?	JN=	/CS	/TI
57	PHILOSOPHER'S INDEX	PY=1940	AU=NAME, I?	JN=	-	/TI
58	GEOARCHIVE	PY=1974	AU=NAME, I?	JN=	-	/TI
59	FROST & SULLIVAN DM^2	DT=75/01/01	-	-	/AN	-
60	USDA/CRIS	-	-	-	PO=	/TI
61	LISA	PY=1969	AU=NAME, I?	JN=	-	/TI
62	SPIN	PY=1975	AU=NAME, I?	JN=	-	/TI
63	MRIS ABS	PY=70	AU=NAME, I?	JN=	CS=	/TI
64	CHILD ABUSE & NEGLECT	-	AU=NAME, I?	-	CS=	/TI
65	SSIE CURRENT RESEARCH	FY=70	-	-	-	/TI
66	GPO MONTHLY CATALOG	CY=1976	AU=NAME, I?	JN=	CS=	/TI
67	WORLD TEXTILES	PY=1970	AU=NAME, I?	JN=	CS=	/TI
68	ENVIRON PERIOD BIBLIOG	PY=1974	AU=NAME, I?	JN=	CS=	/TI
69	ENERGYLINE®	-	AU=NAME I? or AU=NAME, I?	-	/CS	/TI
70	NICSEM/NIMIS	PY=1974	AU=NAME, I?	-	CS=	/TI
71	MLA BIBLIOGRAPHY	PY=1976	AU=NAME, I?	JN=	-	/TI
72	EXCERPTA MEDICA	PY=1975	AU=NAME I?	JN=	CS=	/TI
73	EXCERPTA MEDICA IN PROC	PY=1979	AU=NAME I?	JN=	CS=	/TI
74	INT'L PHARM ABS	PY=1970	AU=NAME, I?	JN=	CS=	/TI
75	MANAGEMENT CONTENTS®	PY=1974	AU=NAME, I?	JN=	-	/TI
77	CONF PAPERS INDEX	CY=1973	AU=NAME, I?	-	CS=	/TI
78	NATIONAL FOUNDATIONS	-	-	-	/FN	-
79	FOODS ADLIBRA	PY=1974	-	JN=	-	/TI
81	PTS U.S. STATISTICAL ABS	DT=71/01	AU=NAME, I?	JO=	-	-
82	PTS U.S. ANNUAL TIME SER	YR=1971	-	JO=	-	-
86	PTS INT'L STATISTICAL ABS	DT=71/01	AU=NAME, I?	JO=	CS=	-
87	PTS INT'L TIME SER	YR=1972	-	JO=	-	-
90	ECONOMICS ABS INT'L	PY=1974	AU=NAME, I?	JN=	CS=	/TI
92	EIS NON MFG ESTAB	-	-	-	-	-
93	USPSD	PY=1975	AU=NAME, I?	JN=	-	/TI
94	SCISEARCH® (1974-1977)	-	AU=NAME I?	JO=	/CS	/TI
95	RAPRA ABS	PY=1978 or CY=1978	AU=NAME I?	JN=	CS=	/TI
97	RILM ABS	PY=1972	AU=NAME, I?	JN=	CS=	/TI
98	PTS F&S IND (1972-1975)	DT=72/01	-	JO=	-	-
99	WELDASEARCH	PY=1967	AU=NAME I?	JN=	-	/TI
100	DISCLOSURE	-	-	-	-	-
105	FOREIGN TRADERS INDEX	-	-	-	-	-
111	NAT'L NEWSPAPER INDEX	PY=1979	AU=NAME, I?	JN=	-	/TI
114	ENCYCLOPEDIA OF ASSNS	-	-	-	/OR	-
124	CLAIMS™/CLASS	-	-	-	-	-
125	CLAIMS™/US PAT ABS WKLY	PY=1979	AU=NAME I?	-	AN=	/TI
911	NEWSEARCH	PY=1979	AU=NAME, I?	JN=	-	/TI

- Means not applicable

** The use of punctuation in the author field as shown in this chart is important. The name followed by the first initial truncated may be the most efficient method. DIALOG recommends EXPANDing author name and initial (EXPAND NAME, I).

† Where it is not possible to select year of publication, it may be possible to limit by DIALOG accession number. Check the Guide to DIALOG Databases for correlation of accession number to years. Or type ?LIMITn (n=File #) for a description of the LIMIT capability for that file.

+ The example date in the year column is the beginning date of each file. Inclusive dates for the files that have been divided are listed here.

Index